Garfield hits the big time

BY JIM DAVIS

Ballantine Books • **New York**

2013 Ballantine Books Trade Paperback Edition

Copyright © 1993, 2013 by PAWS, Inc. All rights reserved.
"GARFIELD" and the GARFIELD characters are trademarks of PAWS, Inc.

Published in the United States by Ballantine Books, an imprint of The Random House Publishing Group,
a division of Random House, Inc., New York.

Ballantine and colophon are registered trademarks of Random House, Inc.

Originally published in slightly different form in the United States by Ballantine Books, an imprint of
The Random House Publishing Group, a division of Random House, Inc., in 1993.

ISBN 978-0-345-52589-5

Printed in the United States of America

www.ballantinebooks.com

9 8 7 6 5 4 3 2 1

First Colorized Edition

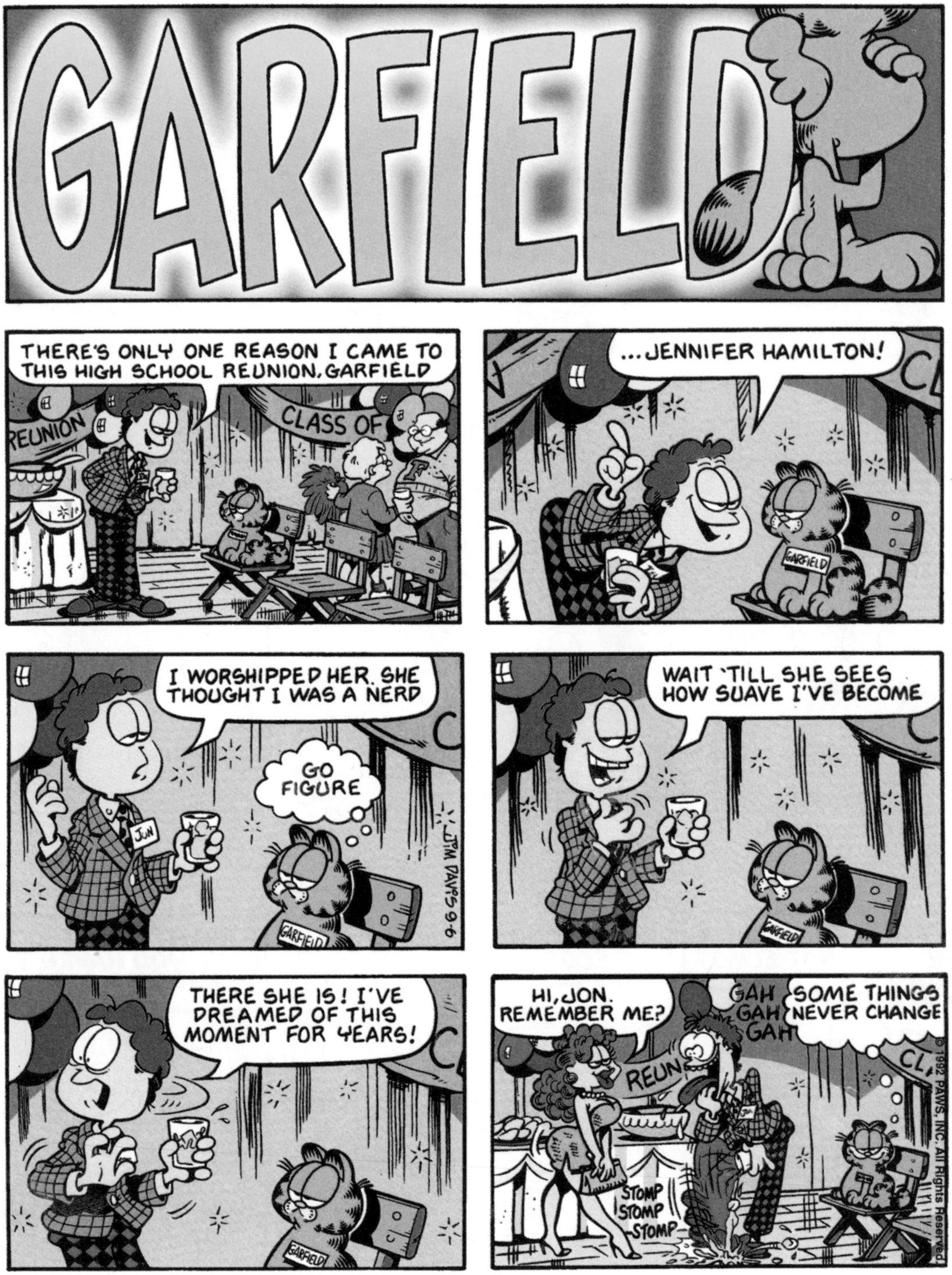
GARFIELD
THERE'S ONLY ONE REASON I CAME TO THIS HIGH SCHOOL REUNION, GARFIELD
REUNION
CLASS OF
...JENNIFER HAMILTON!
GARFIELD
I WORSHIPPED HER. SHE THOUGHT I WAS A NERD
GO FIGURE
JON
JIM DAVIS 9-6
GARFIELD
WAIT 'TILL SHE SEES HOW SUAVE I'VE BECOME
GARFIELD
THERE SHE IS! I'VE DREAMED OF THIS MOMENT FOR YEARS!
GARFIELD
HI, JON. REMEMBER ME?
GAH GAH GAH
SOME THINGS NEVER CHANGE
REUN
STOMP STOMP STOMP
© 1992 PAWS, INC. All Rights Reserved.

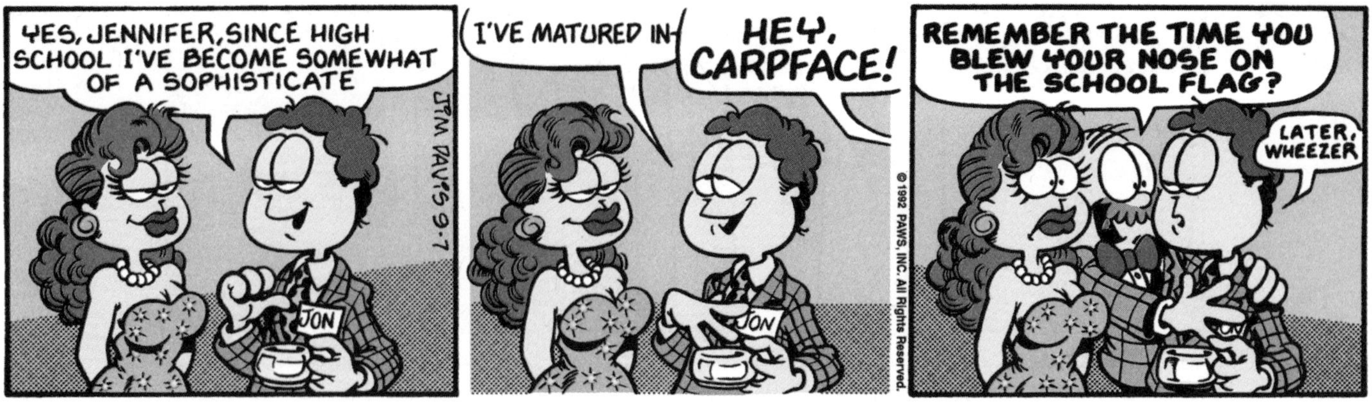
YES, JENNIFER, SINCE HIGH SCHOOL I'VE BECOME SOMEWHAT OF A SOPHISTICATE
JIM DAVIS 9-7
I'VE MATURED IN-
HEY, CARPFACE!
© 1992 PAWS, INC. All Rights Reserved.
REMEMBER THE TIME YOU BLEW YOUR NOSE ON THE SCHOOL FLAG?
LATER, WHEEZER

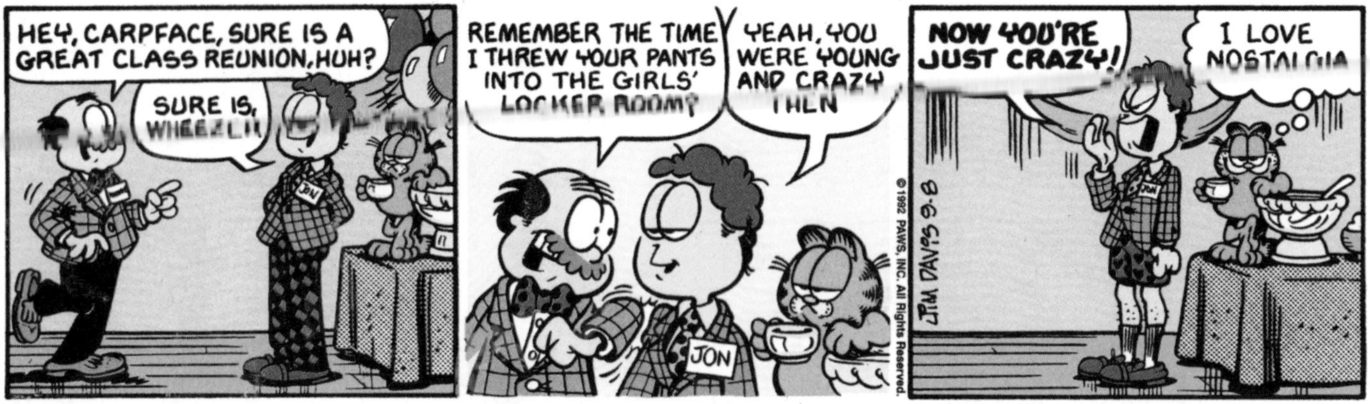
HEY, CARPFACE, SURE IS A GREAT CLASS REUNION, HUH?
SURE IS, WHEEZER
REMEMBER THE TIME I THREW YOUR PANTS INTO THE GIRLS' LOCKER ROOM?
YEAH, YOU WERE YOUNG AND CRAZY THEN
© 1992 PAWS, INC. All Rights Reserved.
JIM DAVIS 9-8
NOW YOU'RE JUST CRAZY!
I LOVE NOSTALGIA

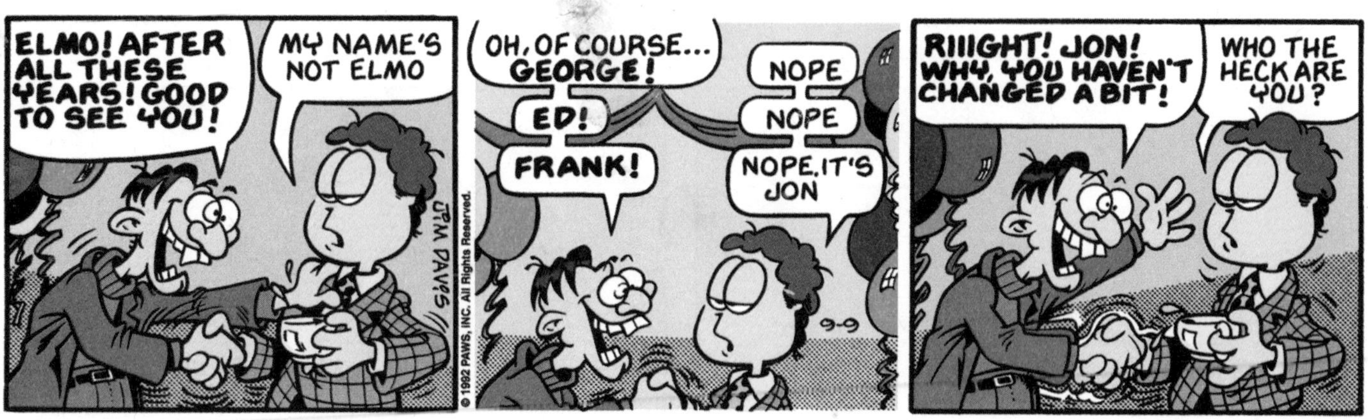
ELMO! AFTER ALL THESE YEARS! GOOD TO SEE YOU!
MY NAME'S NOT ELMO
JIM DAVIS
© 1992 PAWS, INC. All Rights Reserved.
OH, OF COURSE... GEORGE!
NOPE
ED!
NOPE
FRANK!
NOPE, IT'S JON
9-9
RIIIGHT! JON! WHY, YOU HAVEN'T CHANGED A BIT!
WHO THE HECK ARE YOU?

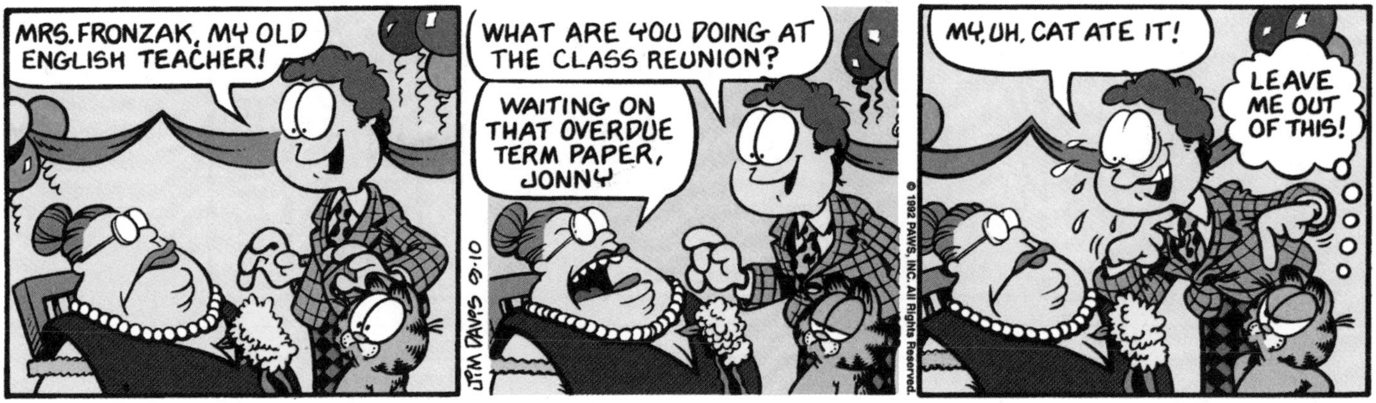
MRS. FRONZAK, MY OLD ENGLISH TEACHER!
JIM DAVIS 9-10
WHAT ARE YOU DOING AT THE CLASS REUNION?
WAITING ON THAT OVERDUE TERM PAPER, JONNY
© 1992 PAWS, INC. All Rights Reserved.
MY, UH, CAT ATE IT!
LEAVE ME OUT OF THIS!

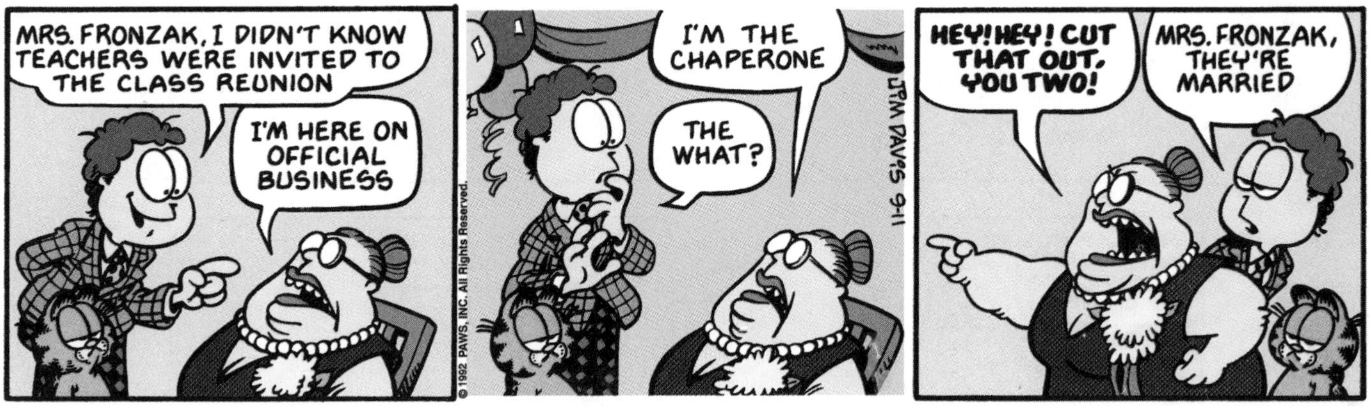
MRS. FRONZAK, I DIDN'T KNOW TEACHERS WERE INVITED TO THE CLASS REUNION
I'M HERE ON OFFICIAL BUSINESS
© 1992 PAWS, INC. All Rights Reserved.
I'M THE CHAPERONE
THE WHAT?
JIM DAVIS 9-11
HEY! HEY! CUT THAT OUT, YOU TWO!
MRS. FRONZAK, THEY'RE MARRIED

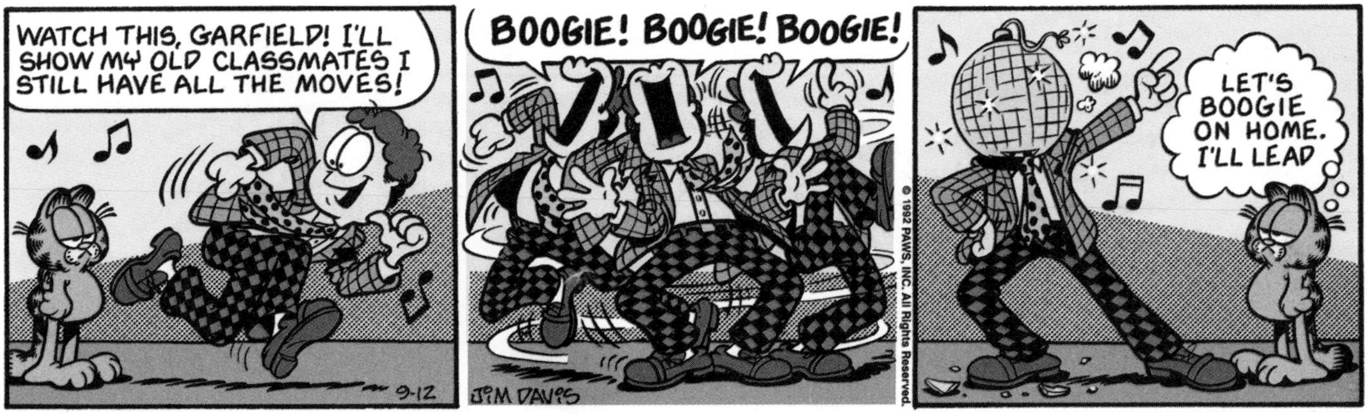
WATCH THIS, GARFIELD! I'LL SHOW MY OLD CLASSMATES I STILL HAVE ALL THE MOVES!
9-12
BOOGIE! BOOGIE! BOOGIE!
JIM DAVIS
© 1992 PAWS, INC. All Rights Reserved.
LET'S BOOGIE ON HOME. I'LL LEAD

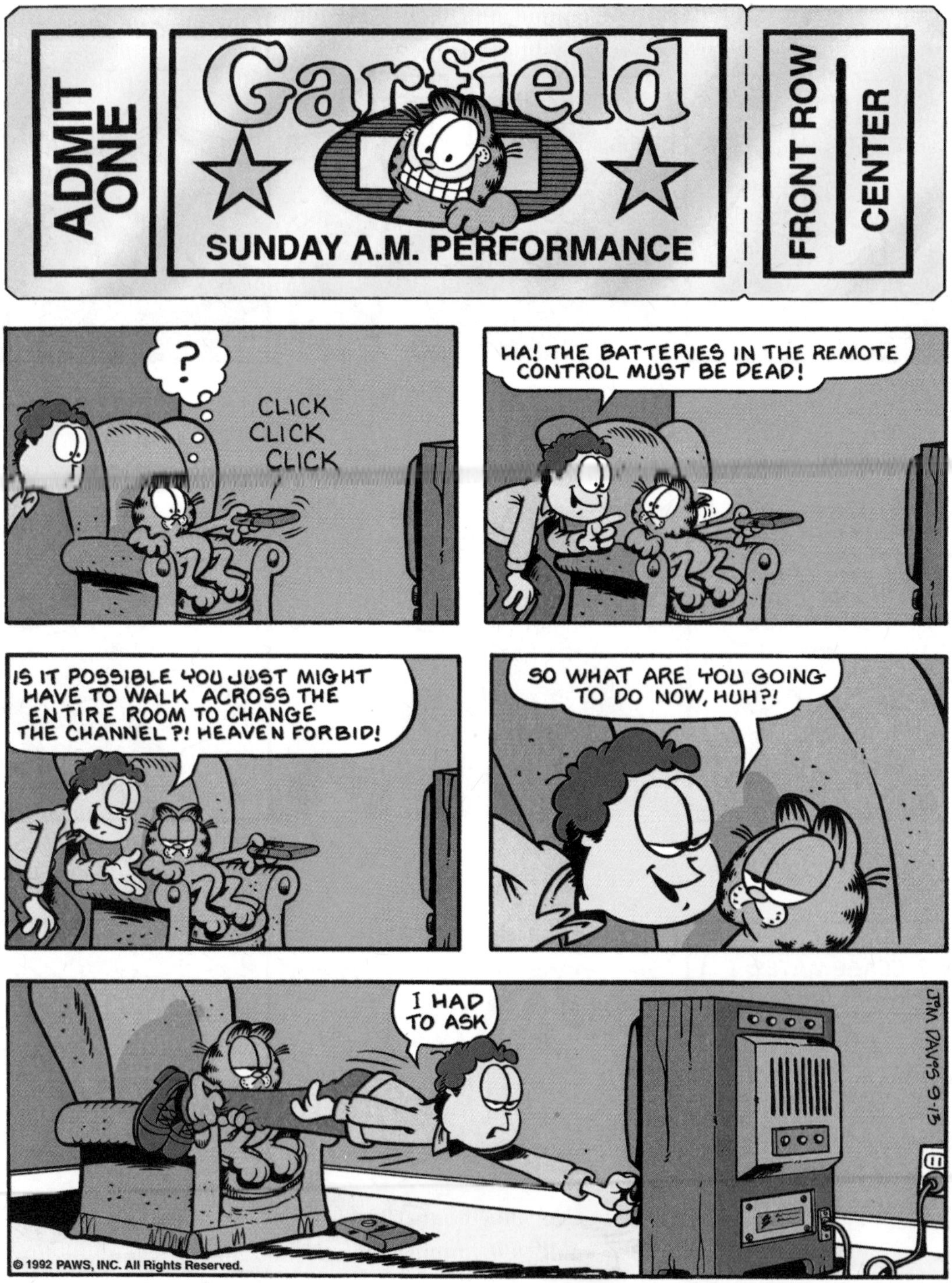
ADMIT ONE
Garfield
SUNDAY A.M. PERFORMANCE
FRONT ROW CENTER
?
CLICK CLICK CLICK
HA! THE BATTERIES IN THE REMOTE CONTROL MUST BE DEAD!
IS IT POSSIBLE YOU JUST MIGHT HAVE TO WALK ACROSS THE ENTIRE ROOM TO CHANGE THE CHANNEL?! HEAVEN FORBID!
SO WHAT ARE YOU GOING TO DO NOW, HUH?!
I HAD TO ASK
JIM DAVIS 9-13

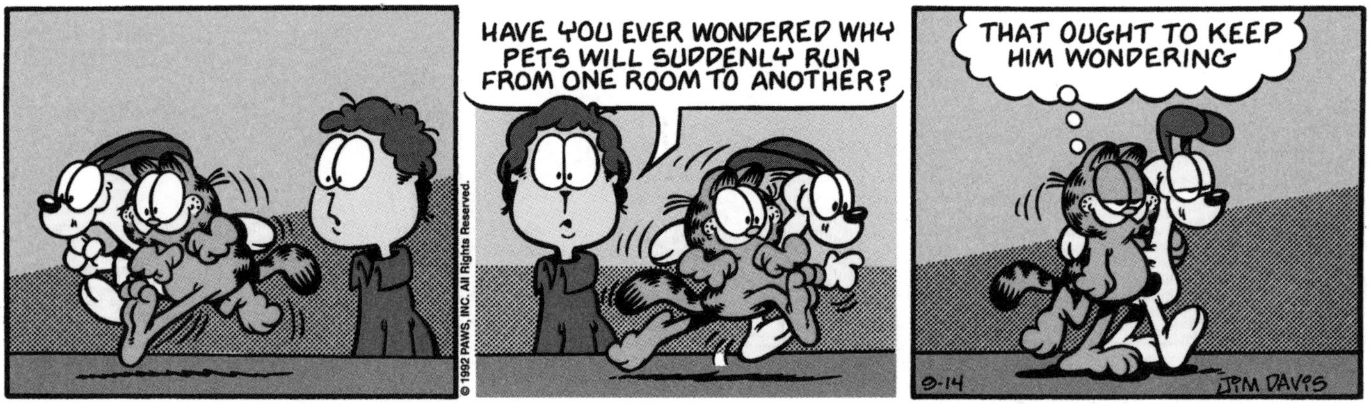
HAVE YOU EVER WONDERED WHY PETS WILL SUDDENLY RUN FROM ONE ROOM TO ANOTHER?
THAT OUGHT TO KEEP HIM WONDERING
9-14
JIM DAVIS

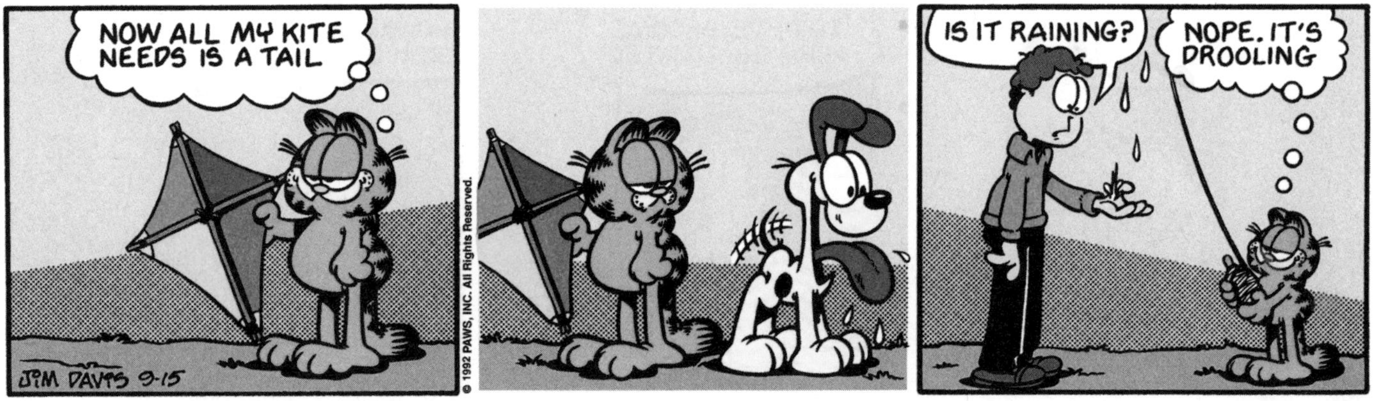
NOW ALL MY KITE NEEDS IS A TAIL
JIM DAVIS 9-15
IS IT RAINING?
NOPE. IT'S DROOLING

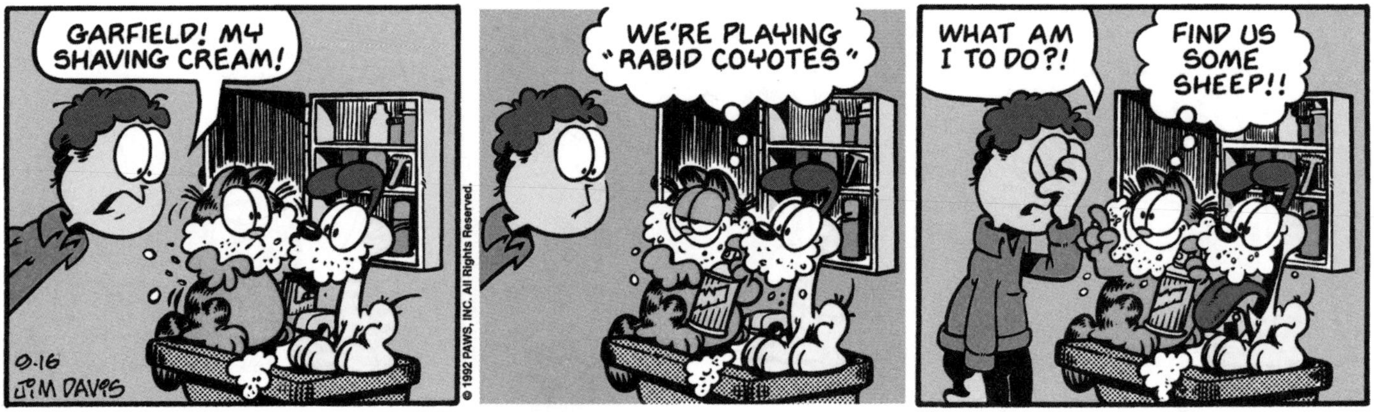
GARFIELD! MY SHAVING CREAM!
9-16
JIM DAVIS
WE'RE PLAYING "RABID COYOTES"
WHAT AM I TO DO?!
FIND US SOME SHEEP!!

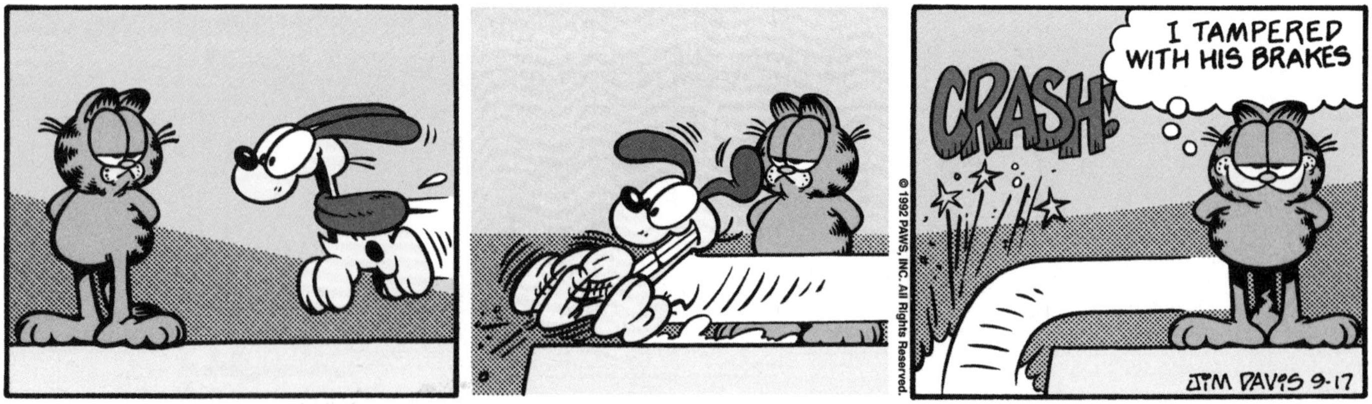
CRASH!
I TAMPERED WITH HIS BRAKES
© 1992 PAWS, INC. All Rights Reserved.
JIM DAVIS 9-17

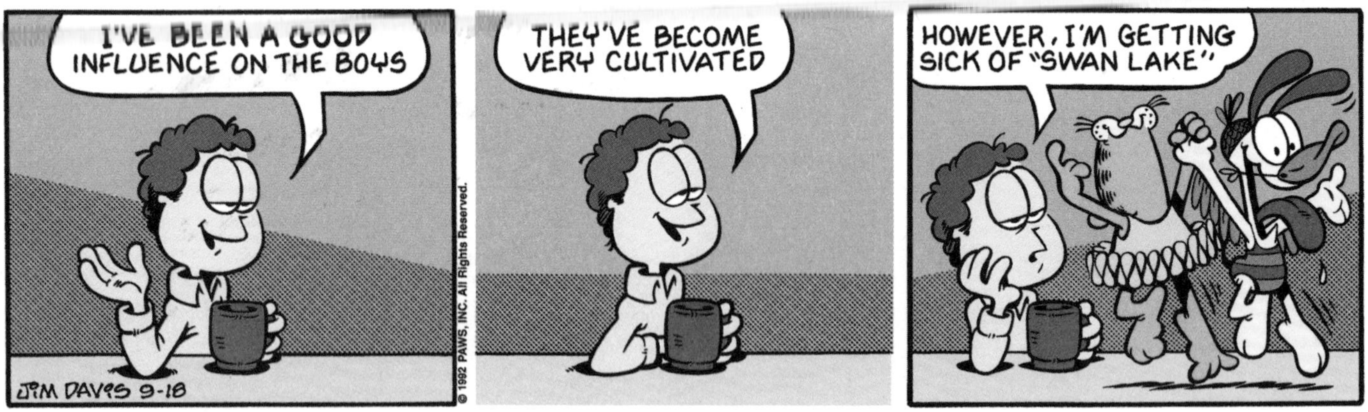
I'VE BEEN A GOOD INFLUENCE ON THE BOYS
THEY'VE BECOME VERY CULTIVATED
HOWEVER, I'M GETTING SICK OF "SWAN LAKE"
© 1992 PAWS, INC. All Rights Reserved.
JIM DAVIS 9-18

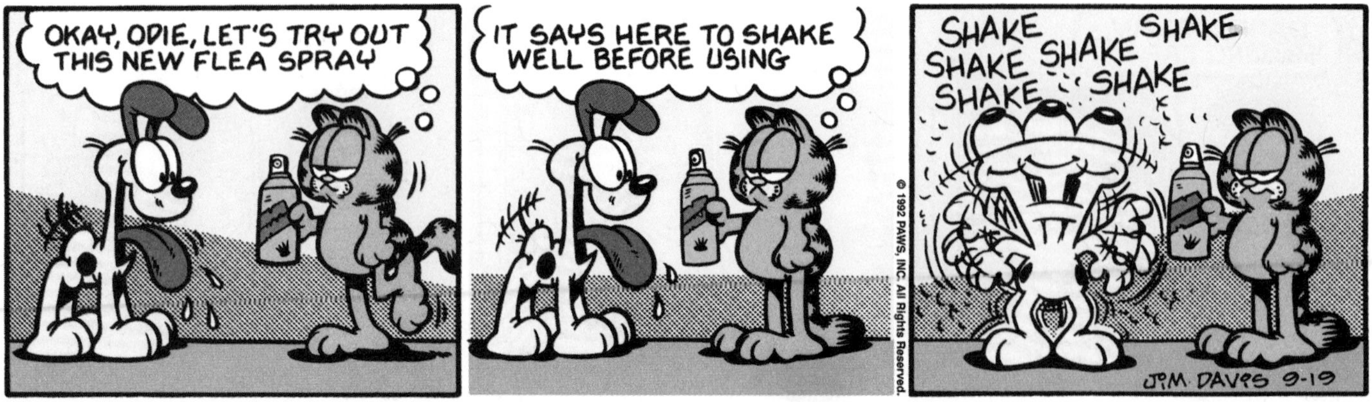
OKAY, ODIE, LET'S TRY OUT THIS NEW FLEA SPRAY
IT SAYS HERE TO SHAKE WELL BEFORE USING
SHAKE SHAKE SHAKE SHAKE SHAKE SHAKE
© 1992 PAWS, INC. All Rights Reserved.
JIM DAVIS 9-19

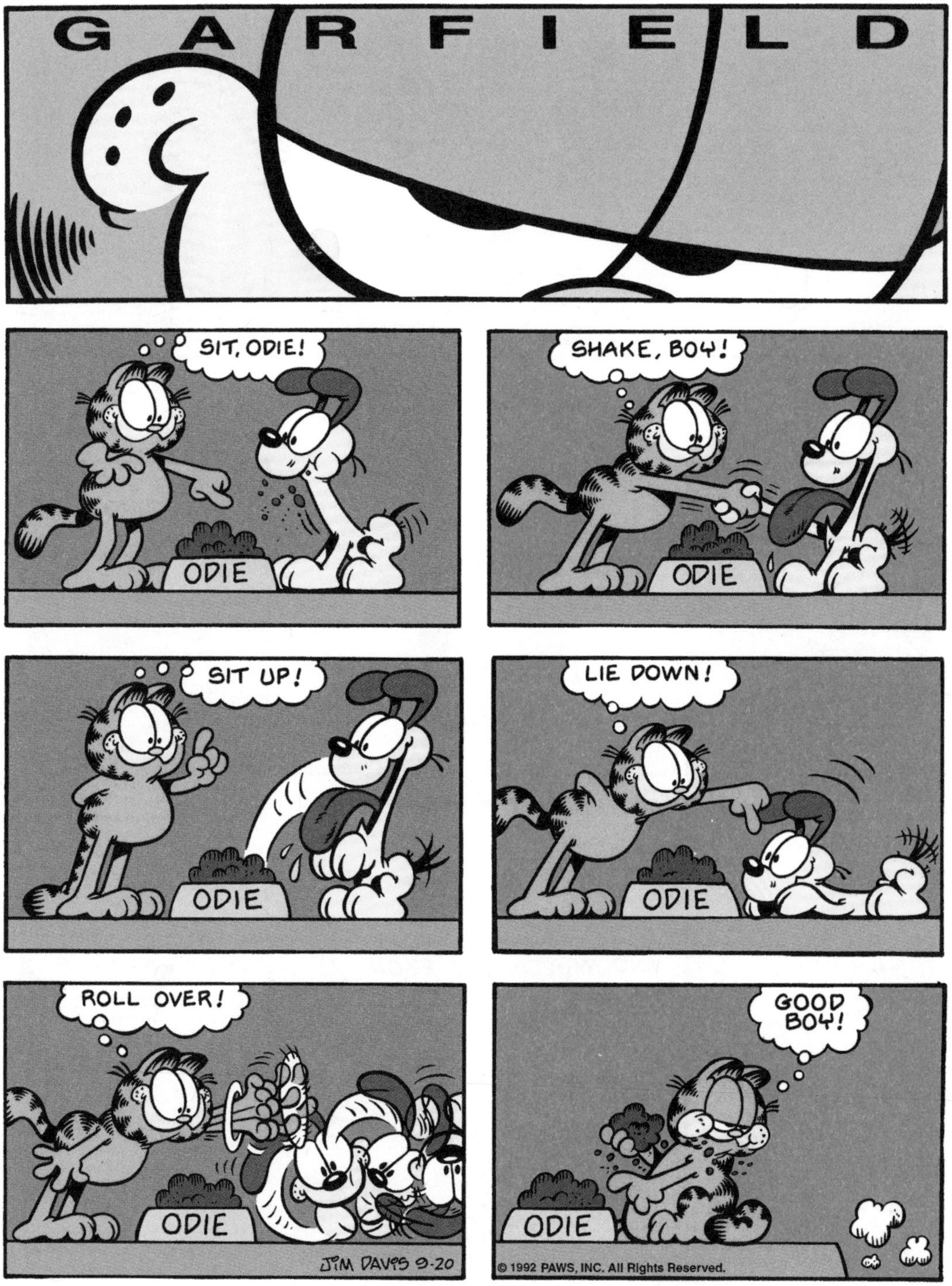
GARFIELD
SIT, ODIE!
ODIE
SHAKE, BOY!
ODIE
SIT UP!
ODIE
LIE DOWN!
ODIE
ROLL OVER!
ODIE
JIM DAVIS 9-20
GOOD BOY!
ODIE
© 1992 PAWS, INC. All Rights Reserved.

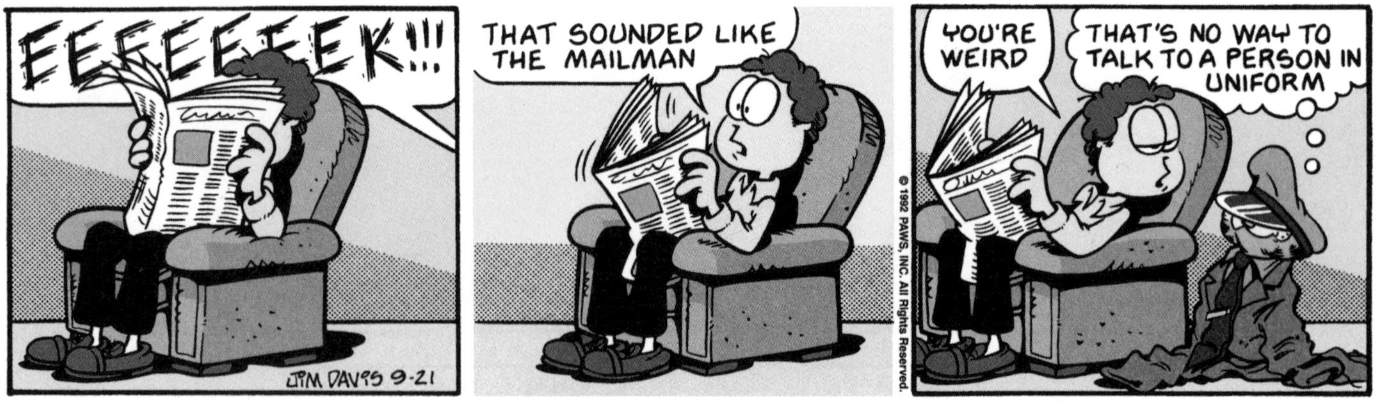
EEEEEEEK!!!
JIM DAVIS 9-21
THAT SOUNDED LIKE THE MAILMAN
© 1992 PAWS, INC. All Rights Reserved.
YOU'RE WEIRD
THAT'S NO WAY TO TALK TO A PERSON IN UNIFORM

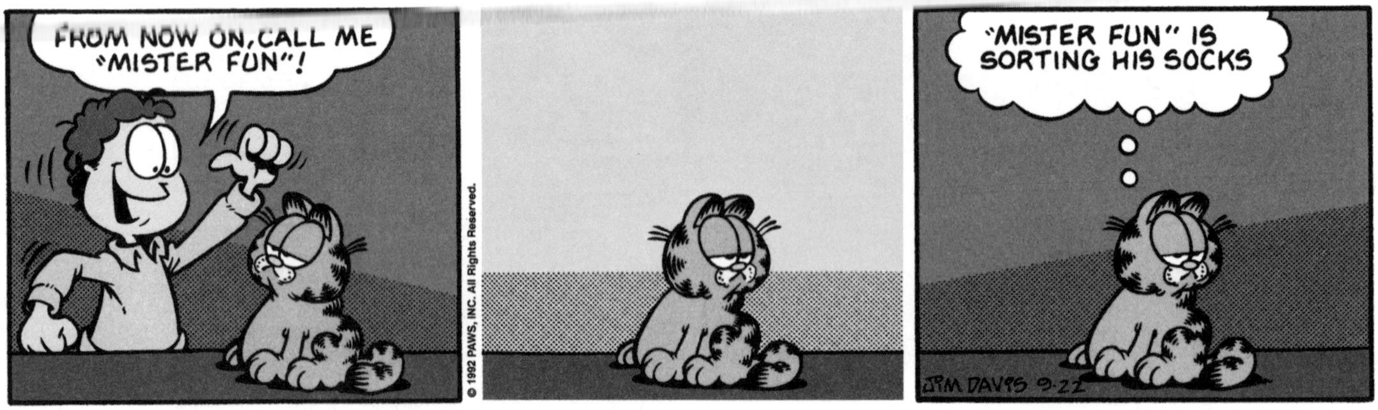
FROM NOW ON, CALL ME "MISTER FUN"!
© 1992 PAWS, INC. All Rights Reserved.
"MISTER FUN" IS SORTING HIS SOCKS
JIM DAVIS 9-22

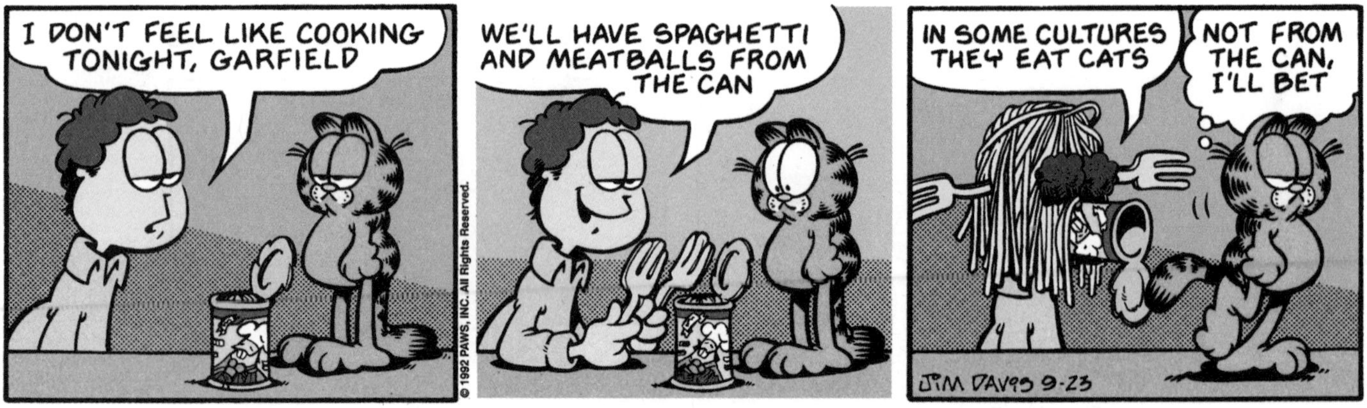
I DON'T FEEL LIKE COOKING TONIGHT, GARFIELD
© 1992 PAWS, INC. All Rights Reserved.
WE'LL HAVE SPAGHETTI AND MEATBALLS FROM THE CAN
IN SOME CULTURES THEY EAT CATS
NOT FROM THE CAN, I'LL BET
JIM DAVIS 9-23

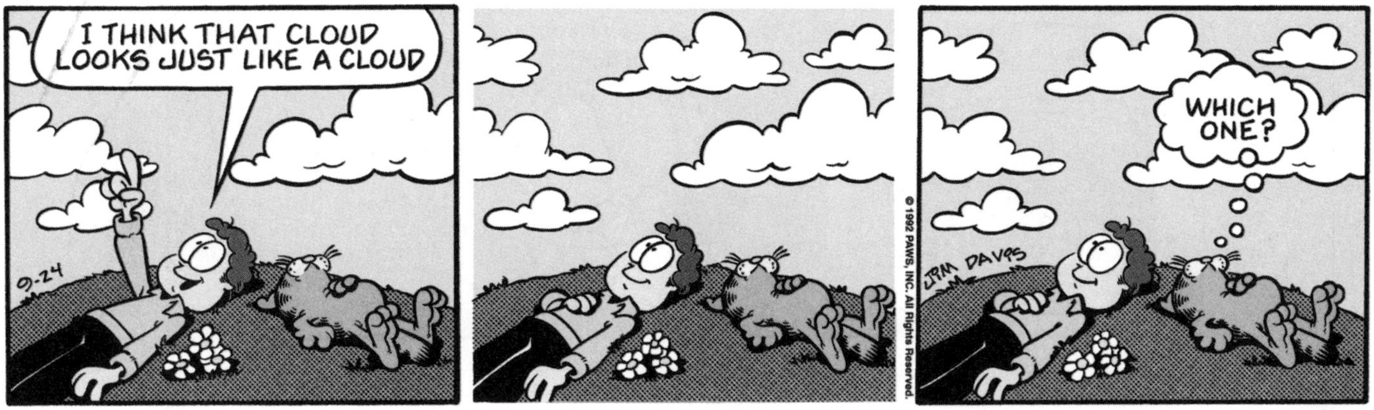
I THINK THAT CLOUD LOOKS JUST LIKE A CLOUD
9-24
© 1992 PAWS, INC. All Rights Reserved.
JIM DAVIS
WHICH ONE?

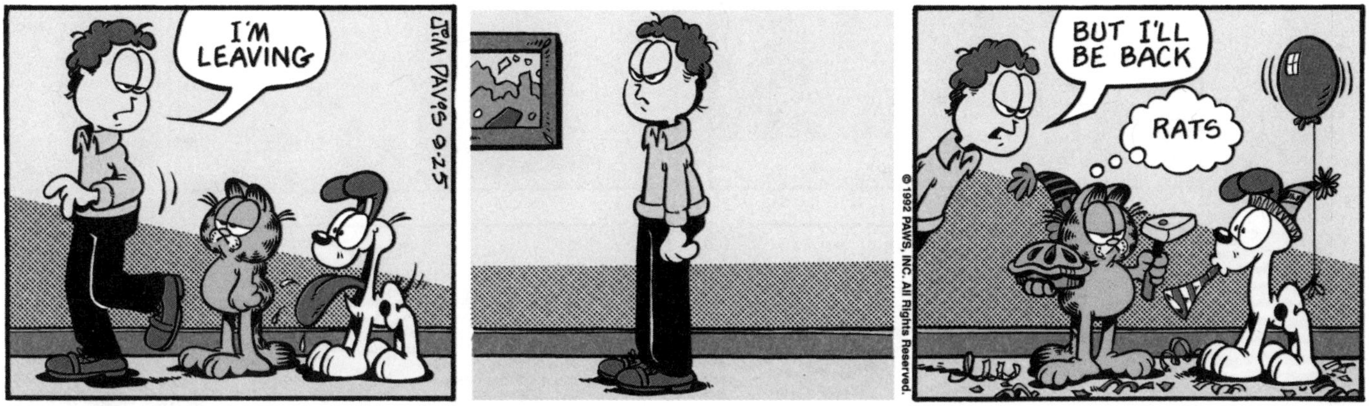
I'M LEAVING
JIM DAVIS 9-25
© 1992 PAWS, INC. All Rights Reserved.
BUT I'LL BE BACK
RATS

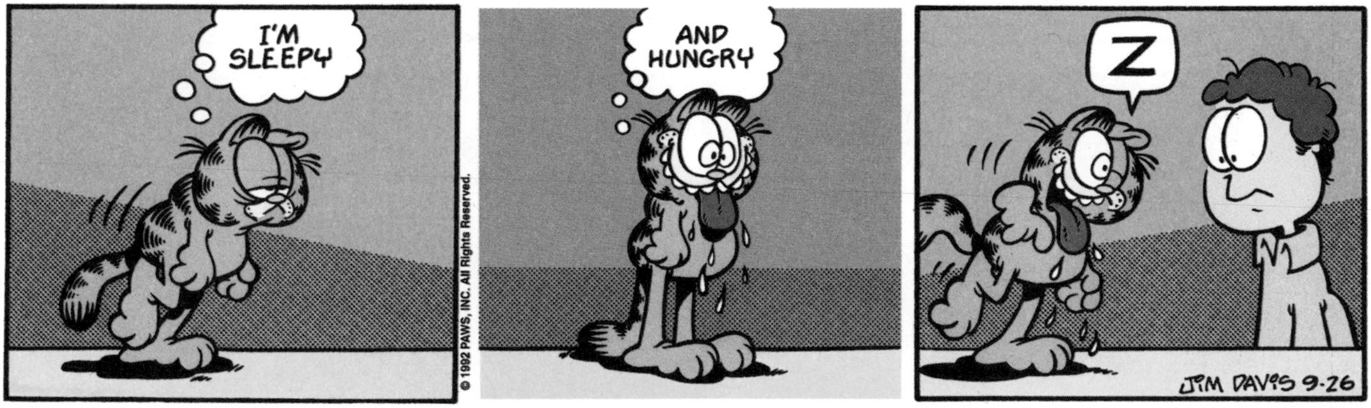
I'M SLEEPY
© 1992 PAWS, INC. All Rights Reserved.
AND HUNGRY
Z
JIM DAVIS 9-26

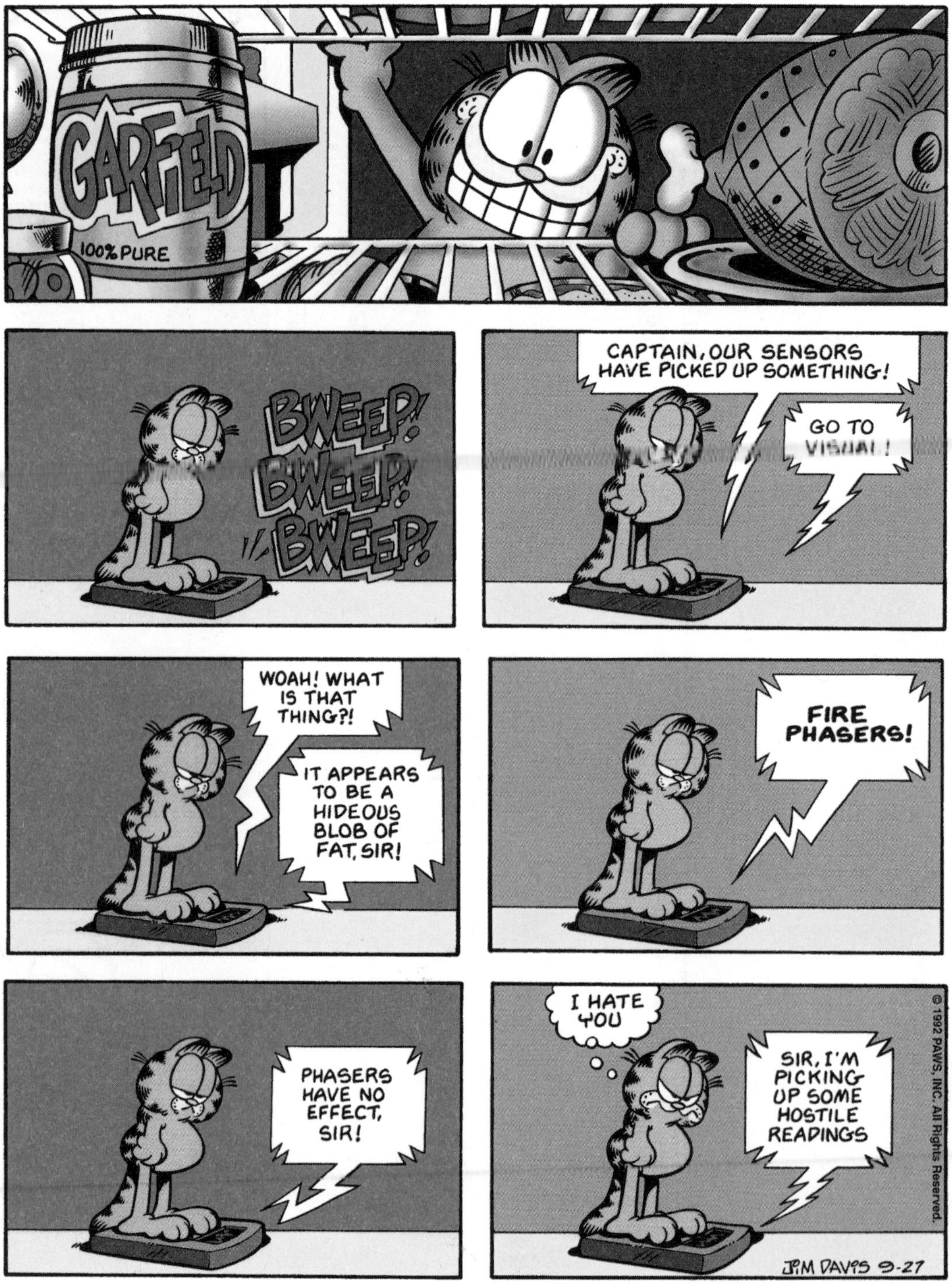
GARFIELD
100% PURE
BWEEP! BWEEP! BWEEP!
CAPTAIN, OUR SENSORS HAVE PICKED UP SOMETHING!
GO TO VISUAL!
WOAH! WHAT IS THAT THING?!
IT APPEARS TO BE A HIDEOUS BLOB OF FAT, SIR!
FIRE PHASERS!
PHASERS HAVE NO EFFECT, SIR!
I HATE YOU
SIR, I'M PICKING UP SOME HOSTILE READINGS
© 1992 PAWS, INC. All Rights Reserved.
JIM DAVIS 9-27

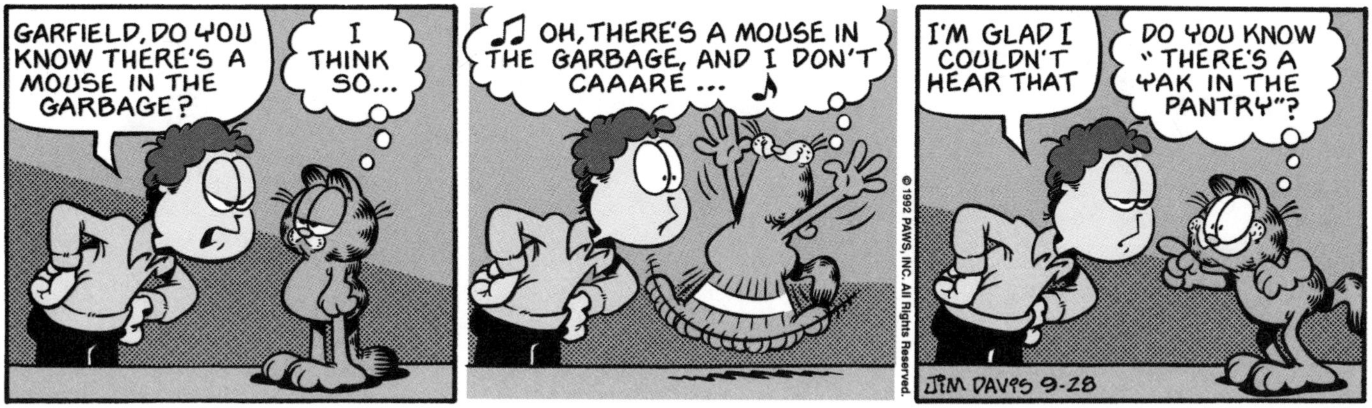
GARFIELD, DO YOU KNOW THERE'S A MOUSE IN THE GARBAGE?
I THINK SO...
♫ OH, THERE'S A MOUSE IN THE GARBAGE, AND I DON'T CAAARE ... ♪
© 1992 PAWS, INC. All Rights Reserved.
I'M GLAD I COULDN'T HEAR THAT
DO YOU KNOW "THERE'S A YAK IN THE PANTRY"?
JIM DAVIS 9-28

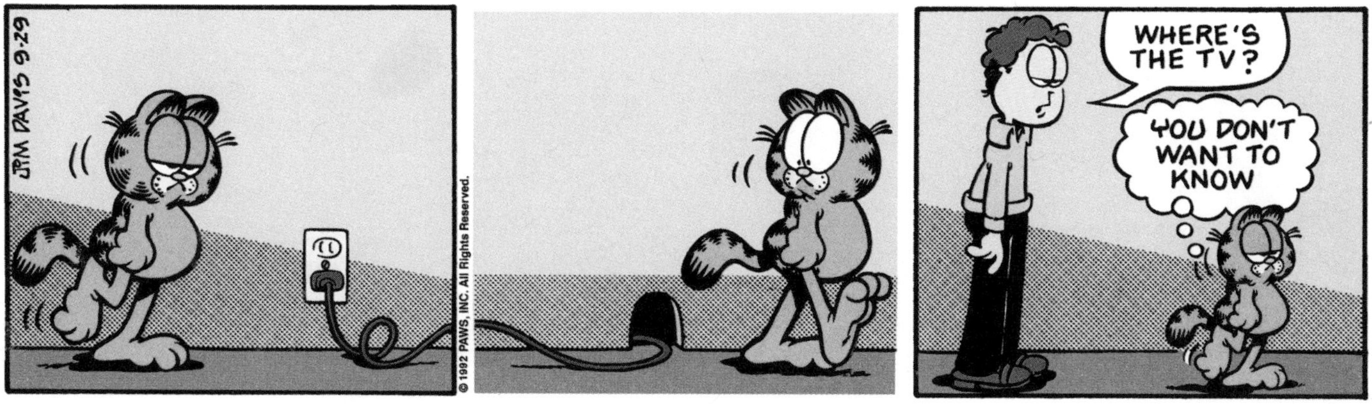
JIM DAVIS 9-29
© 1992 PAWS, INC. All Rights Reserved.
WHERE'S THE TV?
YOU DON'T WANT TO KNOW

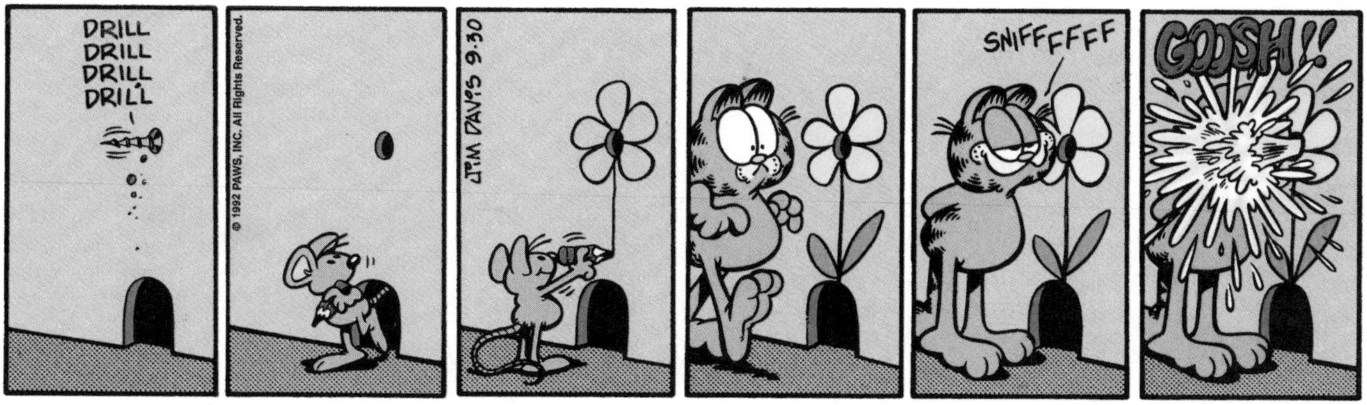
DRILL DRILL DRILL DRILL
© 1992 PAWS, INC. All Rights Reserved.
JIM DAVIS 9-30
SNIFFFFFF
GOOSH!!

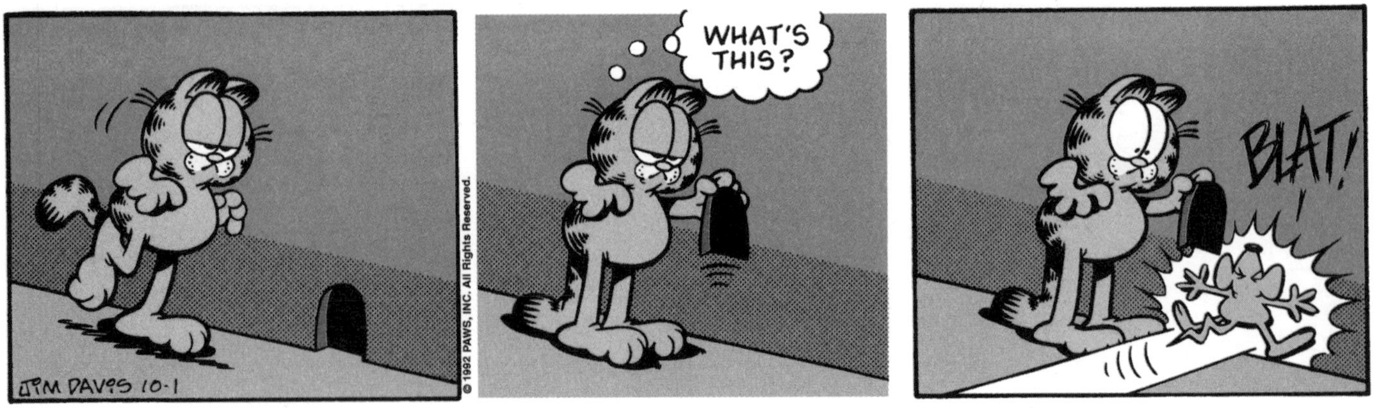
JIM DAVIS 10-1
© 1992 PAWS, INC. All Rights Reserved.
WHAT'S THIS?
BLAT!

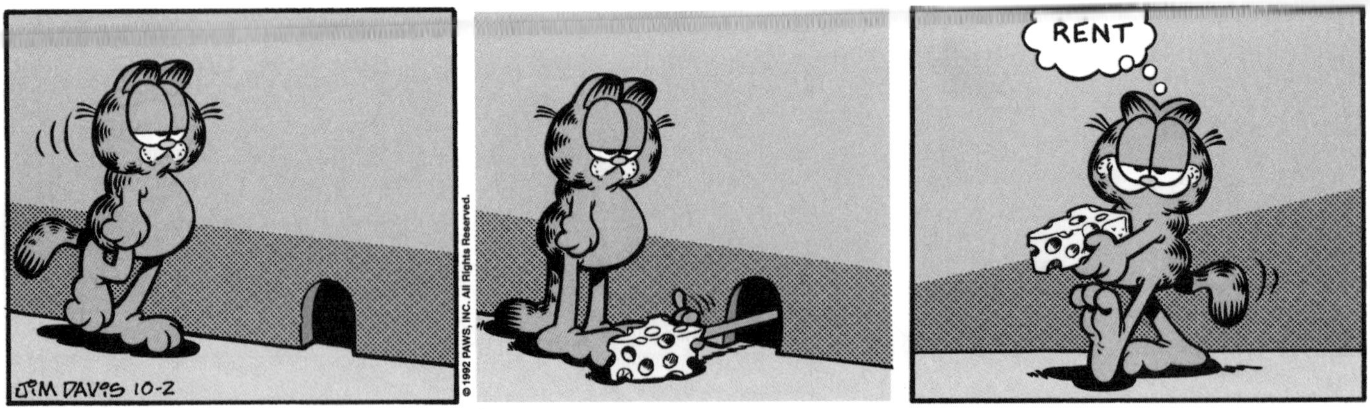
JIM DAVIS 10-2
© 1992 PAWS, INC. All Rights Reserved.
RENT

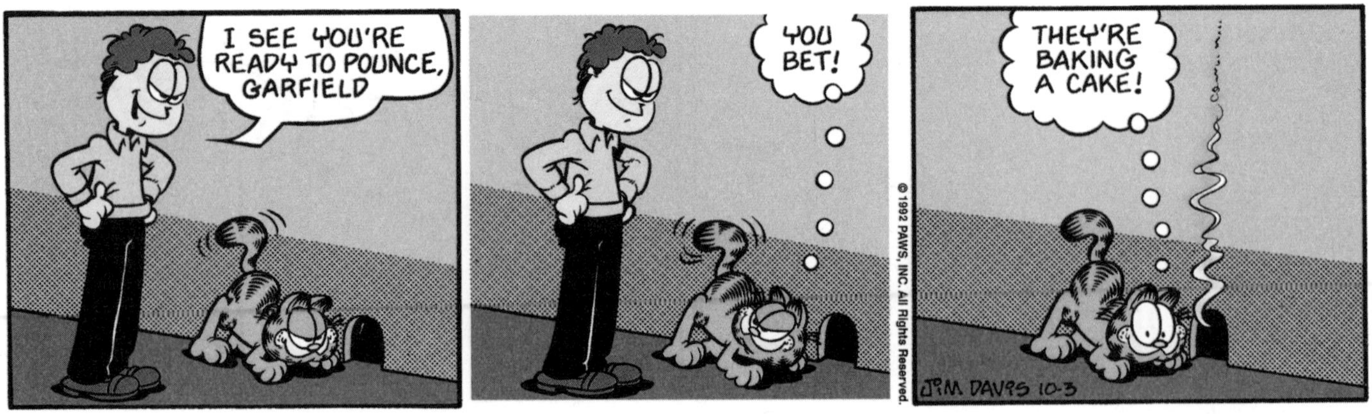
I SEE YOU'RE READY TO POUNCE, GARFIELD
YOU BET!
© 1992 PAWS, INC. All Rights Reserved.
THEY'RE BAKING A CAKE!
JIM DAVIS 10-3

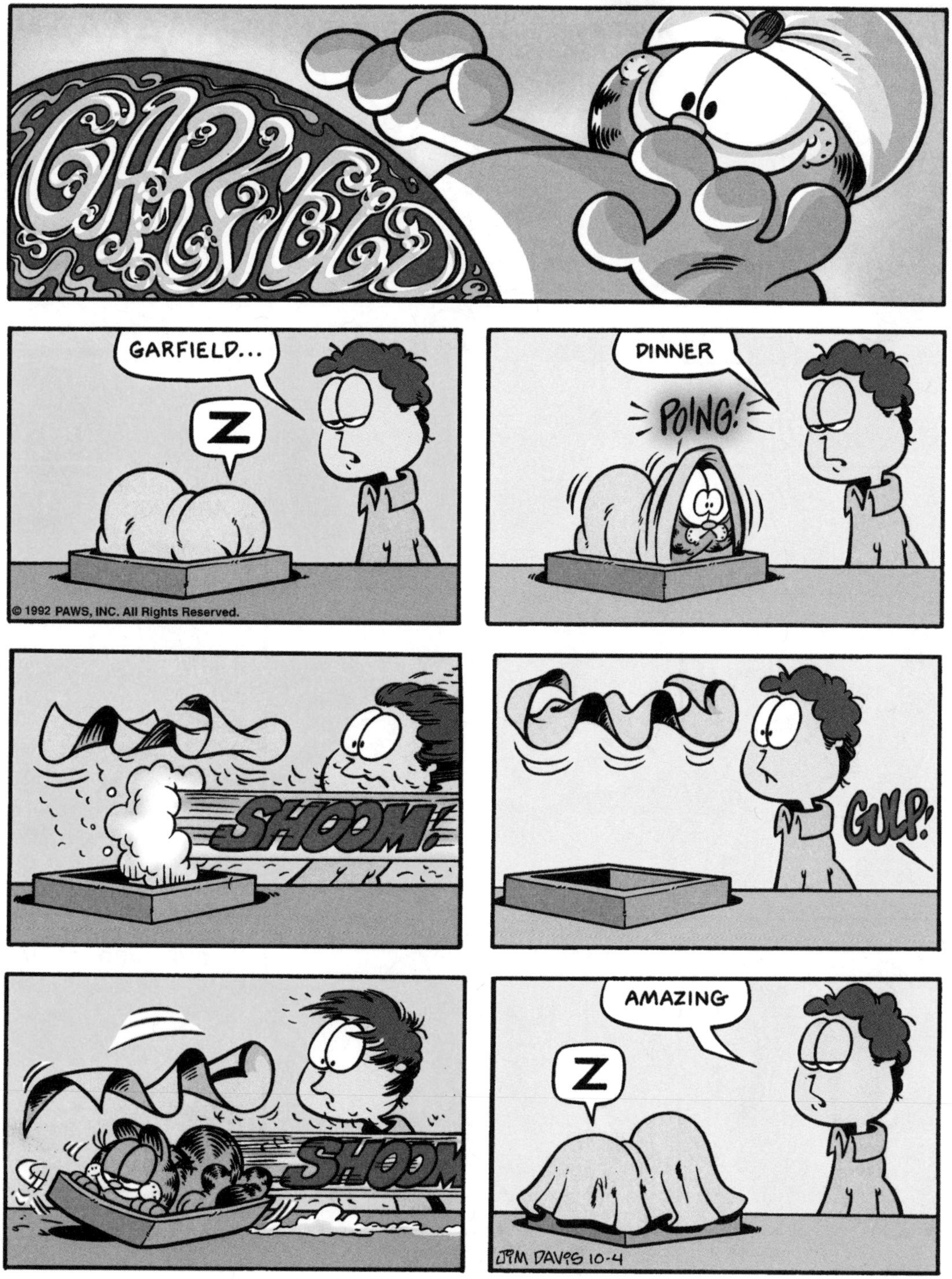
GARFIELD...
Z
© 1992 PAWS, INC. All Rights Reserved.
DINNER
POING!
SHOOM!
GULP!
SHOOM
AMAZING
Z
JIM DAVIS 10-4

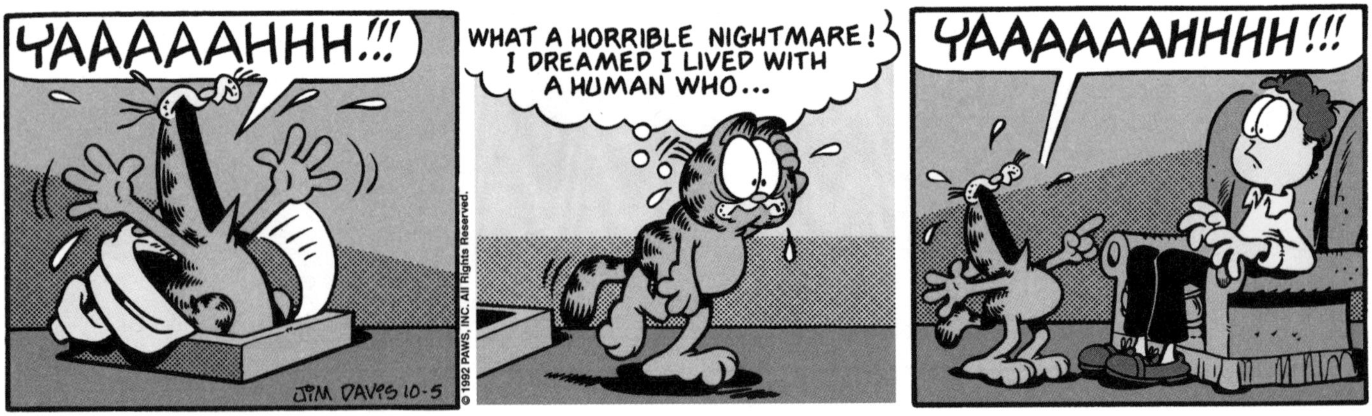
YAAAAAHHH!!!
JIM DAVIS 10-5
© 1992 PAWS, INC. All Rights Reserved.
WHAT A HORRIBLE NIGHTMARE! I DREAMED I LIVED WITH A HUMAN WHO...
YAAAAAAHHHH!!!

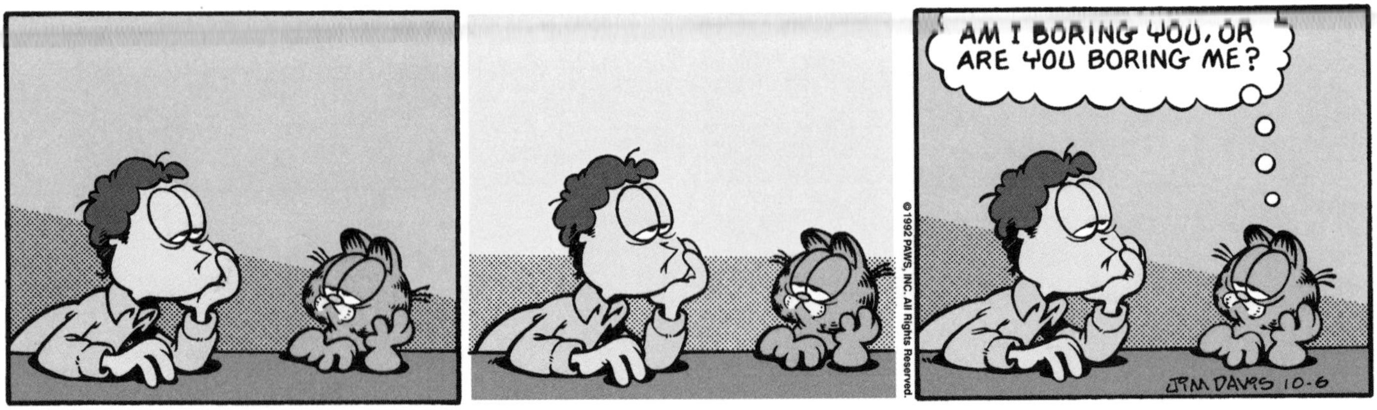
© 1992 PAWS, INC. All Rights Reserved.
AM I BORING YOU, OR ARE YOU BORING ME?
JIM DAVIS 10-6

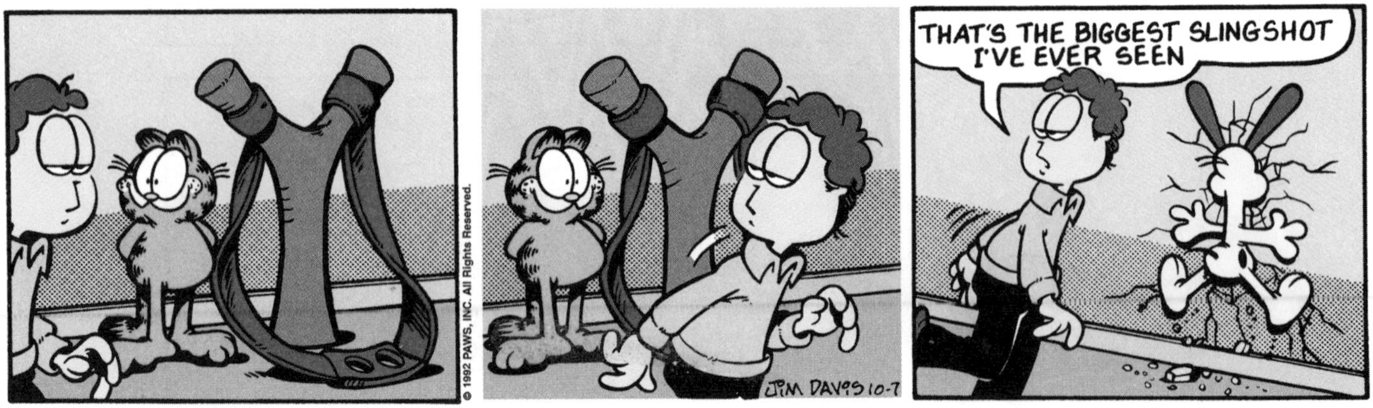
© 1992 PAWS, INC. All Rights Reserved.
JIM DAVIS 10-7
THAT'S THE BIGGEST SLINGSHOT I'VE EVER SEEN

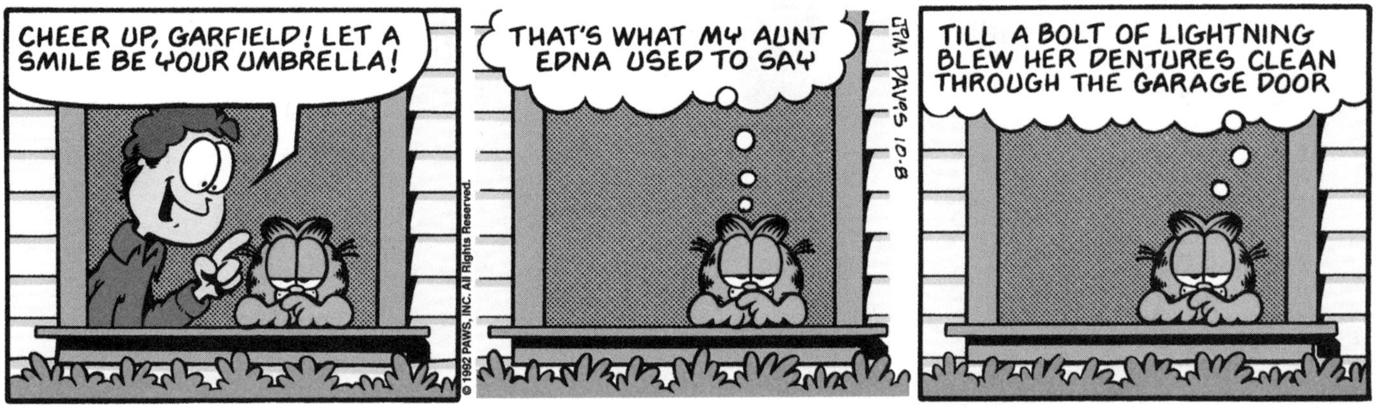
CHEER UP, GARFIELD! LET A SMILE BE YOUR UMBRELLA!
THAT'S WHAT MY AUNT EDNA USED TO SAY
TILL A BOLT OF LIGHTNING BLEW HER DENTURES CLEAN THROUGH THE GARAGE DOOR
JIM DAVIS 10-8
© 1992 PAWS, INC. All Rights Reserved.

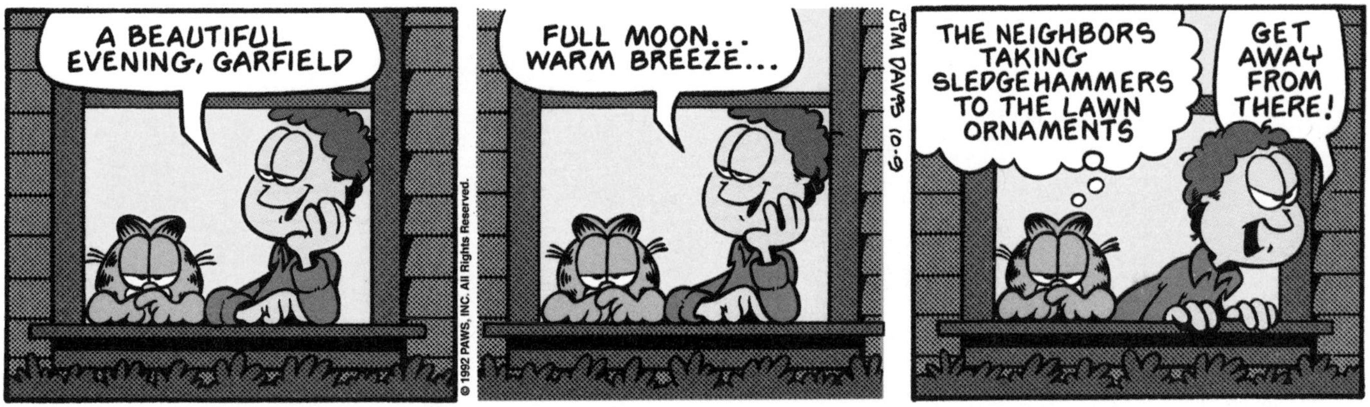
A BEAUTIFUL EVENING, GARFIELD
FULL MOON... WARM BREEZE...
THE NEIGHBORS TAKING SLEDGEHAMMERS TO THE LAWN ORNAMENTS
GET AWAY FROM THERE!
JIM DAVIS 10-9
© 1992 PAWS, INC. All Rights Reserved.

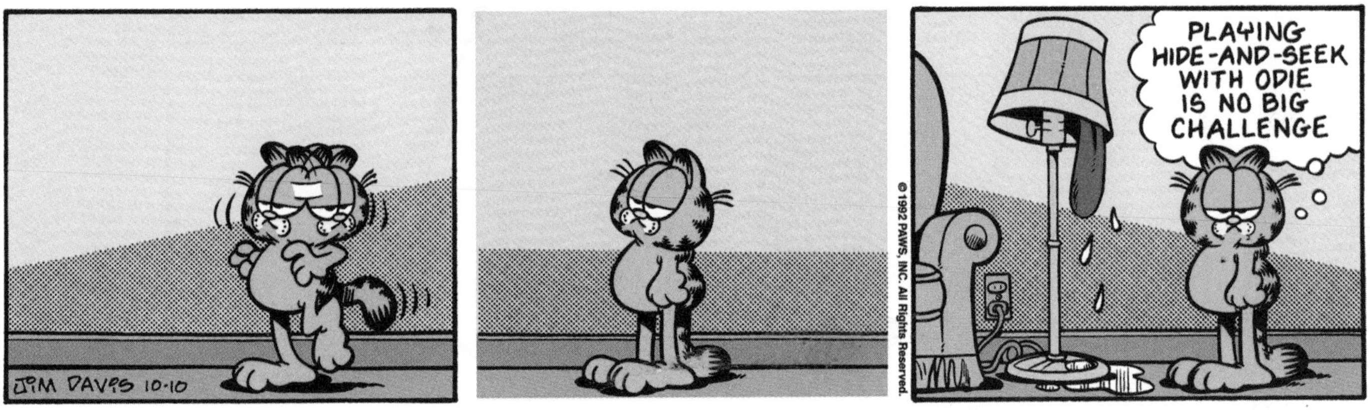
JIM DAVIS 10-10
PLAYING HIDE-AND-SEEK WITH ODIE IS NO BIG CHALLENGE
© 1992 PAWS, INC. All Rights Reserved.

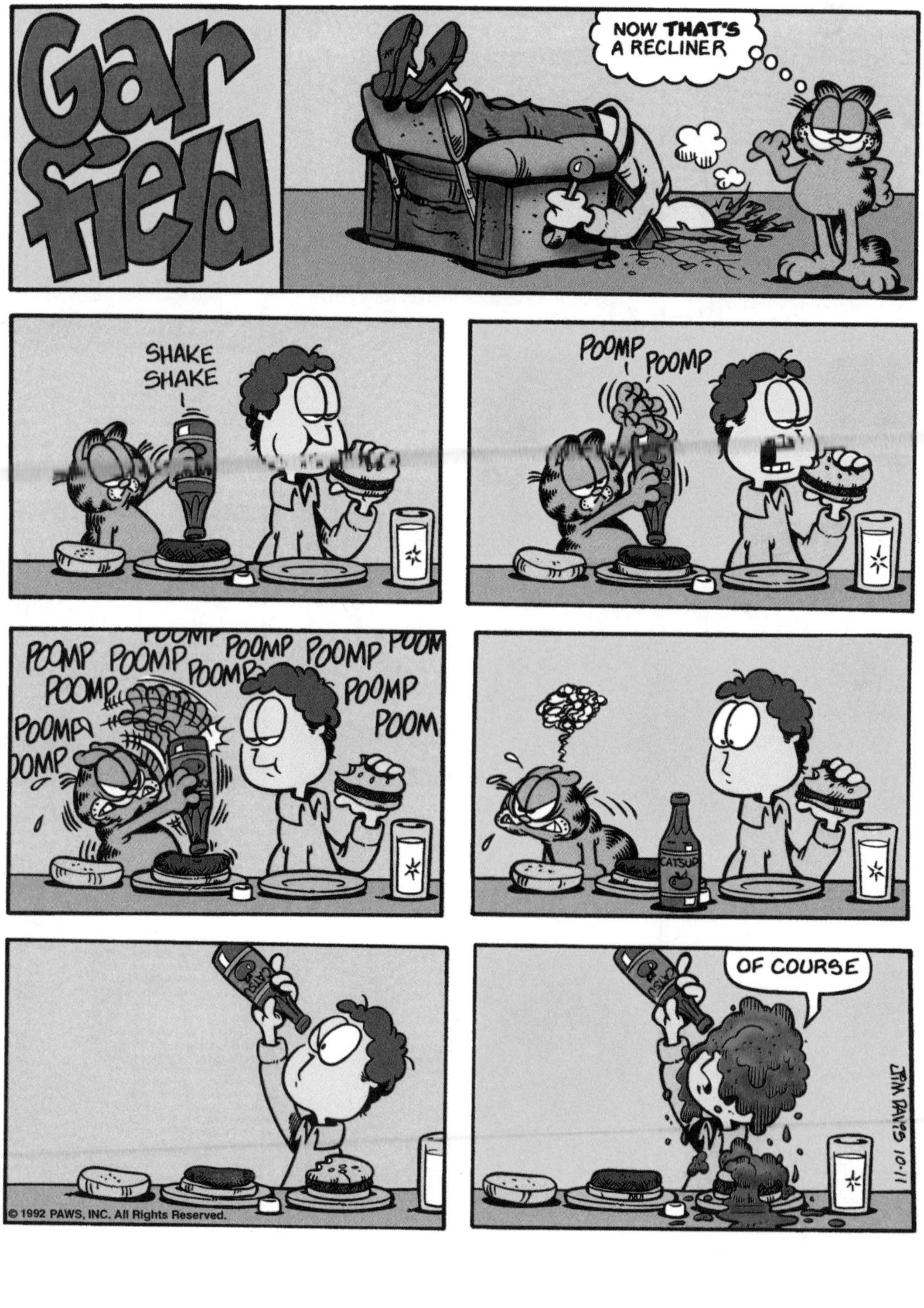
Garfield
NOW THAT'S A RECLINER
SHAKE SHAKE
POOMP POOMP
POOMP POOMP POOMP POOMP POOMP POOM
POOMP POOMP POOMP POOM
POOMP
OMP
CATSUP
OF COURSE
© 1992 PAWS, INC. All Rights Reserved.

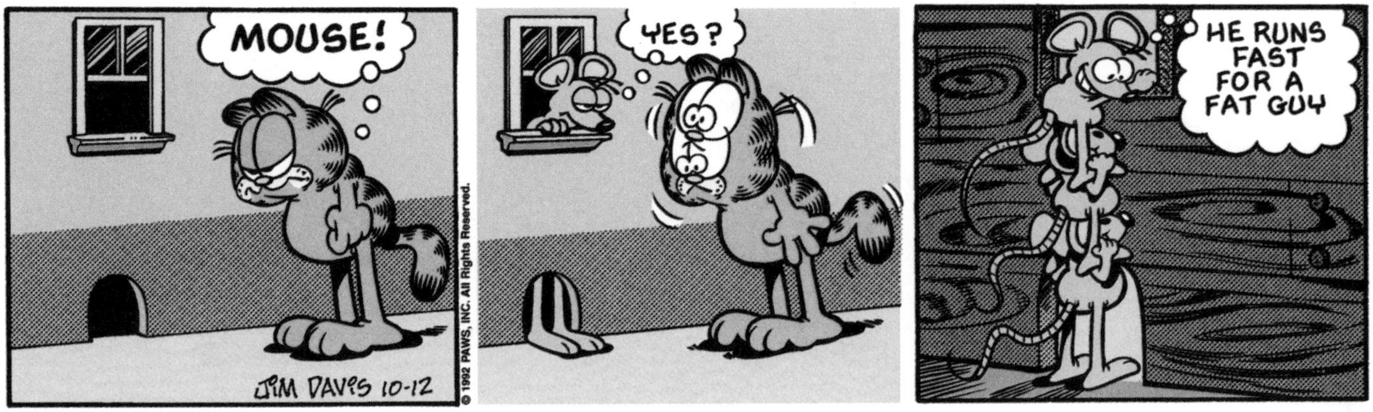
MOUSE!
JIM DAVIS 10-12
© 1992 PAWS, INC. All Rights Reserved.
YES?
HE RUNS FAST FOR A FAT GUY

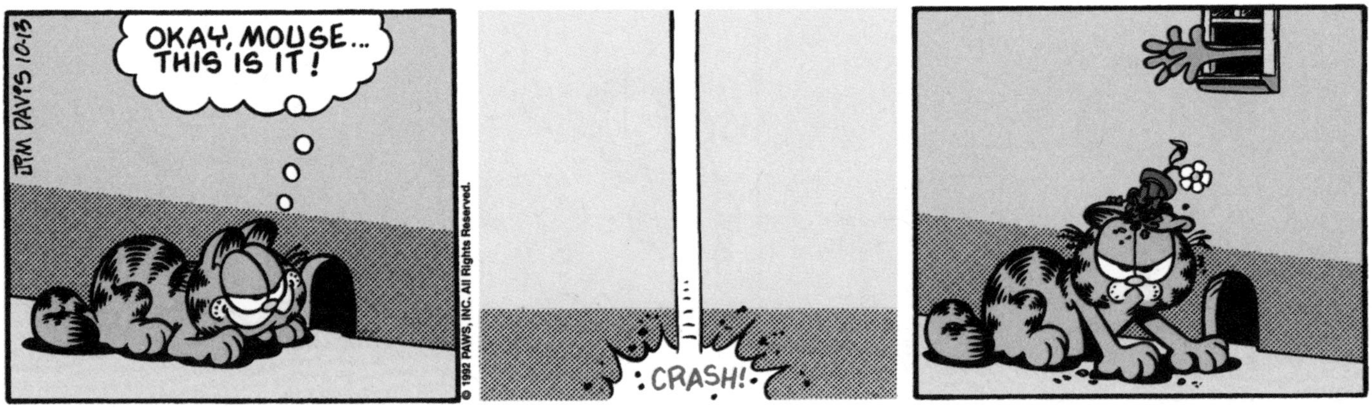
JIM DAVIS 10-13
OKAY, MOUSE... THIS IS IT!
© 1992 PAWS, INC. All Rights Reserved.
CRASH!

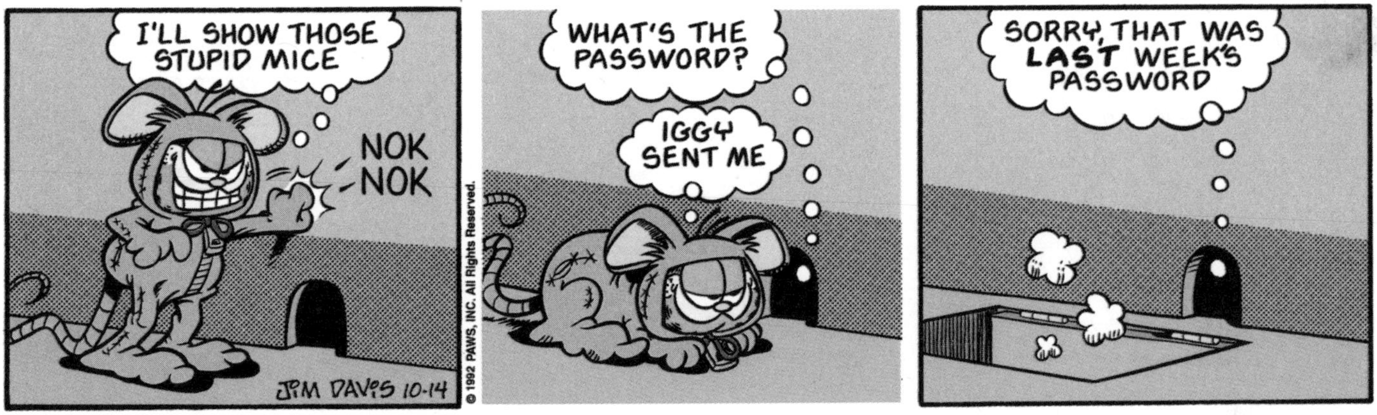
I'LL SHOW THOSE STUPID MICE
NOK NOK
JIM DAVIS 10-14
© 1992 PAWS, INC. All Rights Reserved.
WHAT'S THE PASSWORD?
IGGY SENT ME
SORRY, THAT WAS LAST WEEK'S PASSWORD

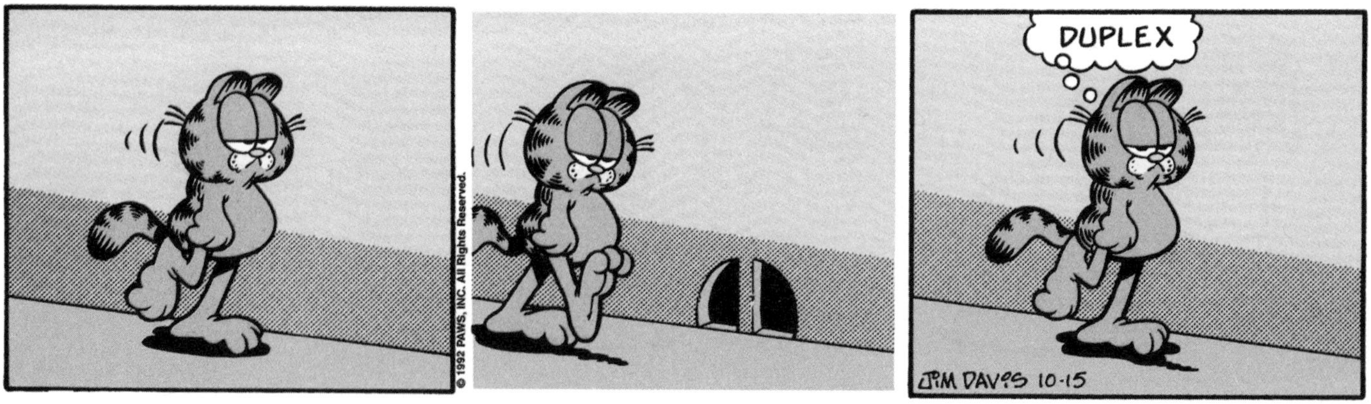
© 1992 PAWS, INC. All Rights Reserved.
DUPLEX
JIM DAVIS 10-15

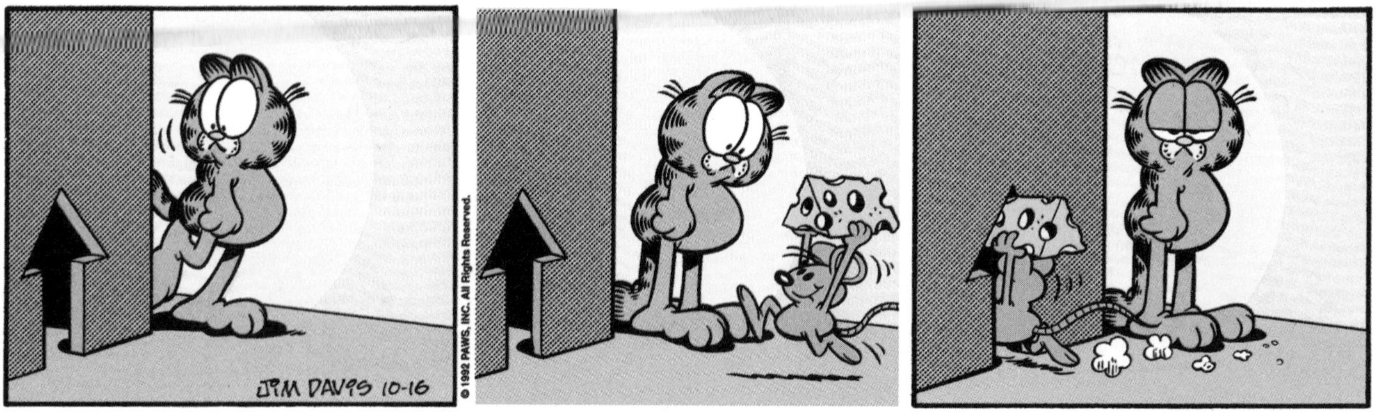
JIM DAVIS 10-16
© 1992 PAWS, INC. All Rights Reserved.

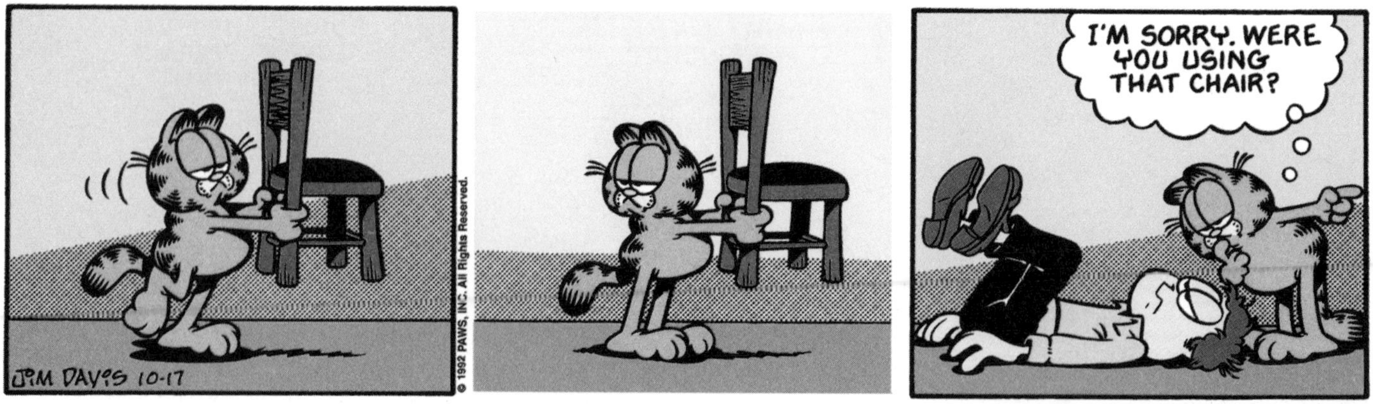
JIM DAVIS 10-17
© 1992 PAWS, INC. All Rights Reserved.
I'M SORRY. WERE YOU USING THAT CHAIR?

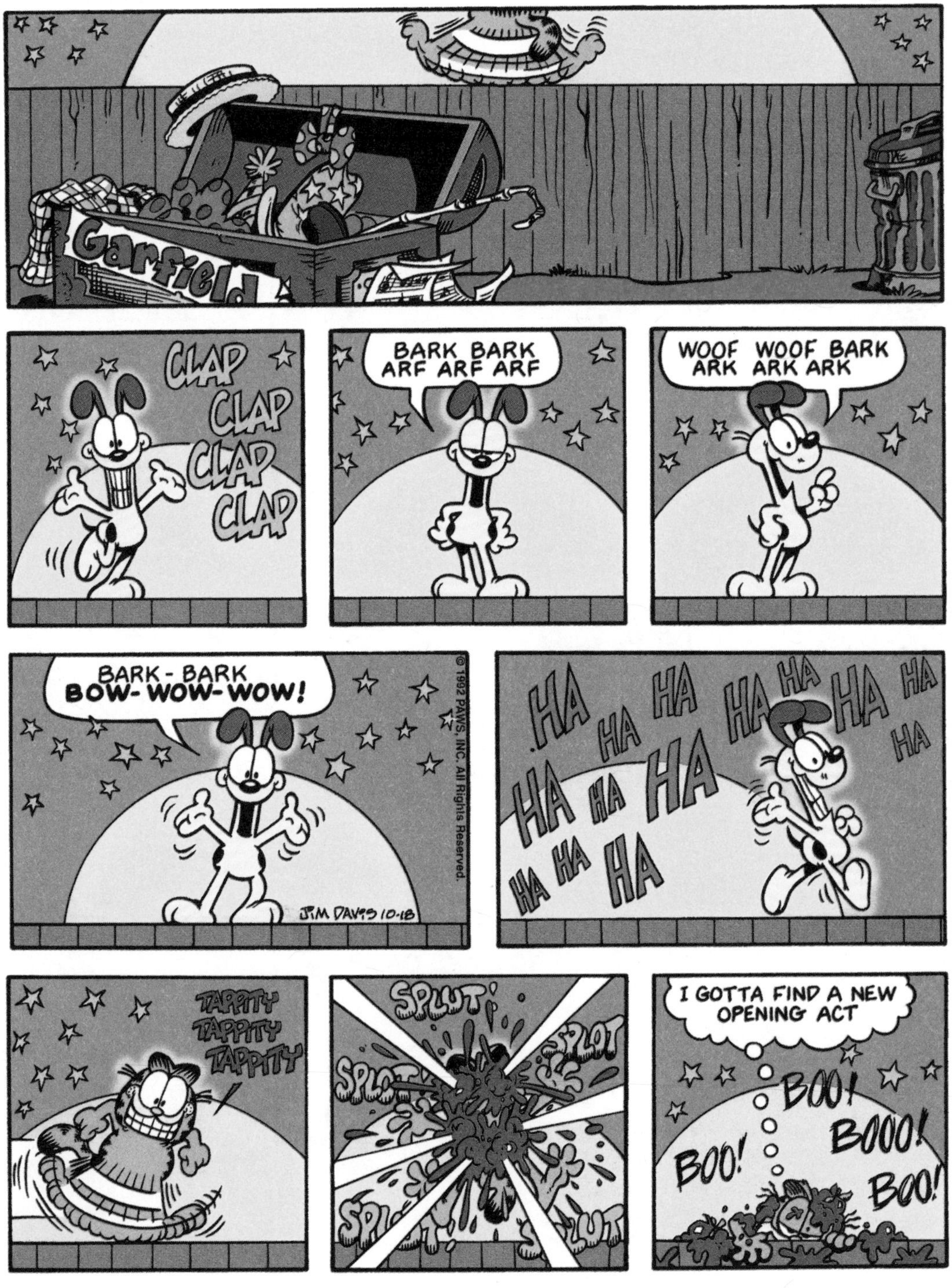

Garfield
CLAP CLAP CLAP CLAP
BARK BARK ARF ARF ARF
WOOF WOOF BARK ARK ARK ARK
BARK - BARK BOW- WOW- WOW!
© 1992 PAWS, INC. All Rights Reserved.
JIM DAVIS 10-18
HA HA HA HA HA HA HA HA HA HA HA HA HA HA HA HA
TAPPITY TAPPITY TAPPITY
SPLUT! SPLOT SPLOT SPLUT SPLUT
I GOTTA FIND A NEW OPENING ACT
BOO! BOO! BOOO! BOO!

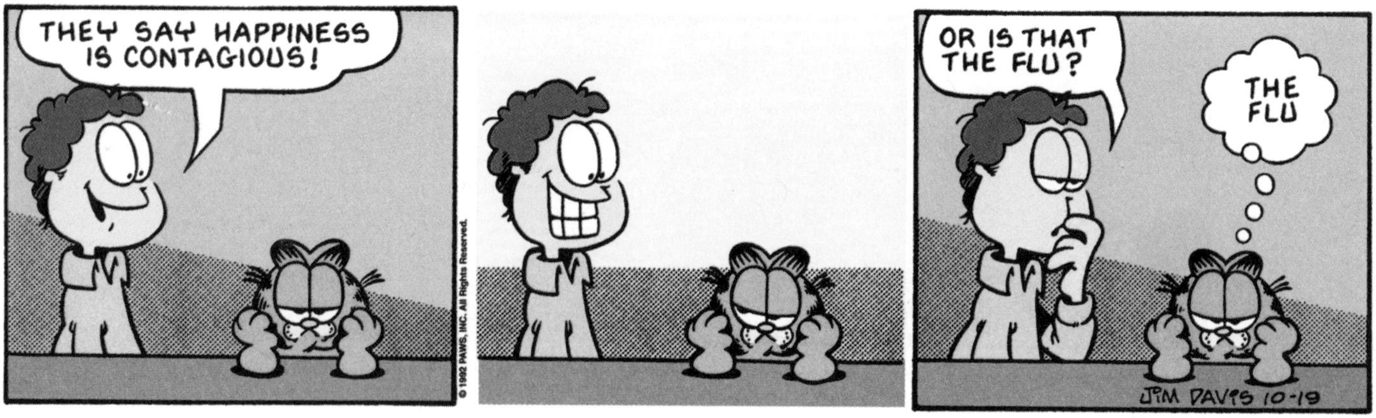
THEY SAY HAPPINESS IS CONTAGIOUS!
© 1992 PAWS, INC. All Rights Reserved.
OR IS THAT THE FLU?
THE FLU
JIM DAVIS 10-19

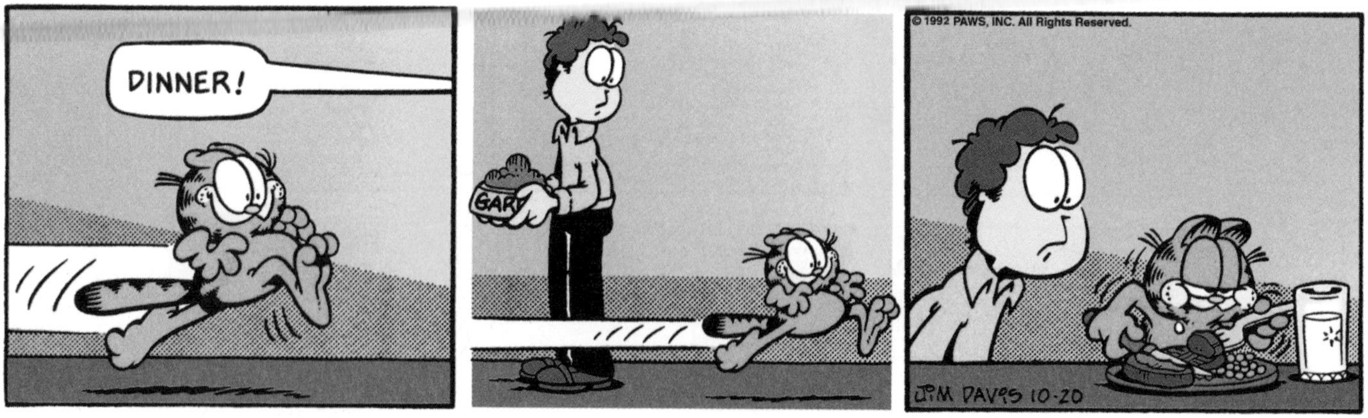
DINNER!
GAR
© 1992 PAWS, INC. All Rights Reserved.
JIM DAVIS 10-20

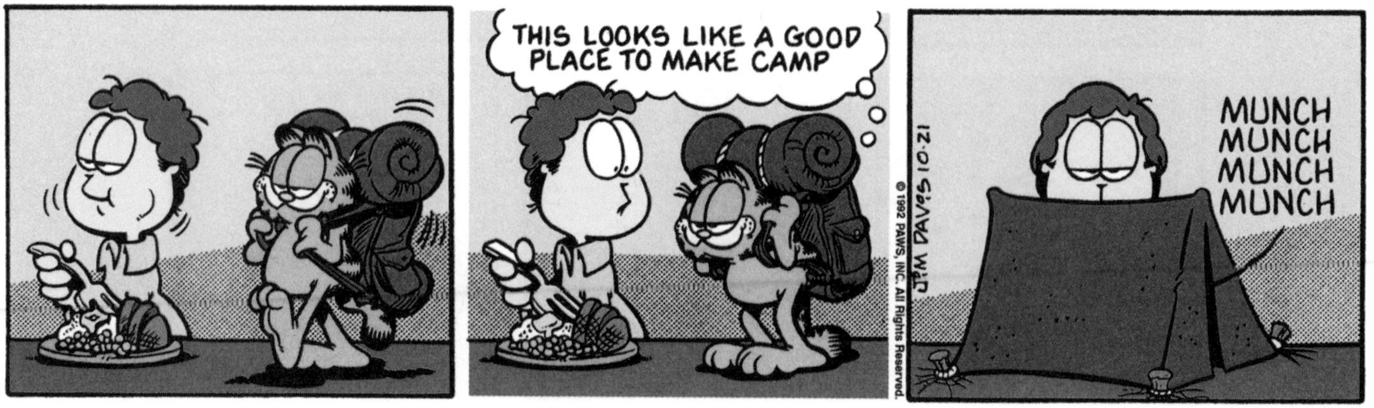
THIS LOOKS LIKE A GOOD PLACE TO MAKE CAMP
© 1992 PAWS, INC. All Rights Reserved.
JIM DAVIS 10-21
MUNCH
MUNCH
MUNCH
MUNCH

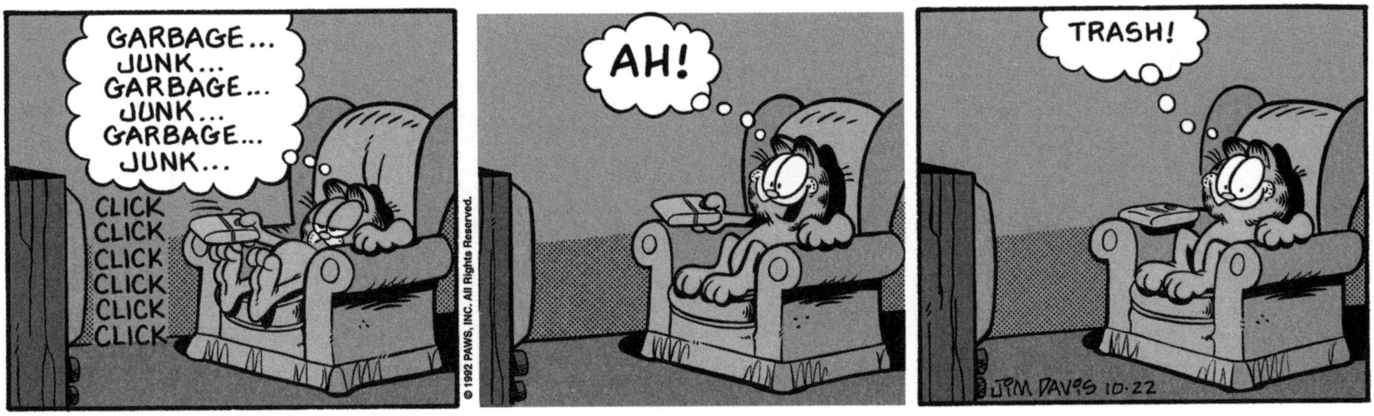
GARBAGE... JUNK... GARBAGE... JUNK... GARBAGE... JUNK...
CLICK CLICK CLICK CLICK CLICK CLICK
© 1992 PAWS, INC. All Rights Reserved.
AH!
TRASH!
JIM DAVIS 10·22

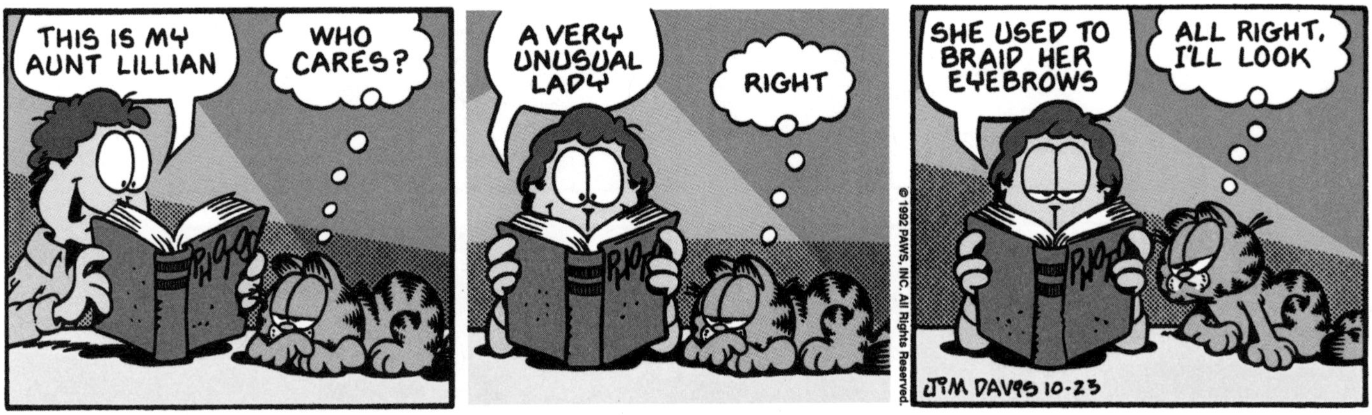
THIS IS MY AUNT LILLIAN
WHO CARES?
PHOTOS
A VERY UNUSUAL LADY
RIGHT
© 1992 PAWS, INC. All Rights Reserved.
SHE USED TO BRAID HER EYEBROWS
ALL RIGHT, I'LL LOOK
JIM DAVIS 10·23

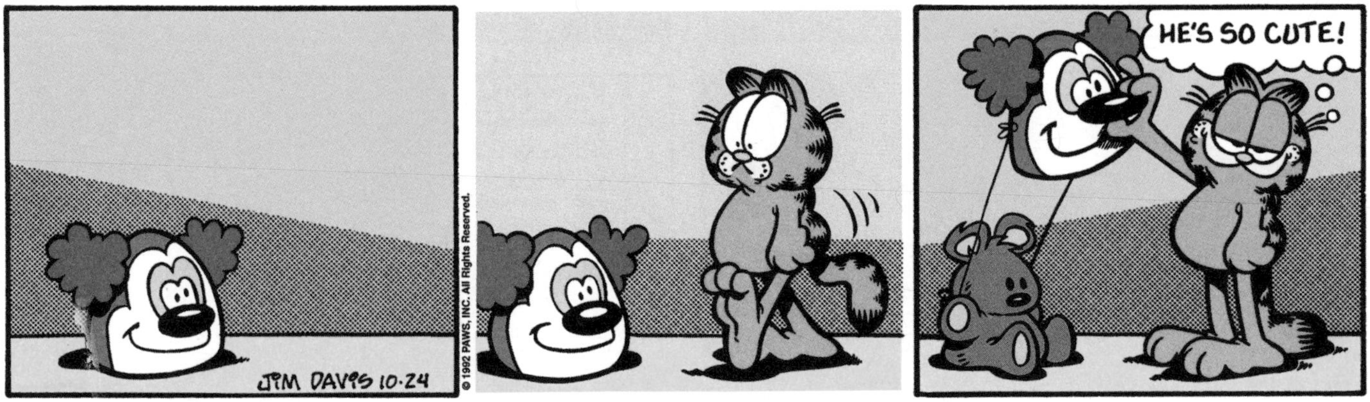
JIM DAVIS 10·24
© 1992 PAWS, INC. All Rights Reserved.
HE'S SO CUTE!

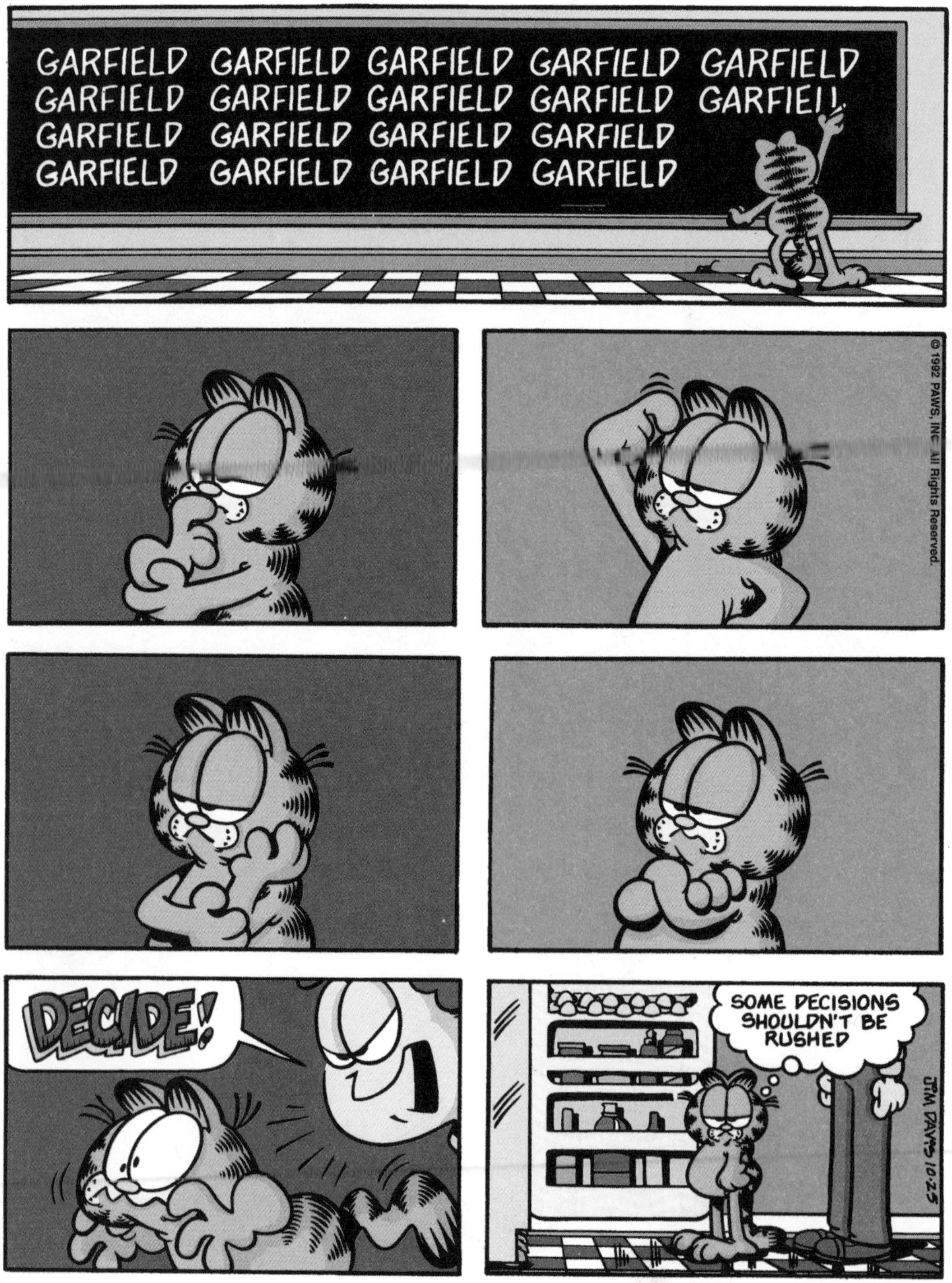
GARFIELD GARFIELD GARFIELD GARFIELD GARFIELD
GARFIELD GARFIELD GARFIELD GARFIELD GARFIEL
GARFIELD GARFIELD GARFIELD GARFIELD
GARFIELD GARFIELD GARFIELD GARFIELD
© 1992 PAWS, INC. All Rights Reserved.
DECIDE!
SOME DECISIONS SHOULDN'T BE RUSHED
JIM DAVIS 10-25

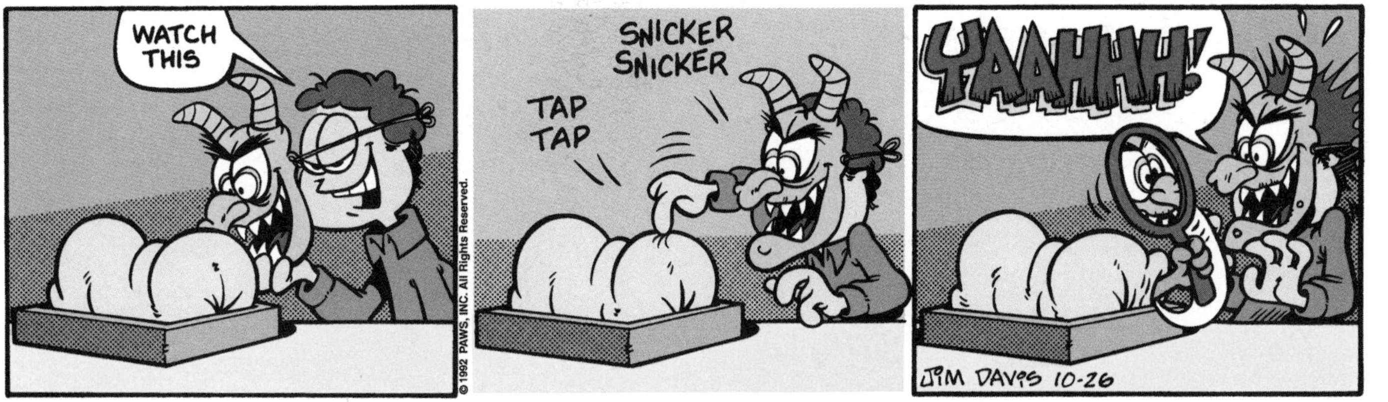
WATCH THIS
TAP TAP
SNICKER SNICKER
YAAHHH!
© 1992 PAWS, INC. All Rights Reserved.
JIM DAVIS 10-26

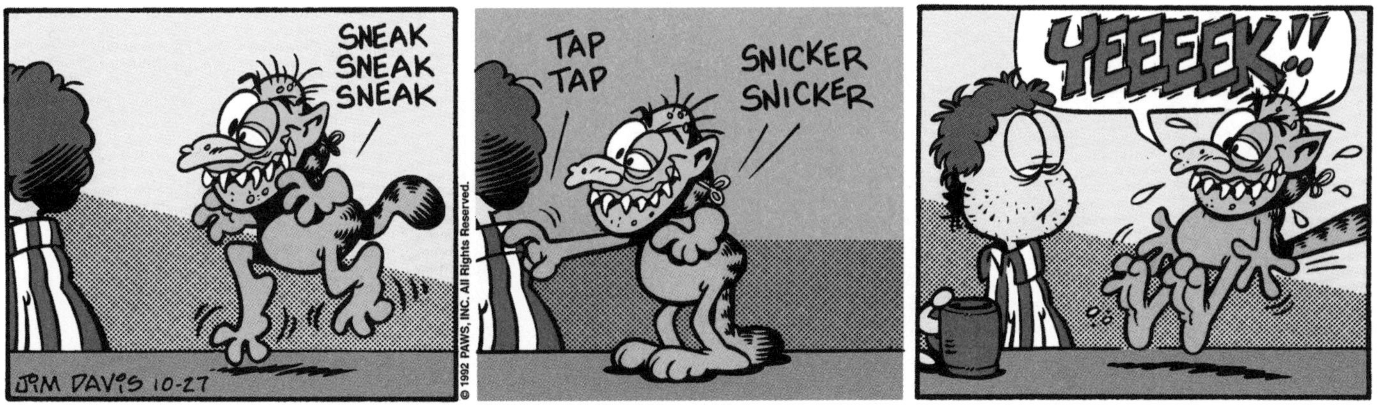
SNEAK SNEAK SNEAK
JIM DAVIS 10-27
TAP TAP
SNICKER SNICKER
YEEEEK!!
© 1992 PAWS, INC. All Rights Reserved.

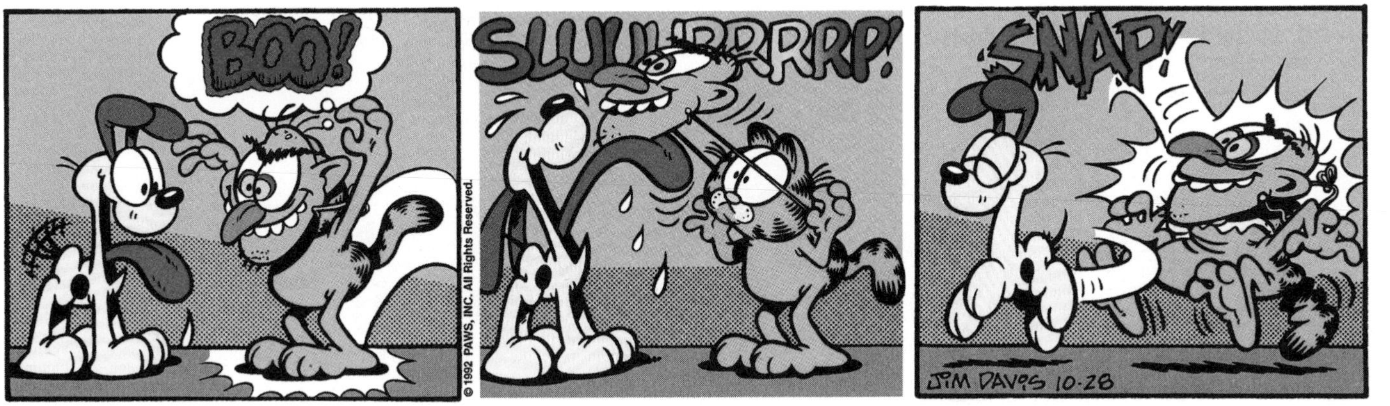
BOO!
SLUUURRRRP!
SNAP!
© 1992 PAWS, INC. All Rights Reserved.
JIM DAVIS 10-28

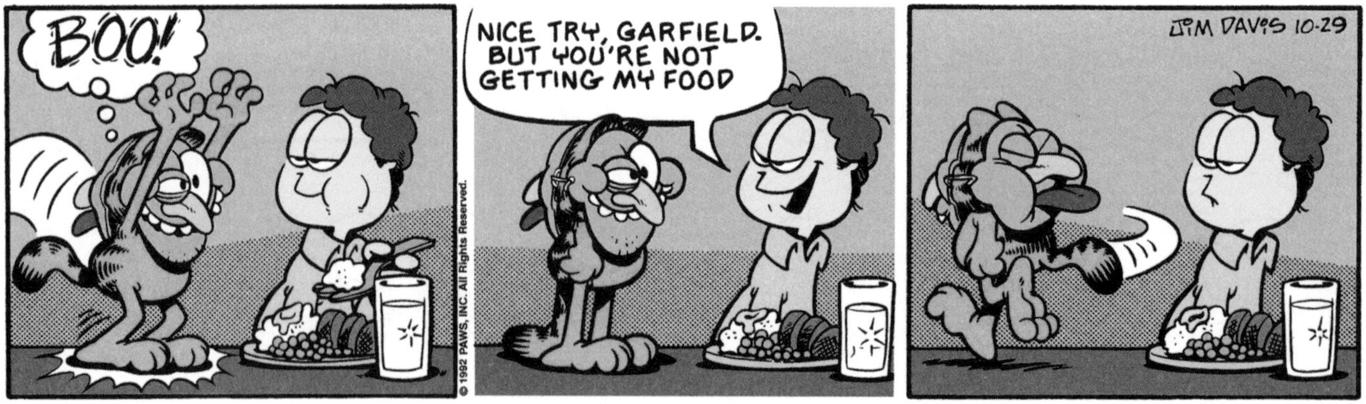
BOO!
NICE TRY, GARFIELD. BUT YOU'RE NOT GETTING MY FOOD
© 1992 PAWS, INC. All Rights Reserved.
JIM DAVIS 10-29

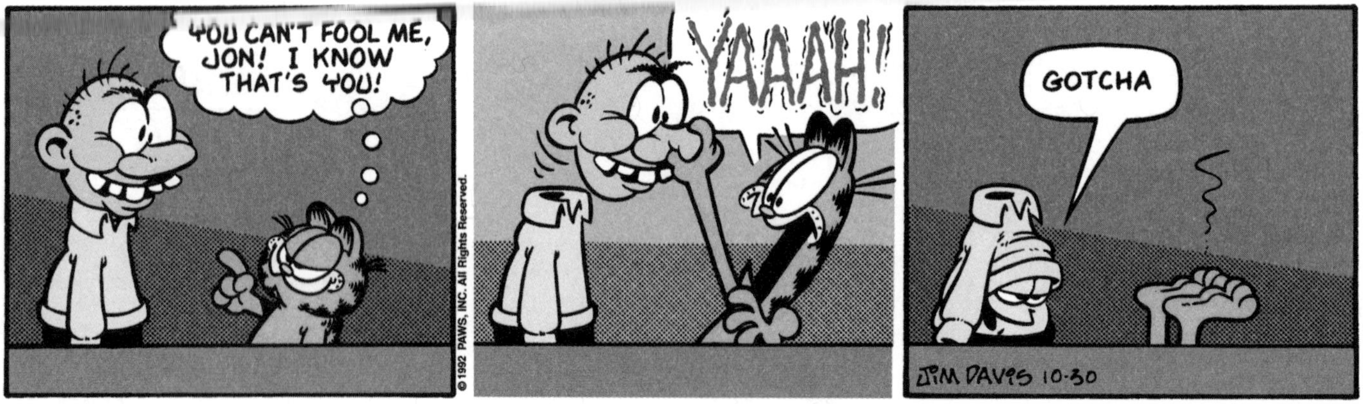
YOU CAN'T FOOL ME, JON! I KNOW THAT'S YOU!
YAAAH!
GOTCHA
© 1992 PAWS, INC. All Rights Reserved.
JIM DAVIS 10-30

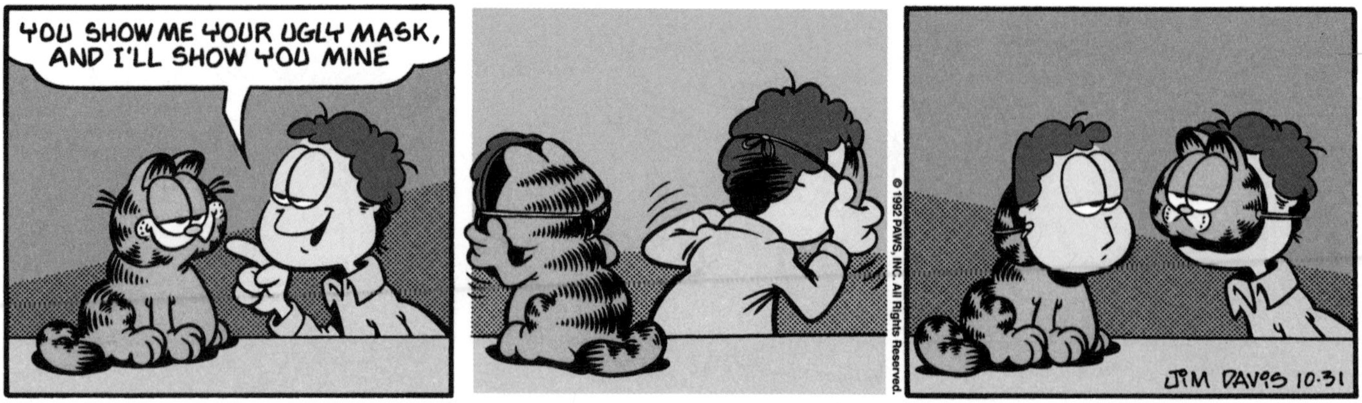
YOU SHOW ME YOUR UGLY MASK, AND I'LL SHOW YOU MINE
© 1992 PAWS, INC. All Rights Reserved.
JIM DAVIS 10-31

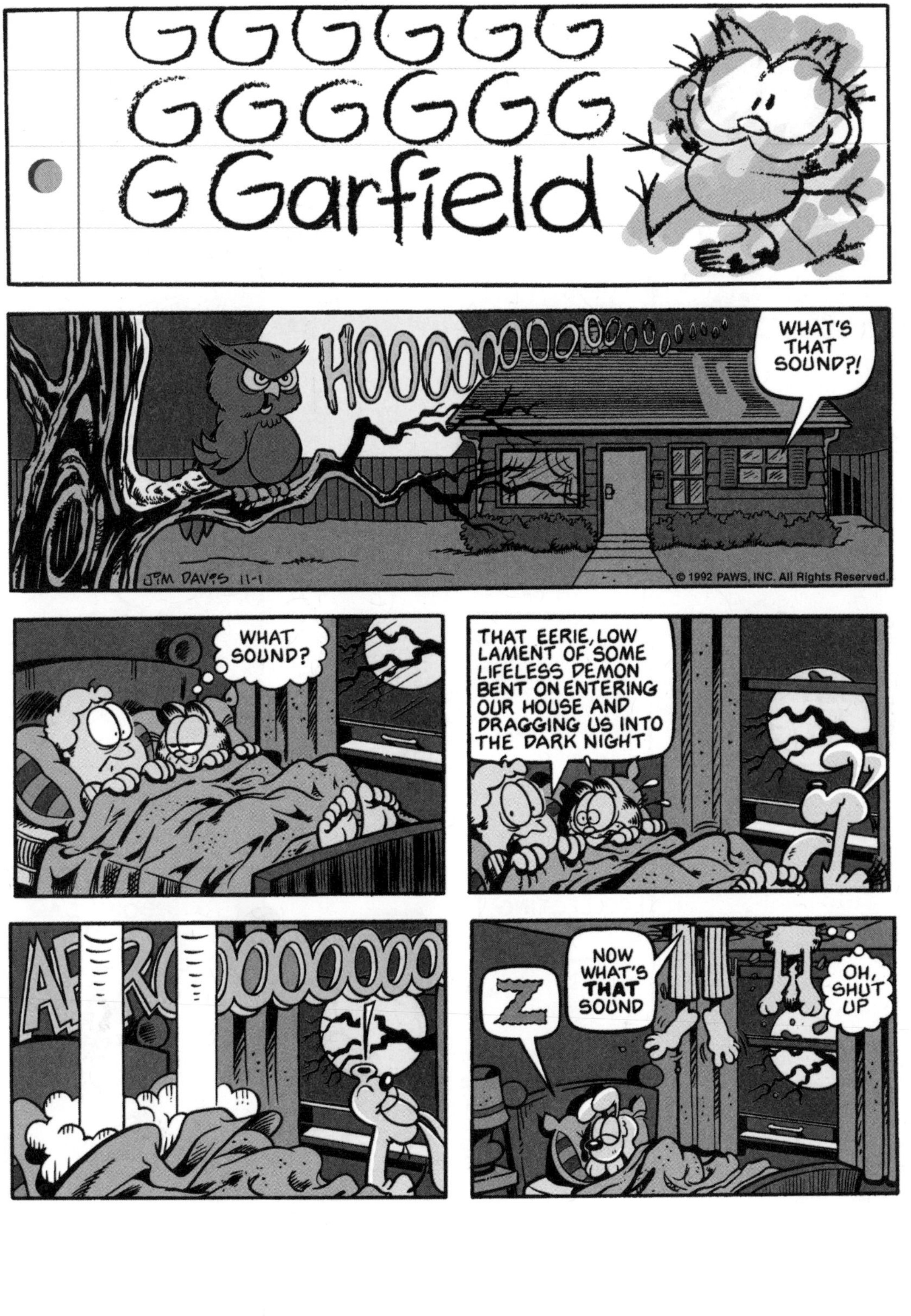
GGGGGG
GGGGGG
G Garfield
HOOOOOOOOOOOOOOOOOO
WHAT'S THAT SOUND?!
JIM DAVIS 11-1
© 1992 PAWS, INC. All Rights Reserved.
WHAT SOUND?
THAT EERIE, LOW LAMENT OF SOME LIFELESS DEMON BENT ON ENTERING OUR HOUSE AND DRAGGING US INTO THE DARK NIGHT
AROOOOOOOOO
Z
NOW WHAT'S THAT SOUND
OH, SHUT UP

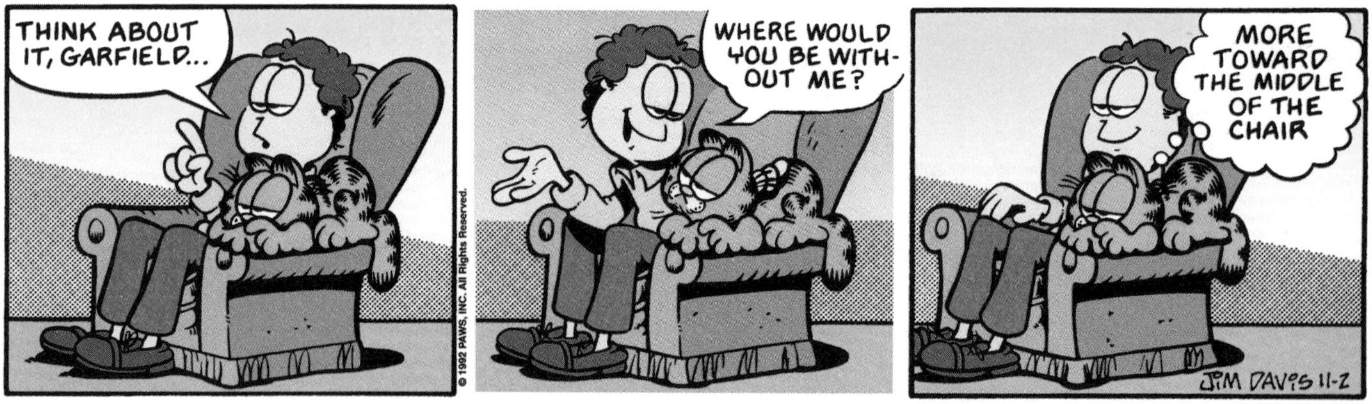
THINK ABOUT IT, GARFIELD...
WHERE WOULD YOU BE WITH-OUT ME?
MORE TOWARD THE MIDDLE OF THE CHAIR
© 1992 PAWS, INC. All Rights Reserved.
JIM DAVIS 11-2

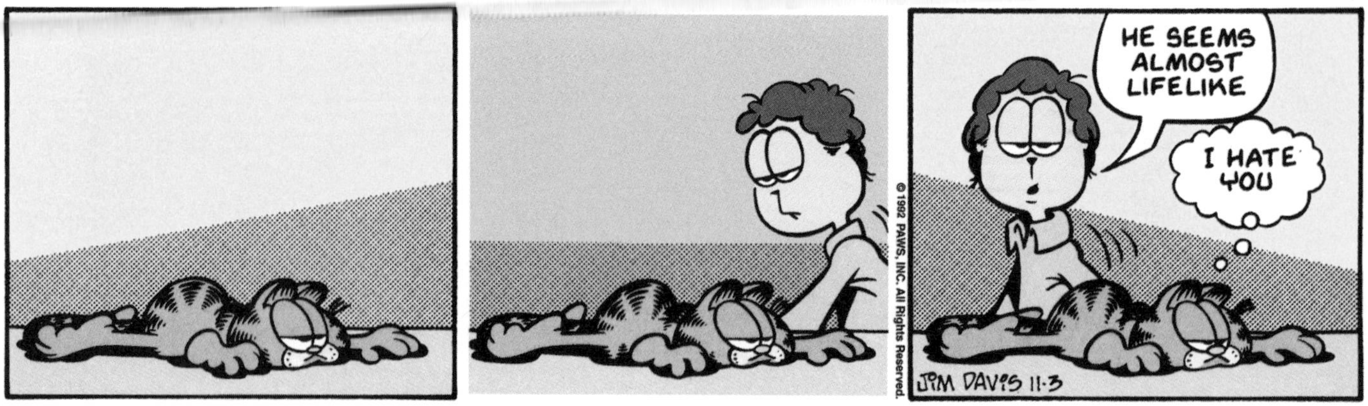
HE SEEMS ALMOST LIFELIKE
I HATE YOU
© 1992 PAWS, INC. All Rights Reserved.
JIM DAVIS 11-3

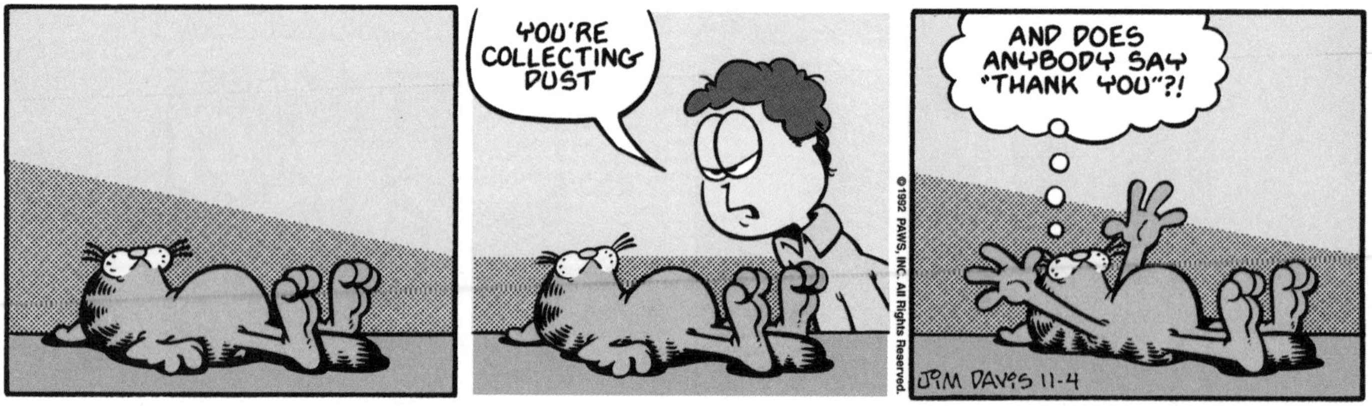
YOU'RE COLLECTING DUST
AND DOES ANYBODY SAY "THANK YOU"?!
© 1992 PAWS, INC. All Rights Reserved.
JIM DAVIS 11-4

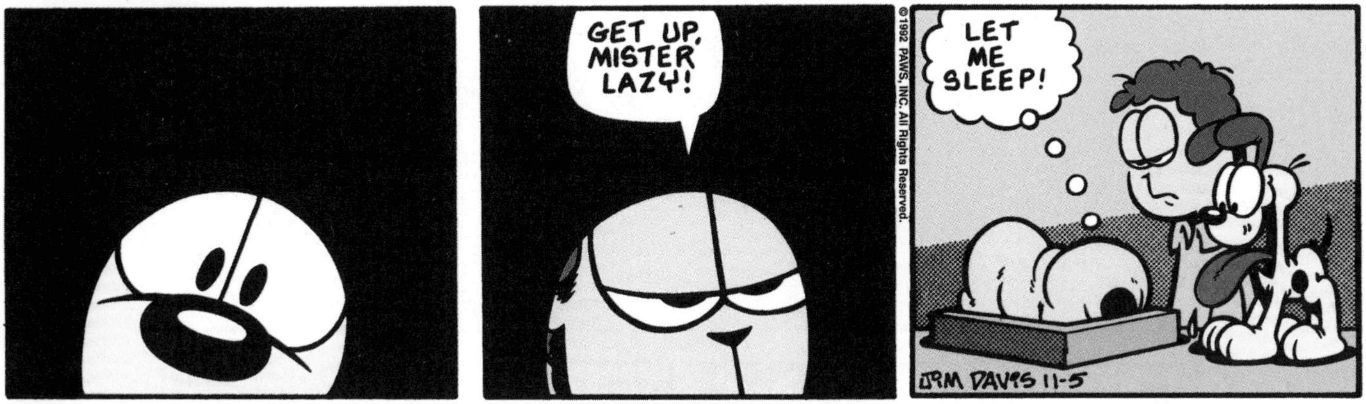
GET UP, MISTER LAZY!
LET ME SLEEP!
JIM DAVIS 11-5

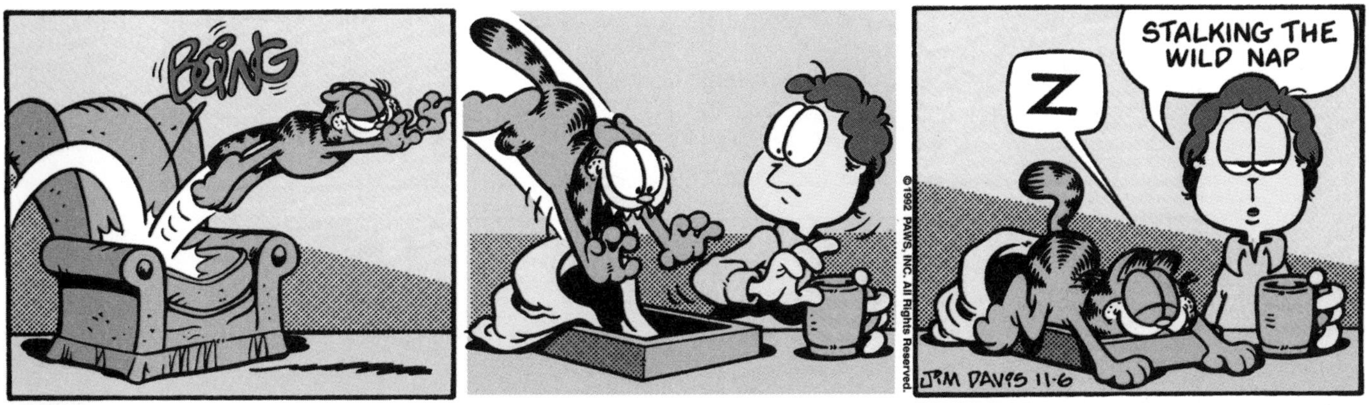
BOING
Z
STALKING THE WILD NAP
JIM DAVIS 11-6

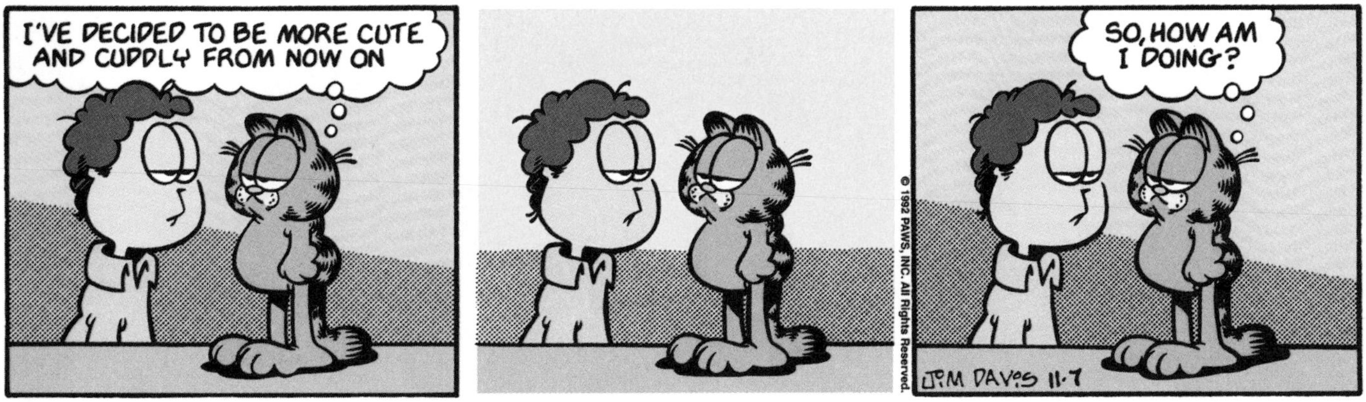
I'VE DECIDED TO BE MORE CUTE AND CUDDLY FROM NOW ON
SO, HOW AM I DOING?
JIM DAVIS 11-7

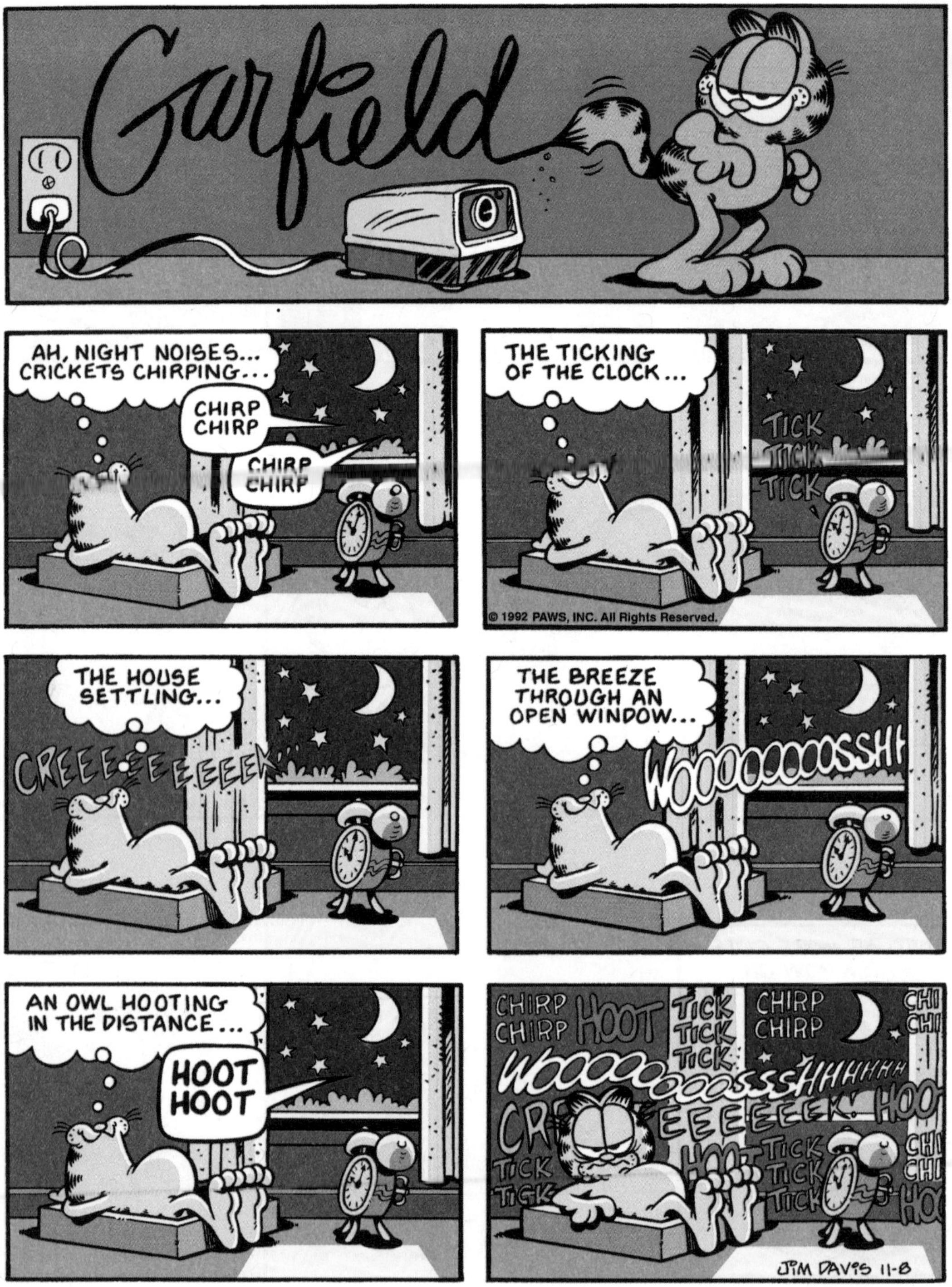
Garfield
AH, NIGHT NOISES... CRICKETS CHIRPING...
CHIRP CHIRP
CHIRP CHIRP
THE TICKING OF THE CLOCK...
TICK TICK TICK
© 1992 PAWS, INC. All Rights Reserved.
THE HOUSE SETTLING...
CREEEEEEEEEK...
THE BREEZE THROUGH AN OPEN WINDOW...
WOOOOOOOOOSSH
AN OWL HOOTING IN THE DISTANCE...
HOOT HOOT
CHIRP CHIRP
HOOT
TICK TICK TICK
CHIRP CHIRP
WOOOOOOOOOSSSHHHHHH
TICK TICK TICK
TICK TICK
JIM DAVIS 11-8

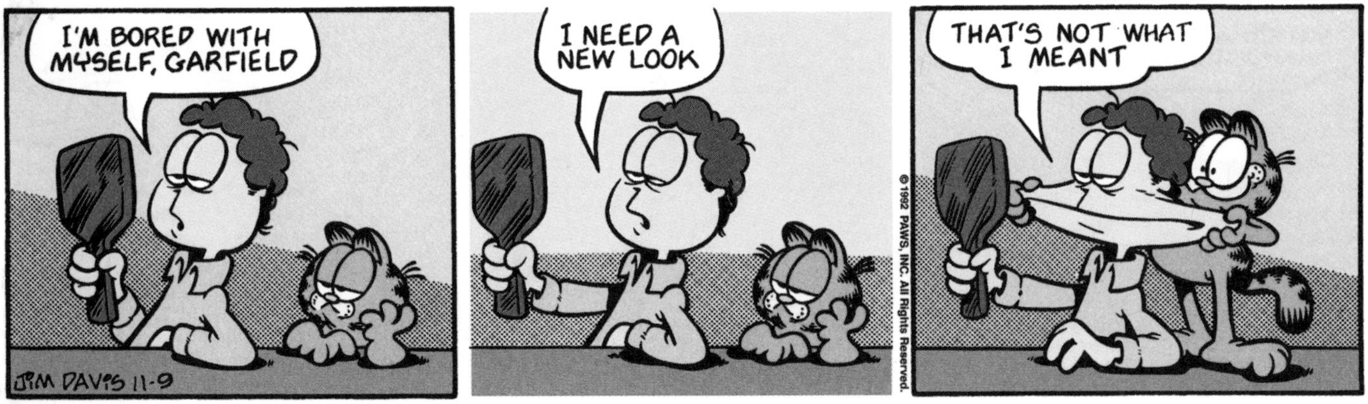
I'M BORED WITH MYSELF, GARFIELD
JIM DAVIS 11-9
I NEED A NEW LOOK
© 1992 PAWS, INC. All Rights Reserved.
THAT'S NOT WHAT I MEANT

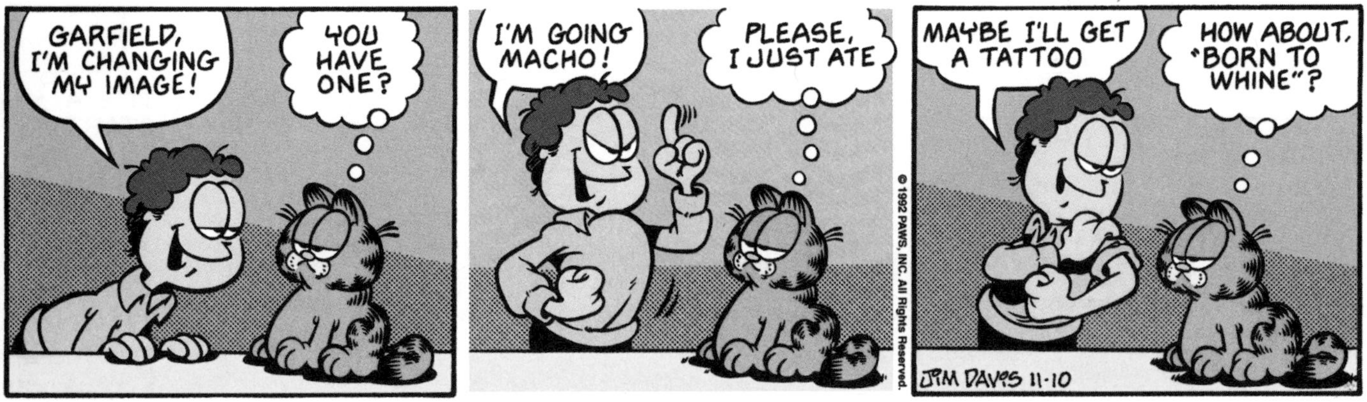
GARFIELD, I'M CHANGING MY IMAGE!
YOU HAVE ONE?
I'M GOING MACHO!
PLEASE, I JUST ATE
© 1992 PAWS, INC. All Rights Reserved.
MAYBE I'LL GET A TATTOO
HOW ABOUT, "BORN TO WHINE"?
JIM DAVIS 11-10

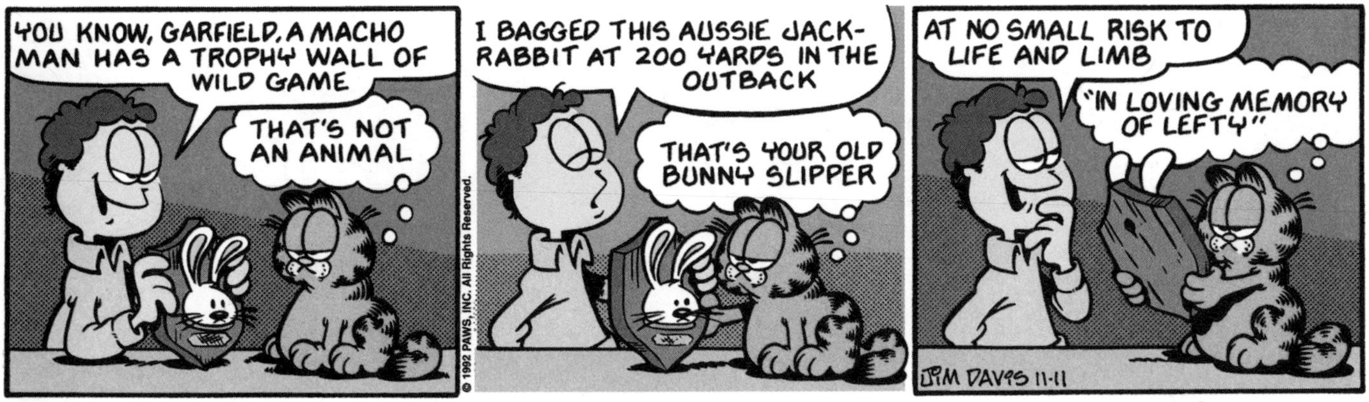
YOU KNOW, GARFIELD, A MACHO MAN HAS A TROPHY WALL OF WILD GAME
THAT'S NOT AN ANIMAL
© 1992 PAWS, INC. All Rights Reserved.
I BAGGED THIS AUSSIE JACK-RABBIT AT 200 YARDS IN THE OUTBACK
THAT'S YOUR OLD BUNNY SLIPPER
AT NO SMALL RISK TO LIFE AND LIMB
"IN LOVING MEMORY OF LEFTY"
JIM DAVIS 11-11

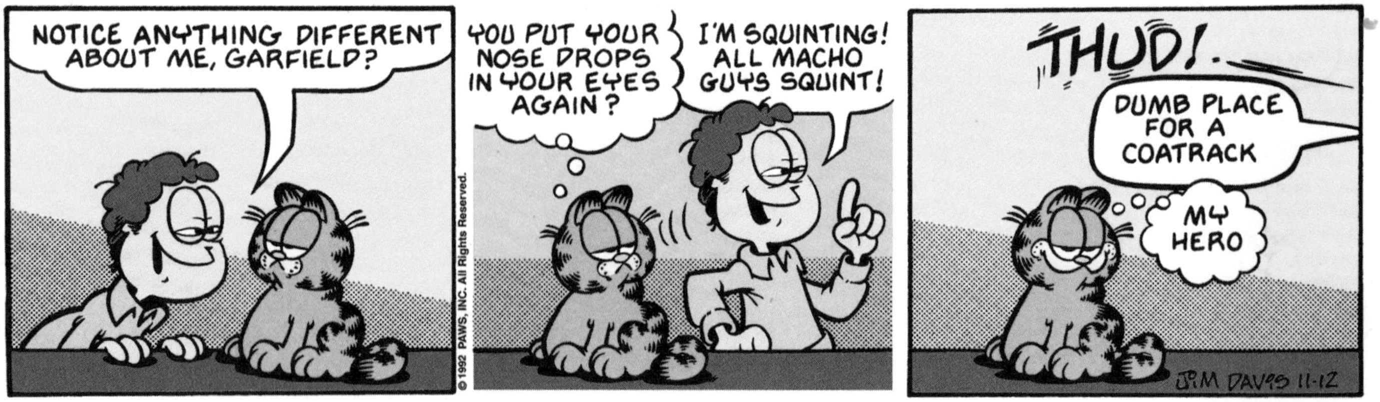
NOTICE ANYTHING DIFFERENT ABOUT ME, GARFIELD?
YOU PUT YOUR NOSE DROPS IN YOUR EYES AGAIN?
I'M SQUINTING! ALL MACHO GUYS SQUINT!
© 1992 PAWS, INC. All Rights Reserved.
THUD!
DUMB PLACE FOR A COATRACK
MY HERO
JIM DAVIS 11-12

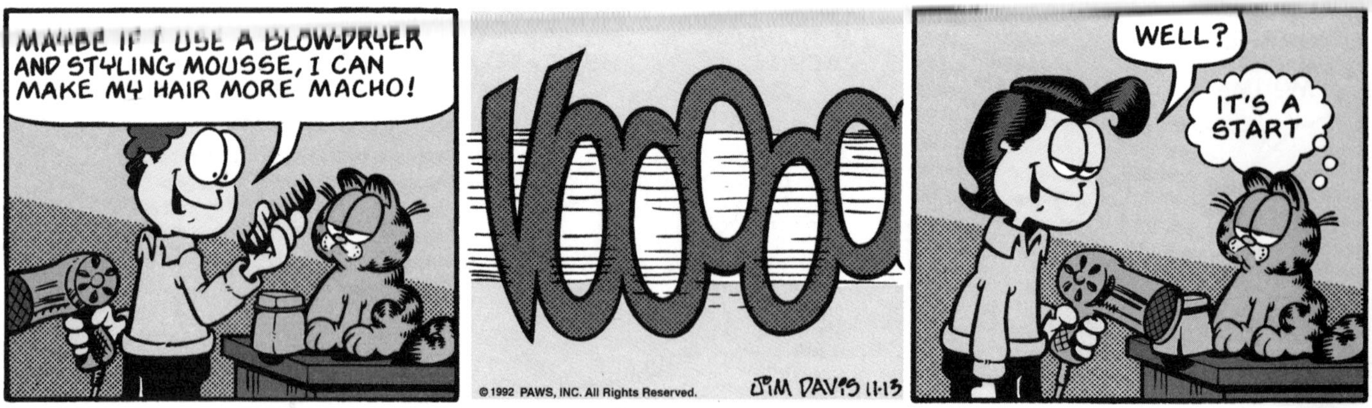
MAYBE IF I USE A BLOW-DRYER AND STYLING MOUSSE, I CAN MAKE MY HAIR MORE MACHO!
VOOOOO
© 1992 PAWS, INC. All Rights Reserved.
JIM DAVIS 11-13
WELL?
IT'S A START

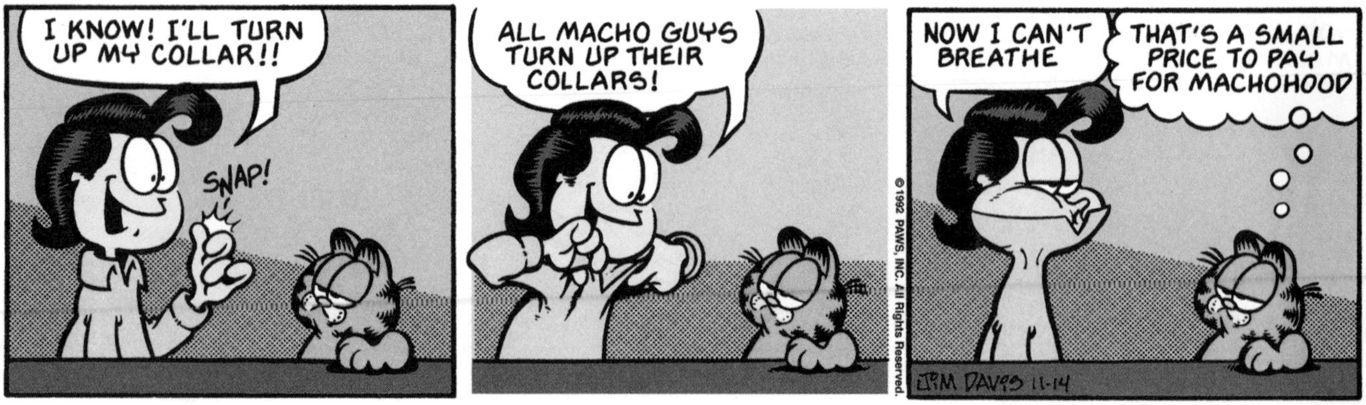
I KNOW! I'LL TURN UP MY COLLAR!!
SNAP!
ALL MACHO GUYS TURN UP THEIR COLLARS!
© 1992 PAWS, INC. All Rights Reserved.
NOW I CAN'T BREATHE
THAT'S A SMALL PRICE TO PAY FOR MACHOHOOD
JIM DAVIS 11-14

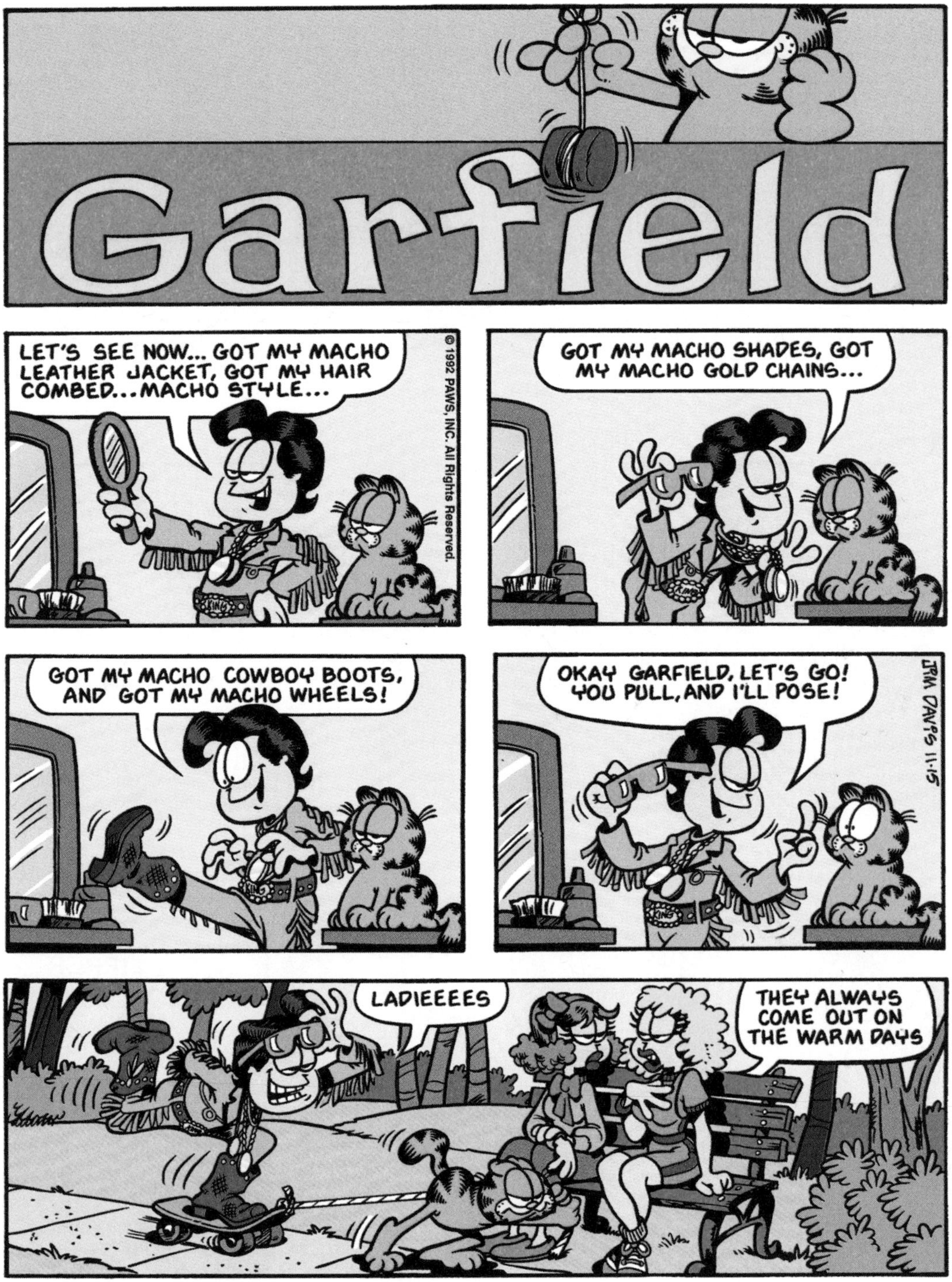
Garfield
LET'S SEE NOW... GOT MY MACHO LEATHER JACKET, GOT MY HAIR COMBED...MACHO STYLE...
© 1992 PAWS, INC. All Rights Reserved.
GOT MY MACHO SHADES, GOT MY MACHO GOLD CHAINS...
GOT MY MACHO COWBOY BOOTS, AND GOT MY MACHO WHEELS!
OKAY GARFIELD, LET'S GO! YOU PULL, AND I'LL POSE!
JPM DAVIS 11-15
LADIEEEES
THEY ALWAYS COME OUT ON THE WARM DAYS

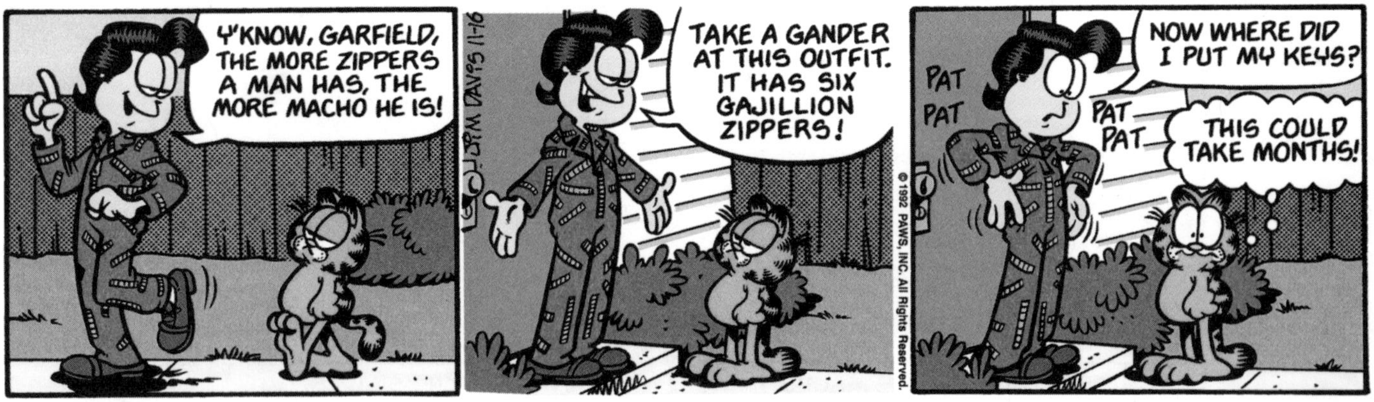

Y'KNOW, GARFIELD, THE MORE ZIPPERS A MAN HAS, THE MORE MACHO HE IS!
JIM DAVIS 11-16
TAKE A GANDER AT THIS OUTFIT. IT HAS SIX GAJILLION ZIPPERS!
© 1992 PAWS, INC. All Rights Reserved.
PAT PAT
NOW WHERE DID I PUT MY KEYS?
PAT PAT
THIS COULD TAKE MONTHS!

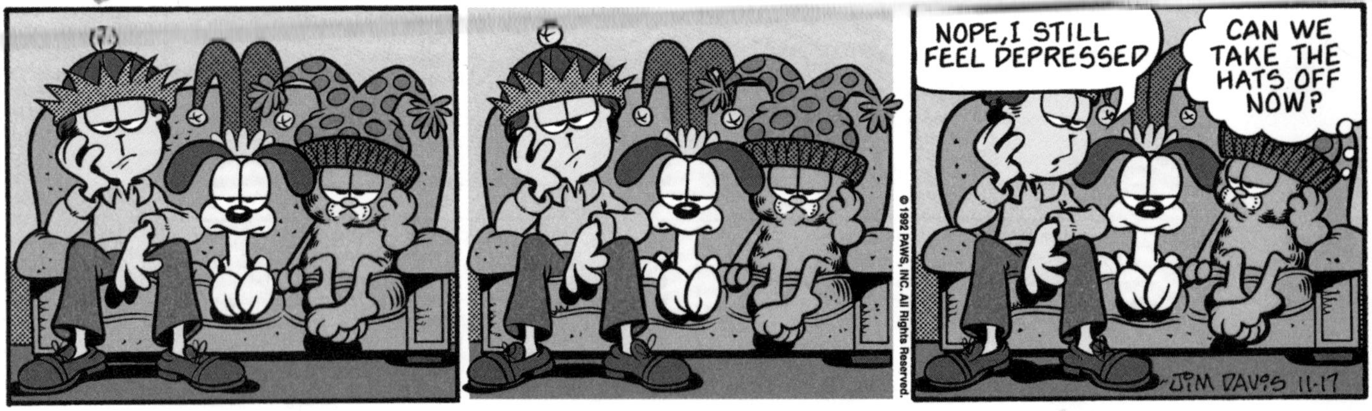

© 1992 PAWS, INC. All Rights Reserved.
NOPE, I STILL FEEL DEPRESSED
CAN WE TAKE THE HATS OFF NOW?
JIM DAVIS 11-17

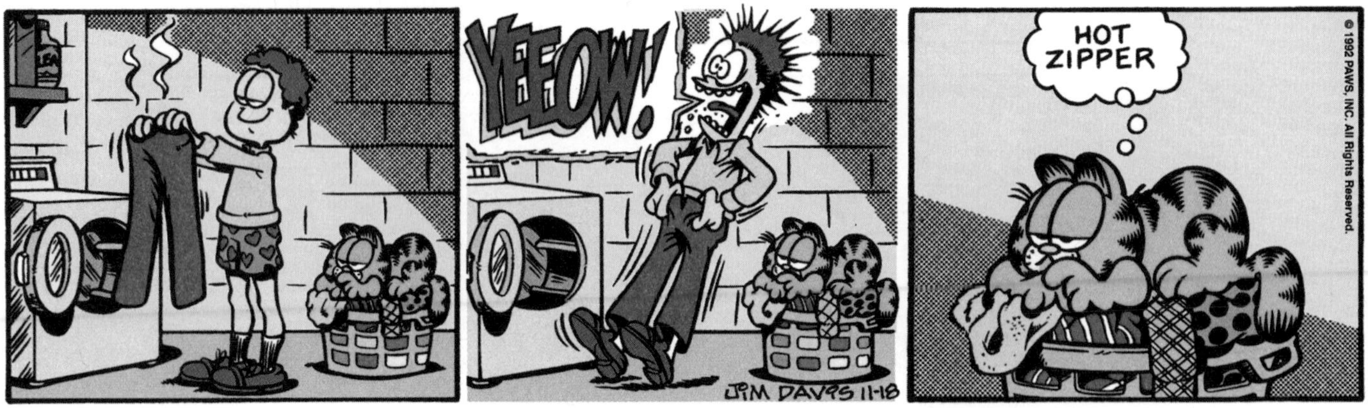

YEEOW!
JIM DAVIS 11-18
HOT ZIPPER
© 1992 PAWS, INC. All Rights Reserved.

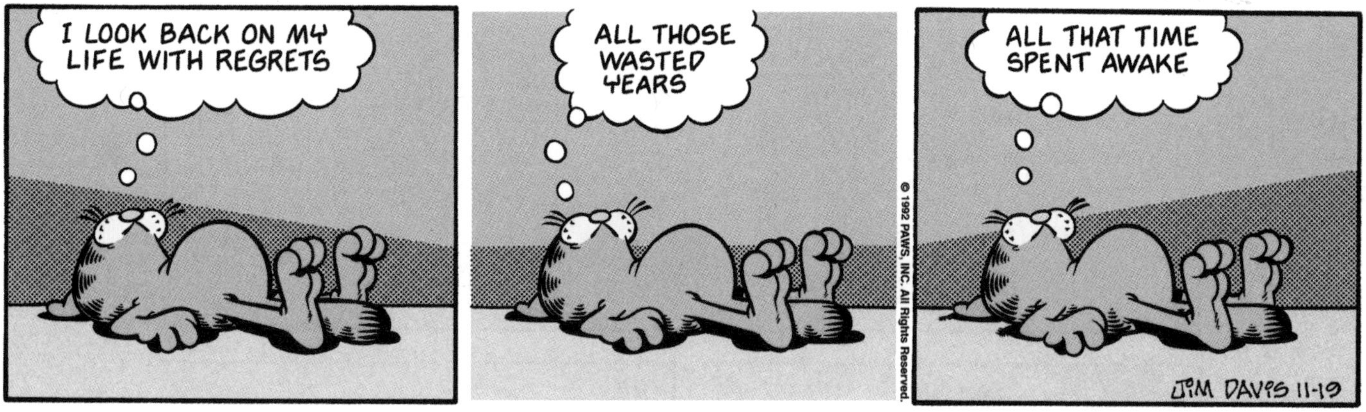
I LOOK BACK ON MY LIFE WITH REGRETS
ALL THOSE WASTED YEARS
© 1992 PAWS, INC. All Rights Reserved.
ALL THAT TIME SPENT AWAKE
JIM DAVIS 11-19

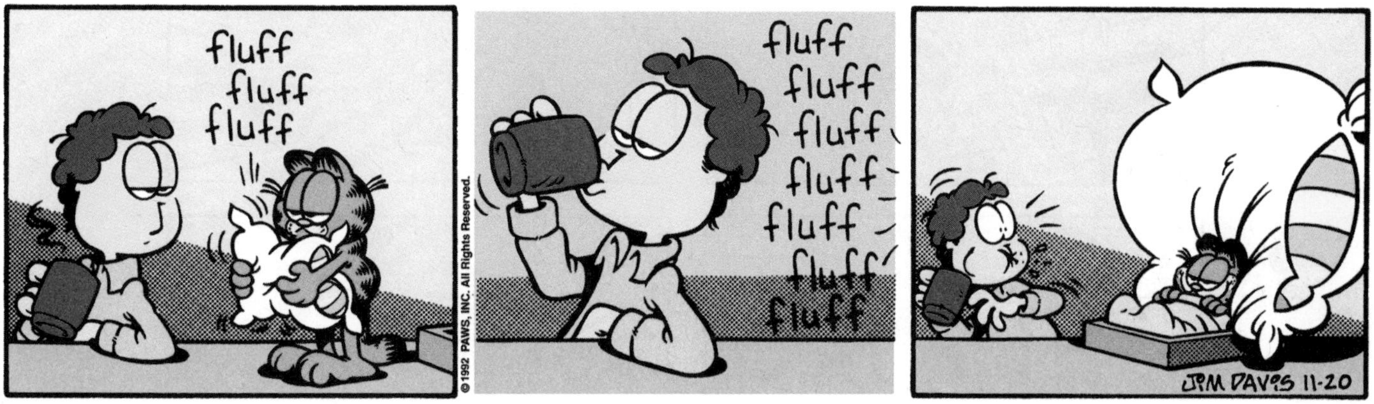
fluff fluff fluff
© 1992 PAWS, INC. All Rights Reserved.
fluff fluff fluff fluff fluff fluff fluff
JIM DAVIS 11-20

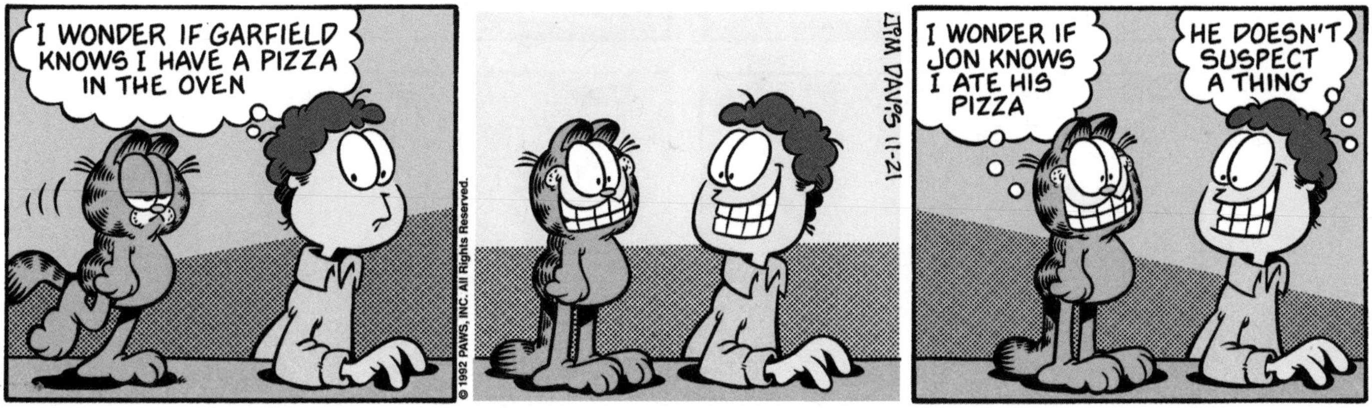
I WONDER IF GARFIELD KNOWS I HAVE A PIZZA IN THE OVEN
© 1992 PAWS, INC. All Rights Reserved.
JIM DAVIS 11-21
I WONDER IF JON KNOWS I ATE HIS PIZZA
HE DOESN'T SUSPECT A THING

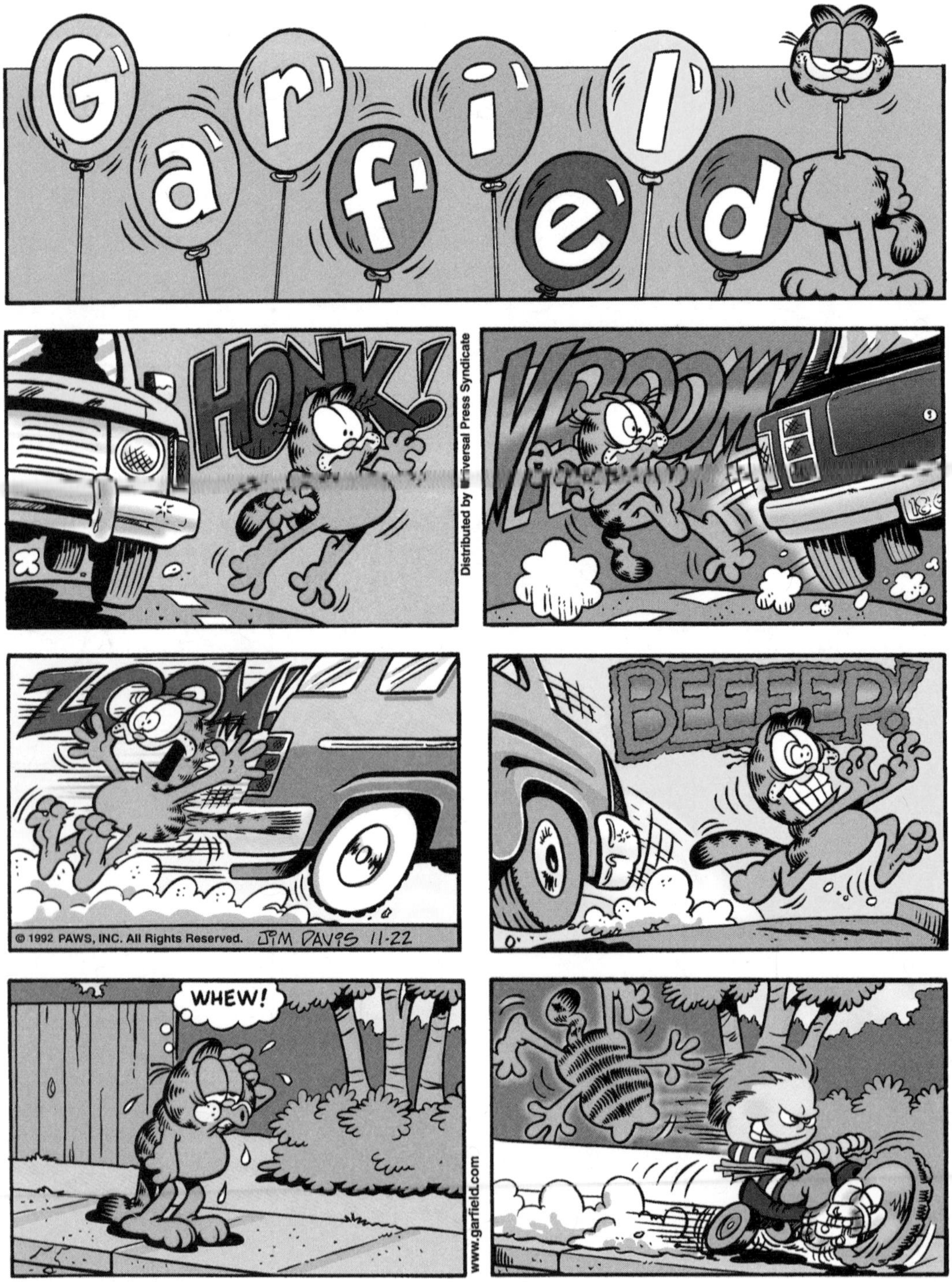
Garfield
HONK!
VROOOM!
ZOOM!
BEEEEP!
WHEW!
Distributed by Universal Press Syndicate
© 1992 PAWS, INC. All Rights Reserved.
JIM DAVIS 11-22
www.garfield.com

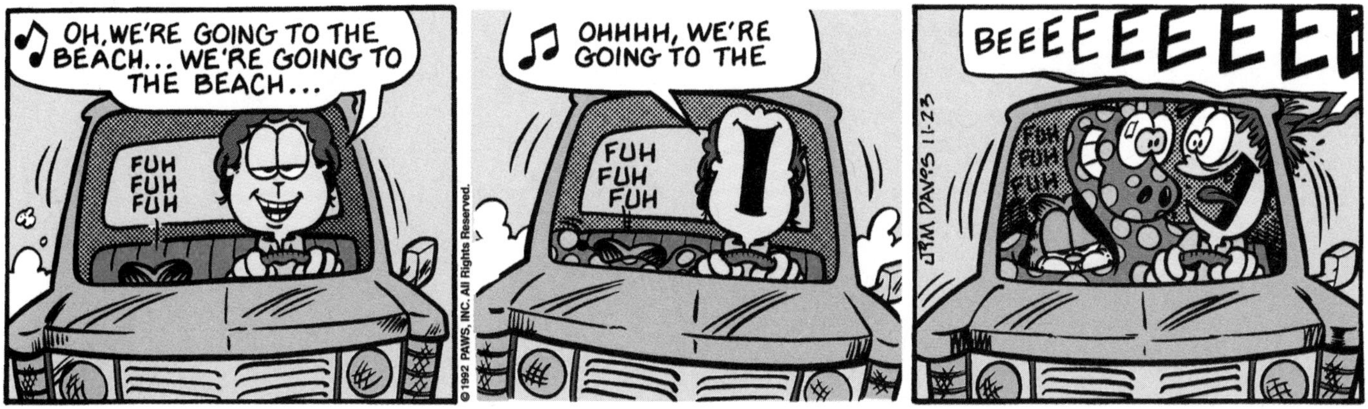
♪ OH, WE'RE GOING TO THE BEACH... WE'RE GOING TO THE BEACH...
FUH FUH FUH
© 1992 PAWS, INC. All Rights Reserved.
♫ OHHHH, WE'RE GOING TO THE
FUH FUH FUH
BEEEEEEEEE
FUH FUH FUH
JIM DAVIS 11-23

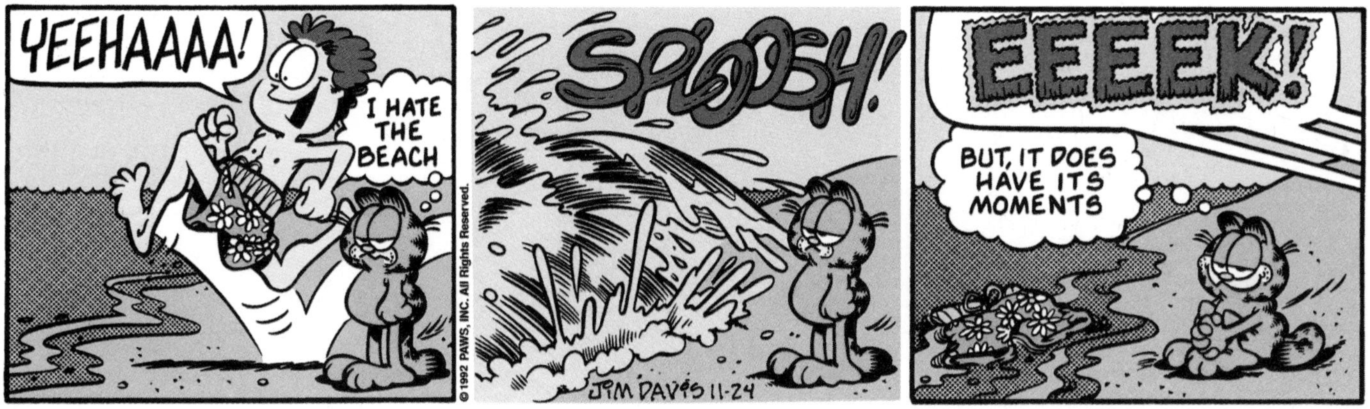
YEEHAAAA!
I HATE THE BEACH
© 1992 PAWS, INC. All Rights Reserved.
SPLOOSH!
JIM DAVIS 11-24
EEEEK!
BUT, IT DOES HAVE ITS MOMENTS

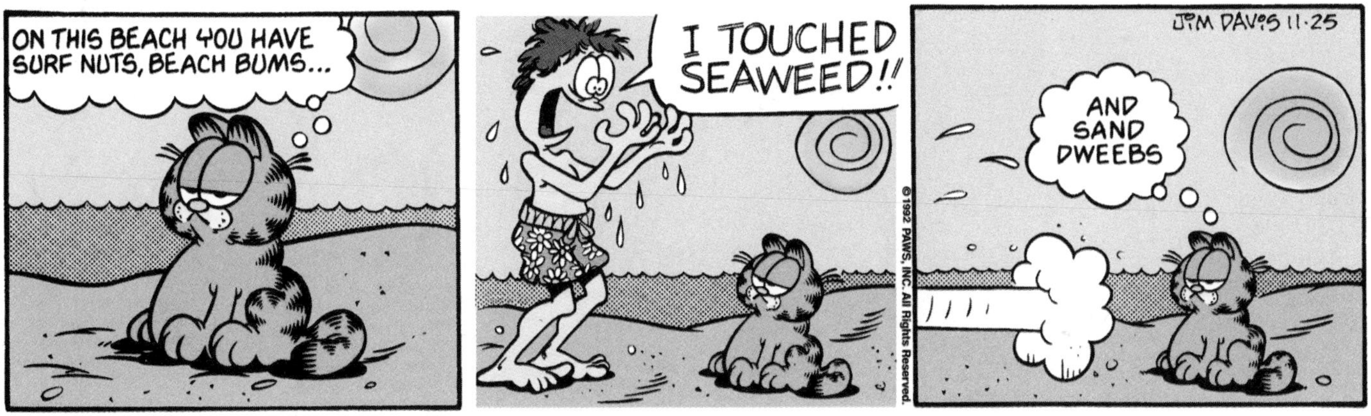
ON THIS BEACH YOU HAVE SURF NUTS, BEACH BUMS...
I TOUCHED SEAWEED!!
© 1992 PAWS, INC. All Rights Reserved.
JIM DAVIS 11-25
AND SAND DWEEBS

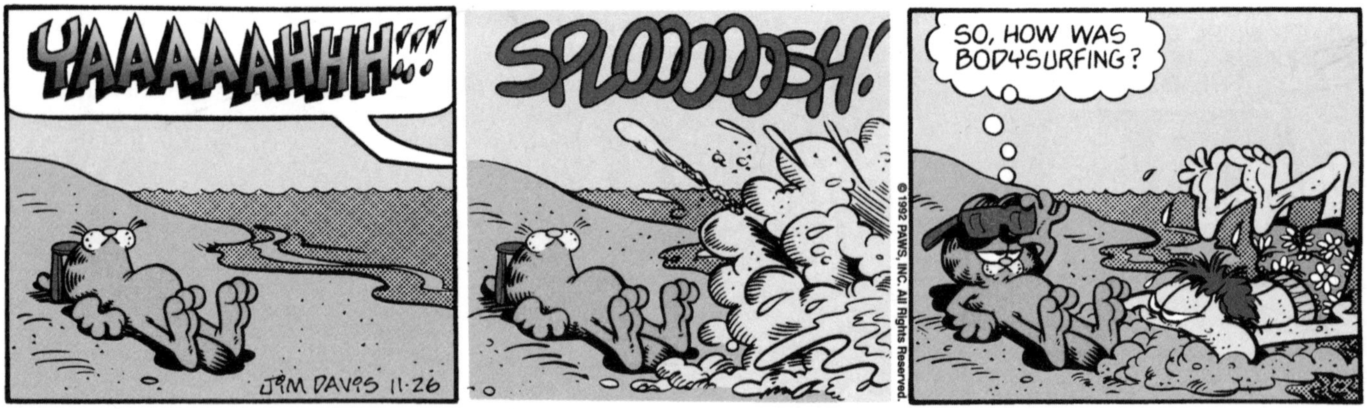
YAAAAAHHH!!!
JIM DAVIS 11-26
SPLOOOOOOSH!
© 1992 PAWS, INC. All Rights Reserved.
SO, HOW WAS BODYSURFING?

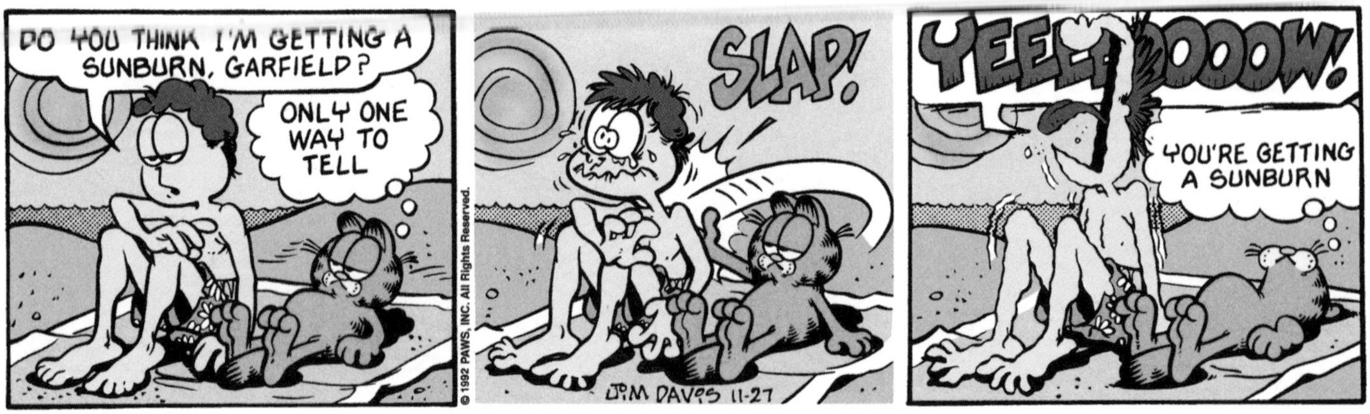
DO YOU THINK I'M GETTING A SUNBURN, GARFIELD?
ONLY ONE WAY TO TELL
© 1992 PAWS, INC. All Rights Reserved.
SLAP!
JIM DAVIS 11-27
YOU'RE GETTING A SUNBURN

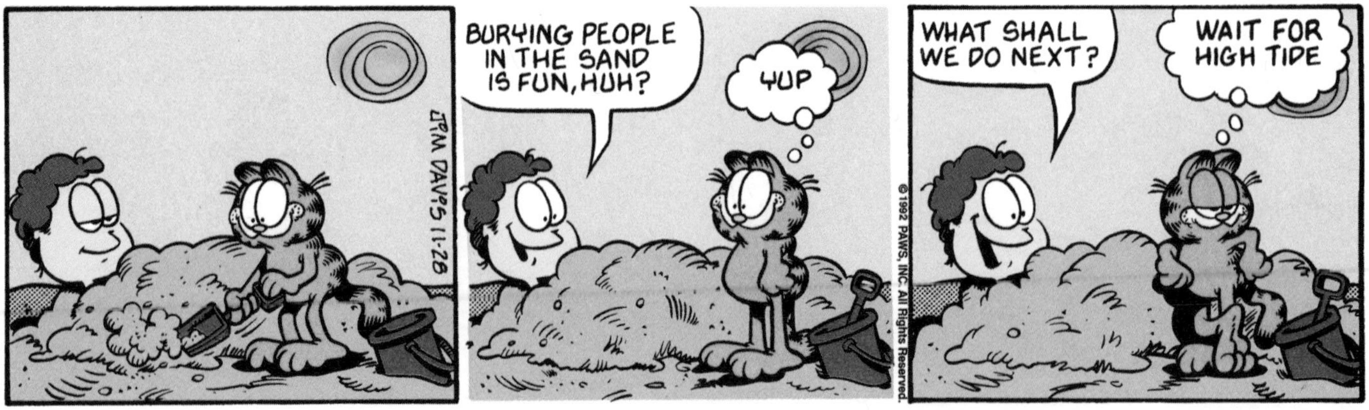
JIM DAVIS 11-28
BURYING PEOPLE IN THE SAND IS FUN, HUH?
YUP
© 1992 PAWS, INC. All Rights Reserved.
WHAT SHALL WE DO NEXT?
WAIT FOR HIGH TIDE

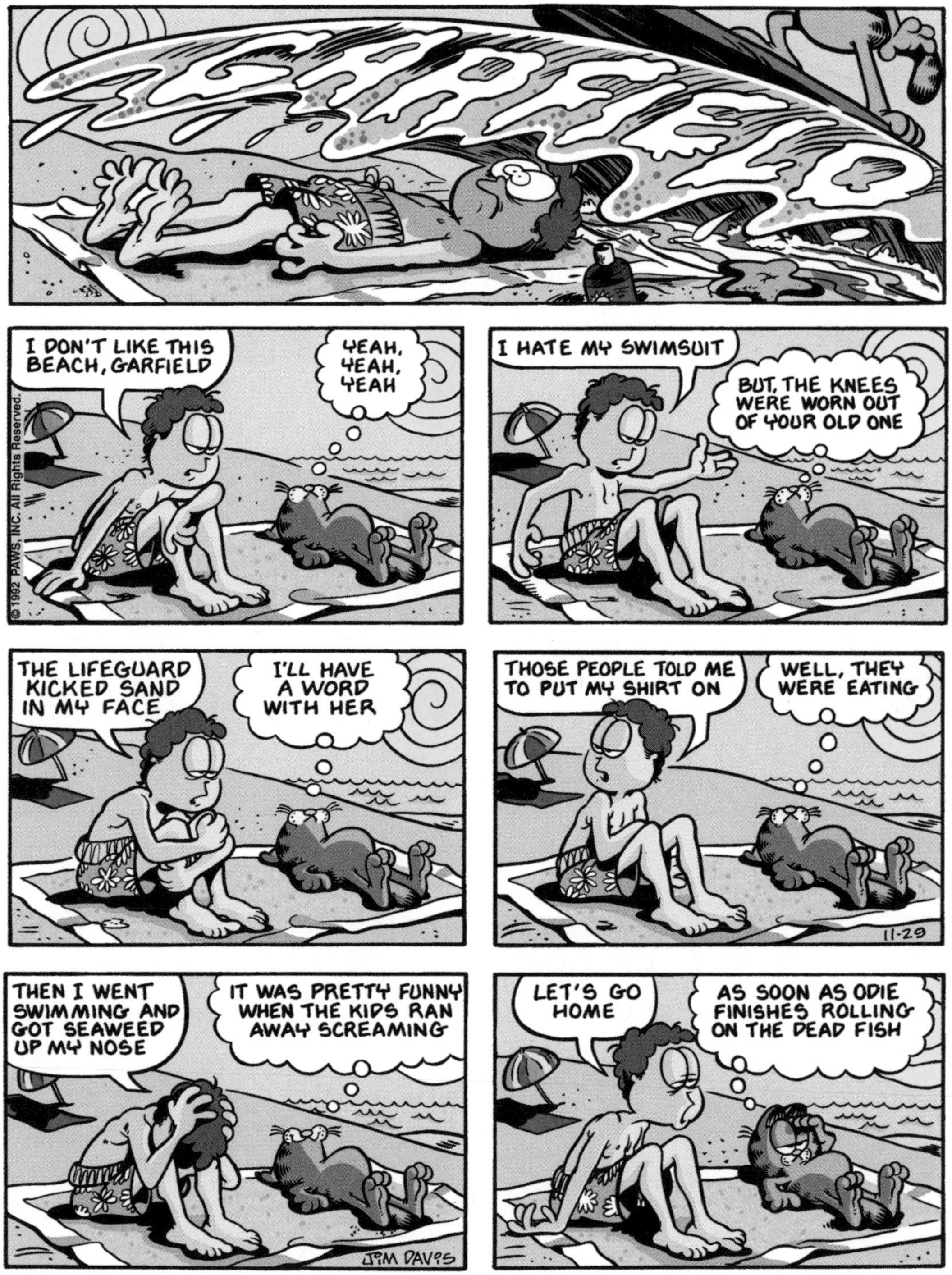
I DON'T LIKE THIS BEACH, GARFIELD
YEAH, YEAH, YEAH
I HATE MY SWIMSUIT
BUT, THE KNEES WERE WORN OUT OF YOUR OLD ONE
THE LIFEGUARD KICKED SAND IN MY FACE
I'LL HAVE A WORD WITH HER
THOSE PEOPLE TOLD ME TO PUT MY SHIRT ON
WELL, THEY WERE EATING
THEN I WENT SWIMMING AND GOT SEAWEED UP MY NOSE
IT WAS PRETTY FUNNY WHEN THE KIDS RAN AWAY SCREAMING
LET'S GO HOME
AS SOON AS ODIE FINISHES ROLLING ON THE DEAD FISH
© 1992 PAWS, INC. All Rights Reserved.
11-29
JIM DAVIS

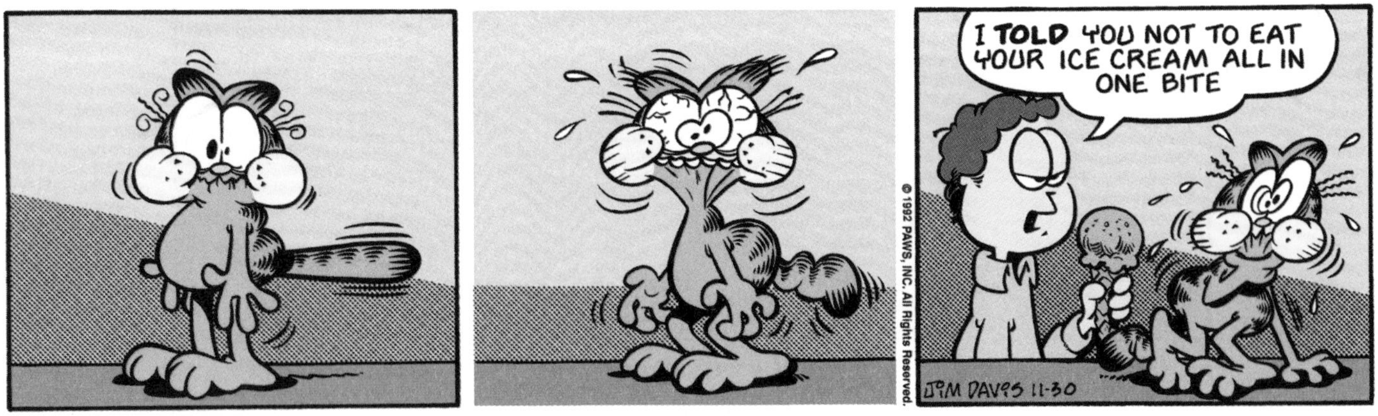
I TOLD YOU NOT TO EAT YOUR ICE CREAM ALL IN ONE BITE
JIM DAVIS 11-30
© 1992 PAWS, INC. All Rights Reserved.

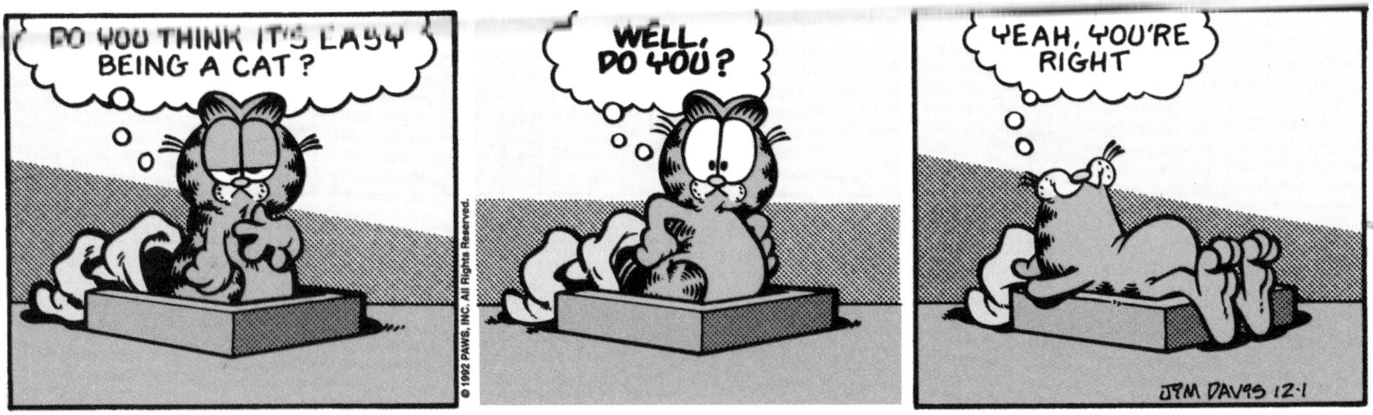
DO YOU THINK IT'S EASY BEING A CAT?
WELL, DO YOU?
YEAH, YOU'RE RIGHT
JIM DAVIS 12-1
© 1992 PAWS, INC. All Rights Reserved.

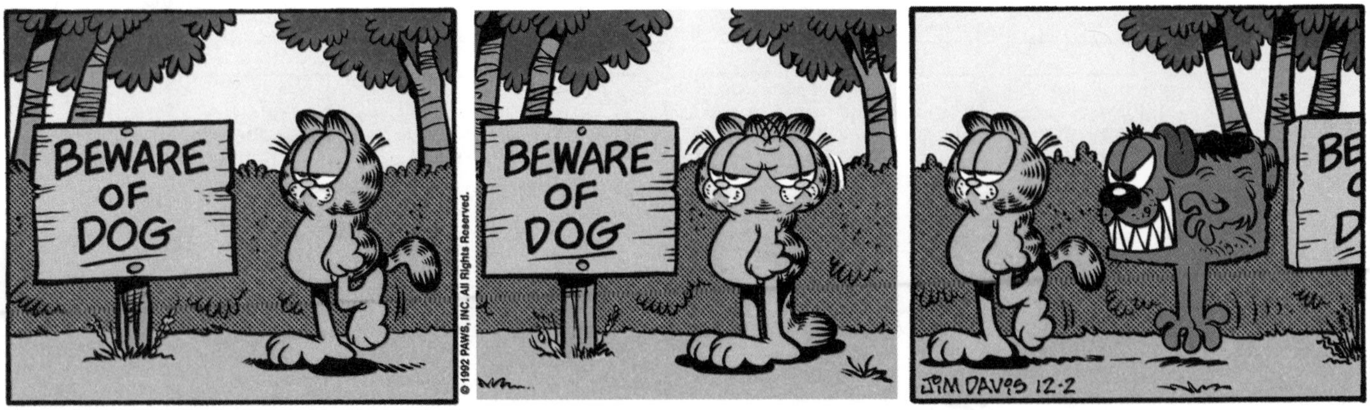
BEWARE OF DOG
BEWARE OF DOG
JIM DAVIS 12-2
© 1992 PAWS, INC. All Rights Reserved.

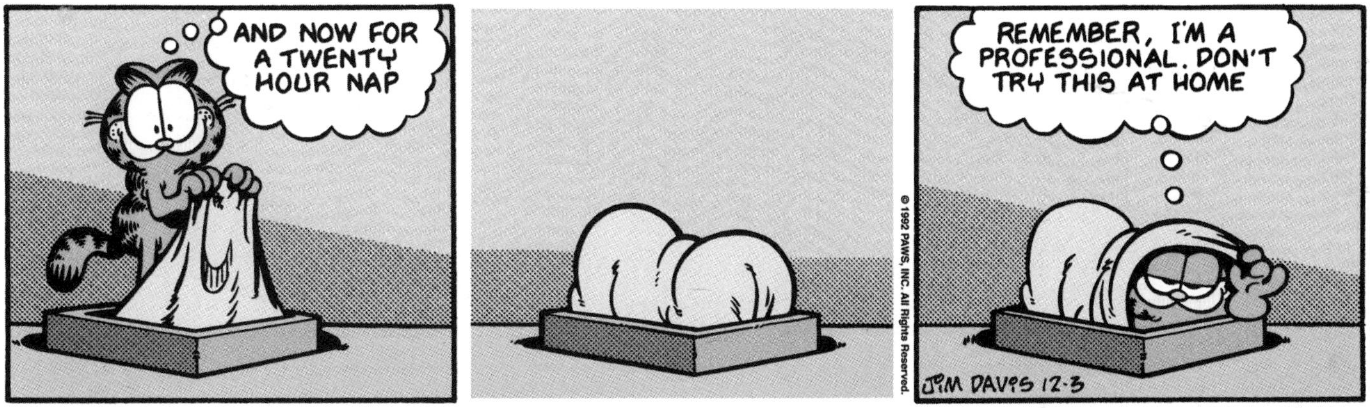
AND NOW FOR A TWENTY HOUR NAP
REMEMBER, I'M A PROFESSIONAL. DON'T TRY THIS AT HOME
© 1992 PAWS, INC. All Rights Reserved.
JIM DAVIS 12-3

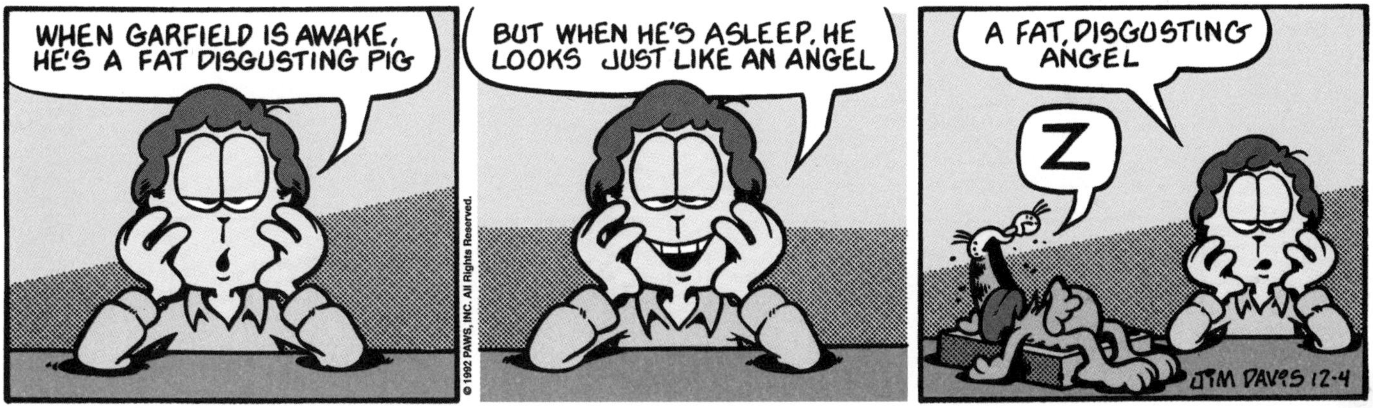
WHEN GARFIELD IS AWAKE, HE'S A FAT DISGUSTING PIG
BUT WHEN HE'S ASLEEP, HE LOOKS JUST LIKE AN ANGEL
A FAT, DISGUSTING ANGEL
Z
© 1992 PAWS, INC. All Rights Reserved.
JIM DAVIS 12-4

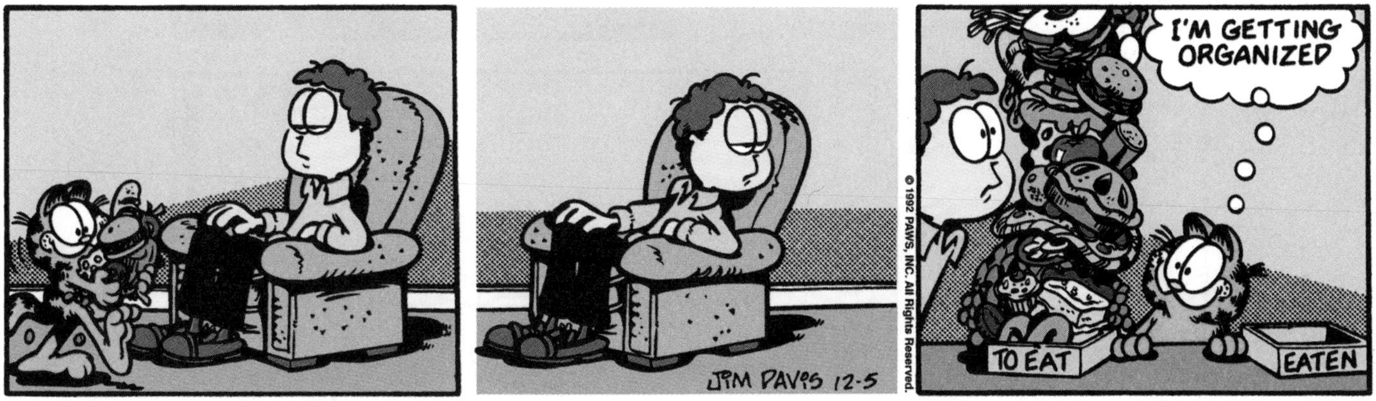
I'M GETTING ORGANIZED
TO EAT
EATEN
© 1992 PAWS, INC. All Rights Reserved.
JIM DAVIS 12-5

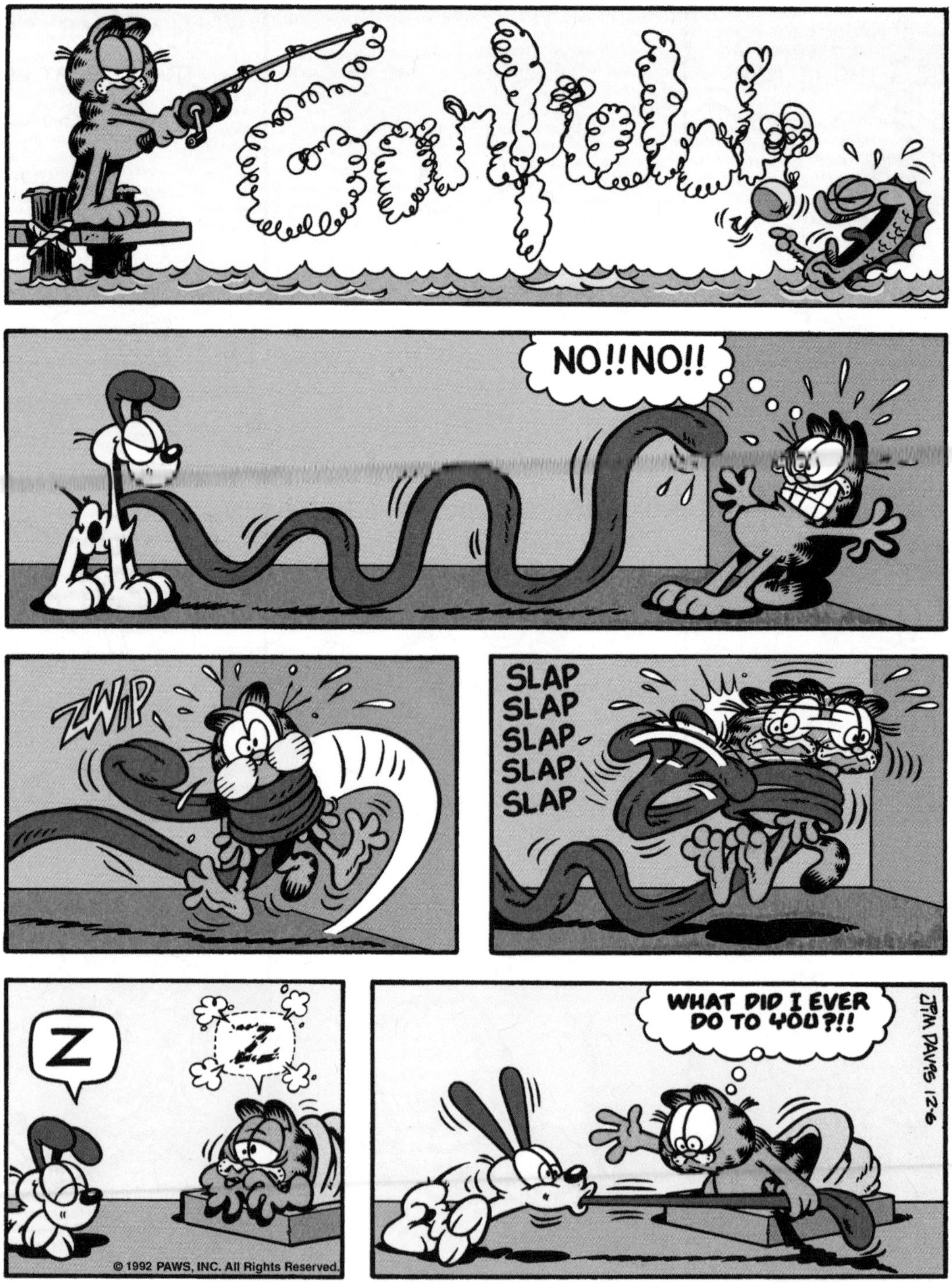
Garfield
NO!!NO!!
ZWIP
SLAP
SLAP
SLAP
SLAP
SLAP
Z
Z
WHAT DID I EVER DO TO YOU?!!
JPM DAVIS 12-6

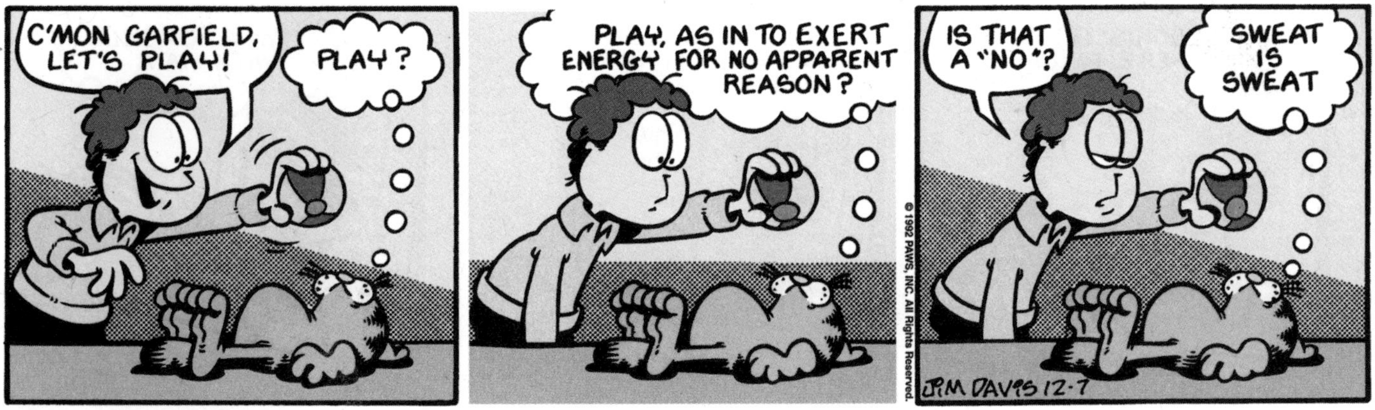
C'MON GARFIELD, LET'S PLAY!
PLAY?
PLAY, AS IN TO EXERT ENERGY FOR NO APPARENT REASON?
© 1992 PAWS, INC. All Rights Reserved.
IS THAT A "NO"?
SWEAT IS SWEAT
JIM DAVIS 12-7

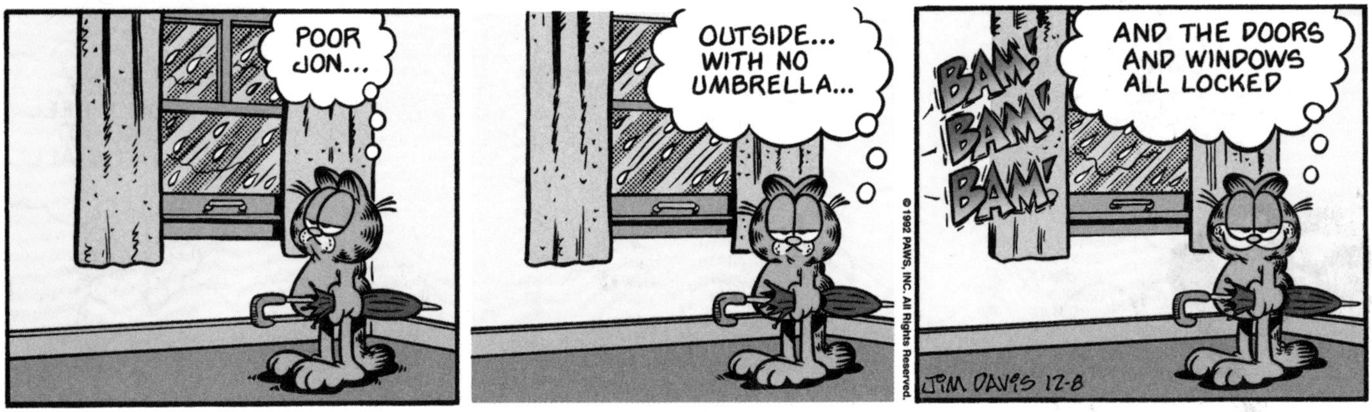
POOR JON...
OUTSIDE... WITH NO UMBRELLA...
© 1992 PAWS, INC. All Rights Reserved.
BAM! BAM! BAM!
AND THE DOORS AND WINDOWS ALL LOCKED
JIM DAVIS 12-8

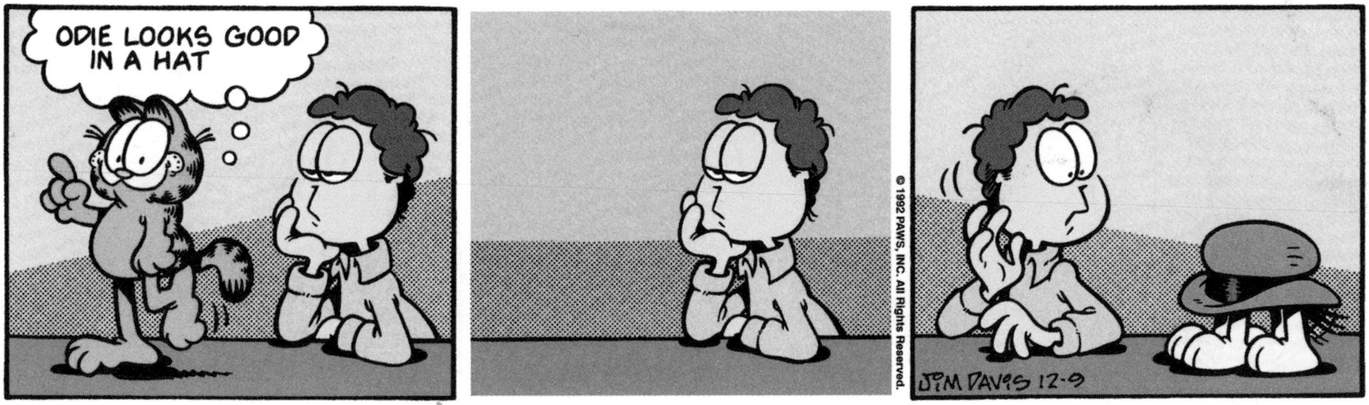
ODIE LOOKS GOOD IN A HAT
© 1992 PAWS, INC. All Rights Reserved.
JIM DAVIS 12-9

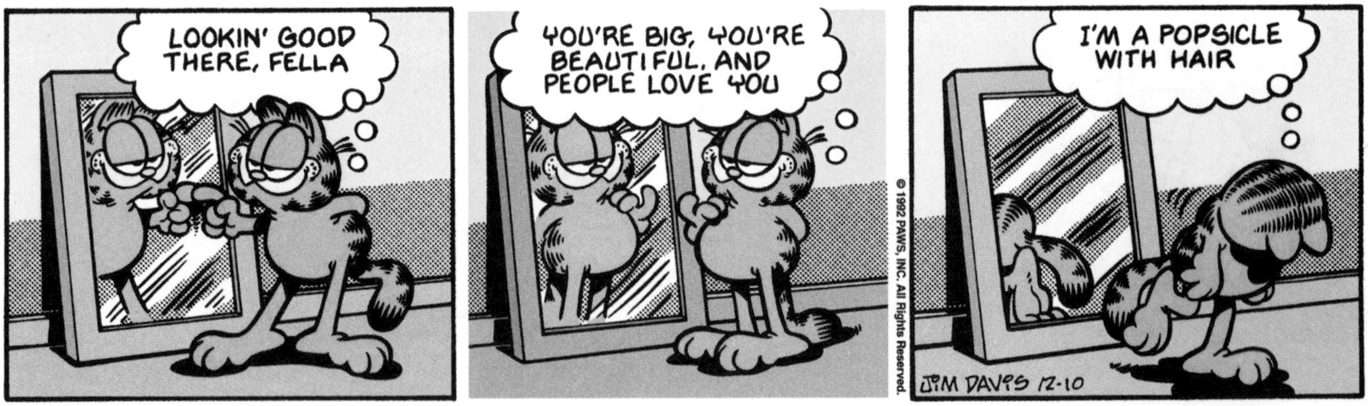
LOOKIN' GOOD THERE, FELLA
YOU'RE BIG, YOU'RE BEAUTIFUL, AND PEOPLE LOVE YOU
© 1992 PAWS, INC. All Rights Reserved.
I'M A POPSICLE WITH HAIR
JIM DAVIS 12-10

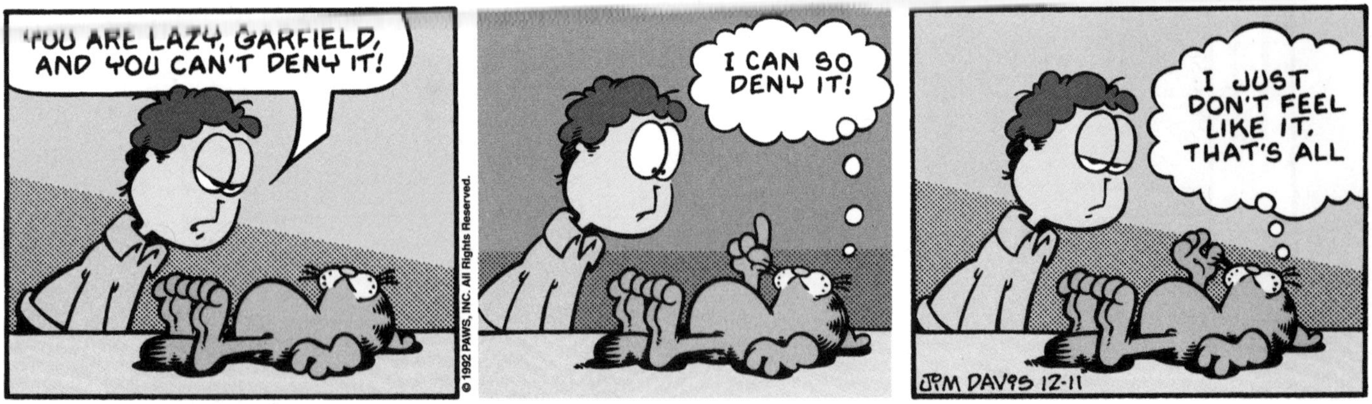
YOU ARE LAZY, GARFIELD, AND YOU CAN'T DENY IT!
© 1992 PAWS, INC. All Rights Reserved.
I CAN SO DENY IT!
I JUST DON'T FEEL LIKE IT, THAT'S ALL
JIM DAVIS 12-11

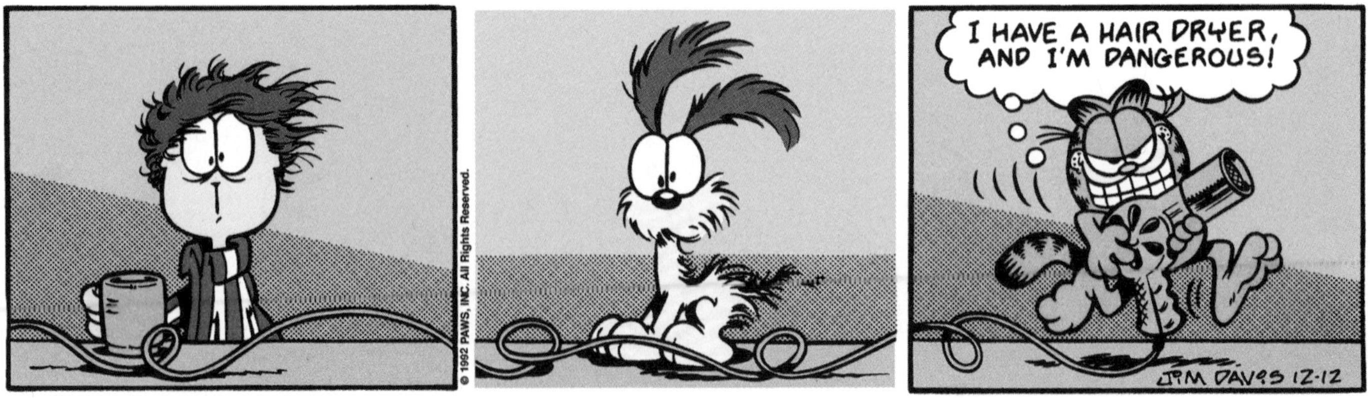
© 1992 PAWS, INC. All Rights Reserved.
I HAVE A HAIR DRYER, AND I'M DANGEROUS!
JIM DAVIS 12-12

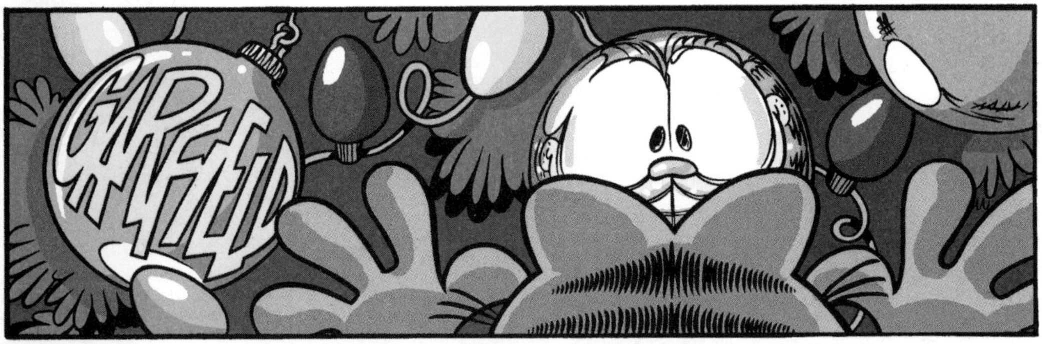
GARFIELD

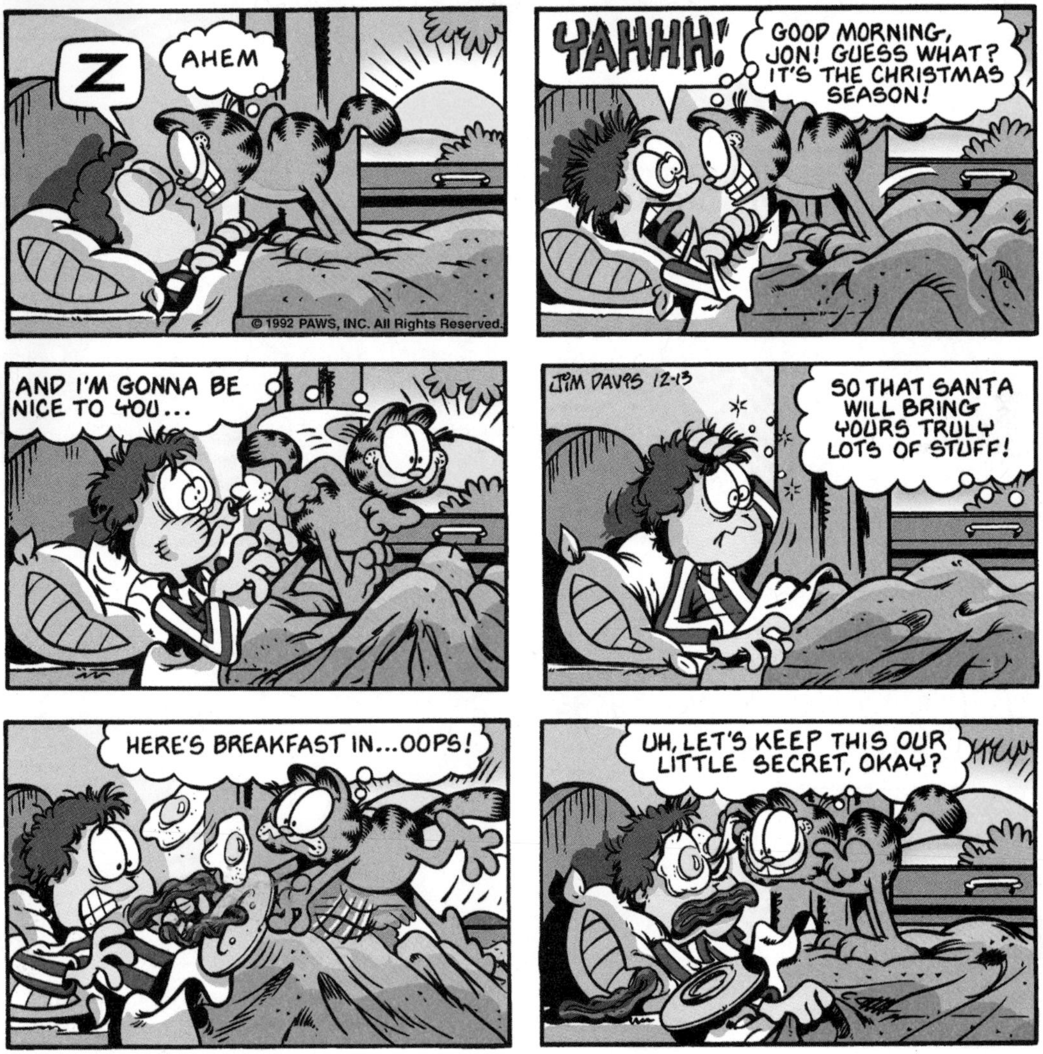
Z
AHEM
© 1992 PAWS, INC. All Rights Reserved.
YAHHH!
GOOD MORNING, JON! GUESS WHAT? IT'S THE CHRISTMAS SEASON!
AND I'M GONNA BE NICE TO YOU...
JIM DAVIS 12-13
SO THAT SANTA WILL BRING YOURS TRULY LOTS OF STUFF!
HERE'S BREAKFAST IN...OOPS!
UH, LET'S KEEP THIS OUR LITTLE SECRET, OKAY?

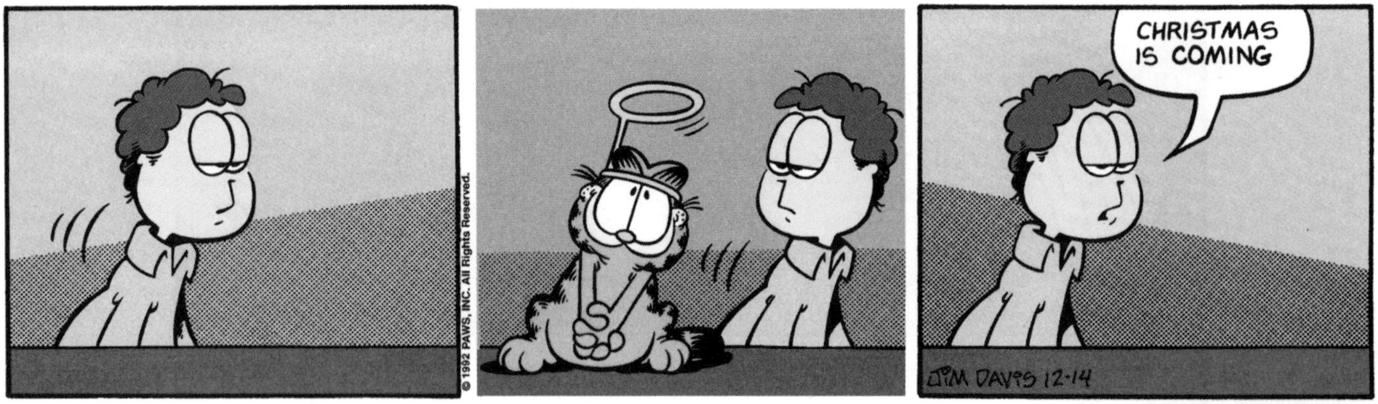

© 1992 PAWS, INC. All Rights Reserved.
CHRISTMAS IS COMING
JIM DAVIS 12-14

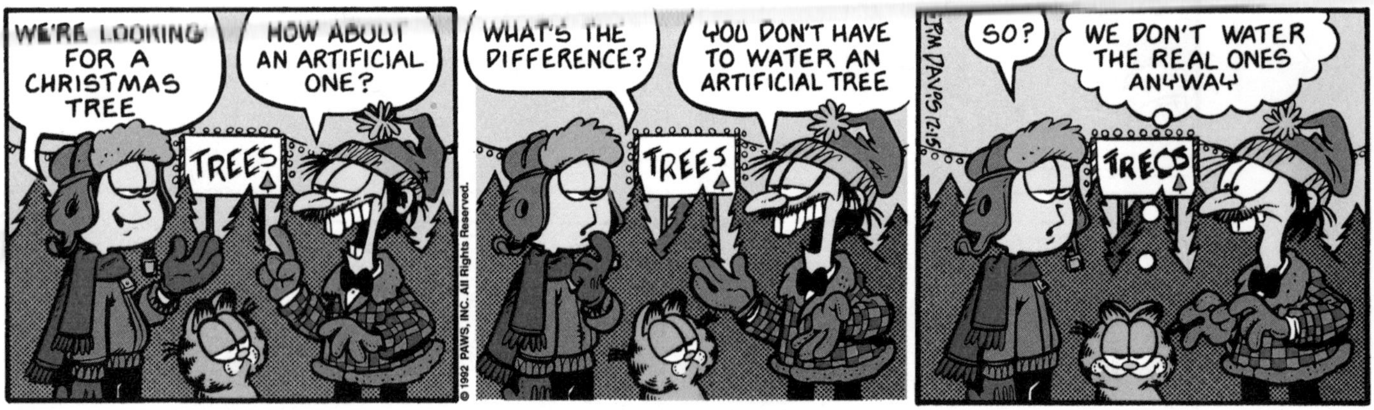

WE'RE LOOKING FOR A CHRISTMAS TREE
HOW ABOUT AN ARTIFICIAL ONE?
TREES
© 1992 PAWS, INC. All Rights Reserved.
WHAT'S THE DIFFERENCE?
YOU DON'T HAVE TO WATER AN ARTIFICIAL TREE
TREES
JIM DAVIS 12-15
SO?
WE DON'T WATER THE REAL ONES ANYWAY

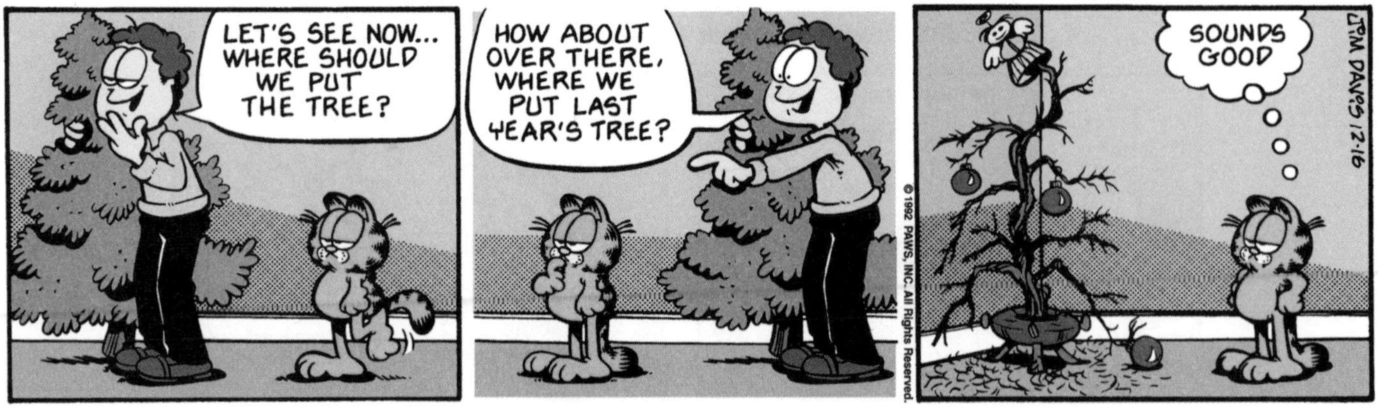

LET'S SEE NOW... WHERE SHOULD WE PUT THE TREE?
HOW ABOUT OVER THERE, WHERE WE PUT LAST YEAR'S TREE?
© 1992 PAWS, INC. All Rights Reserved.
SOUNDS GOOD
JIM DAVIS 12-16

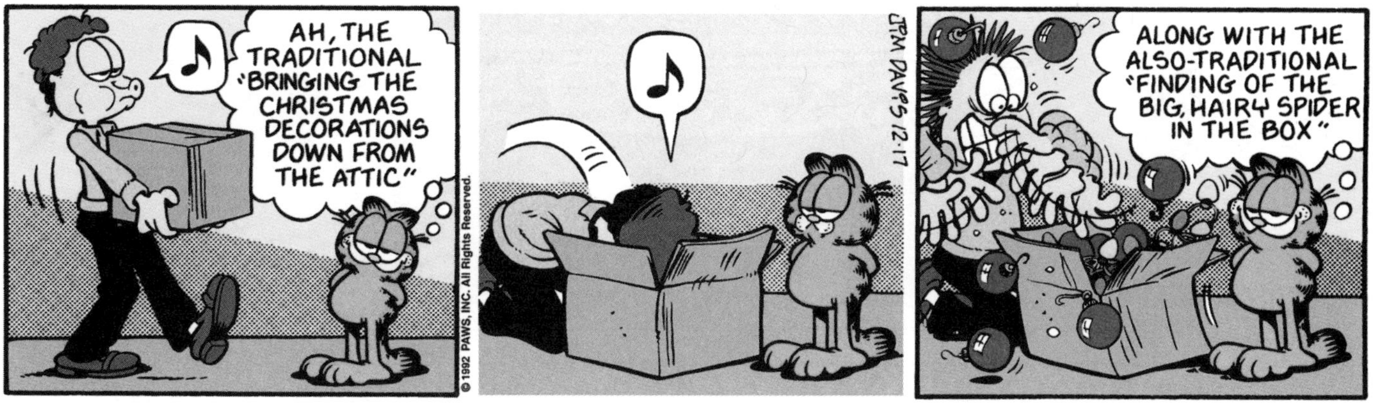
AH, THE TRADITIONAL "BRINGING THE CHRISTMAS DECORATIONS DOWN FROM THE ATTIC"
© 1992 PAWS, INC. All Rights Reserved.
JIM DAVIS 12-17
ALONG WITH THE ALSO-TRADITIONAL "FINDING OF THE BIG, HAIRY SPIDER IN THE BOX"

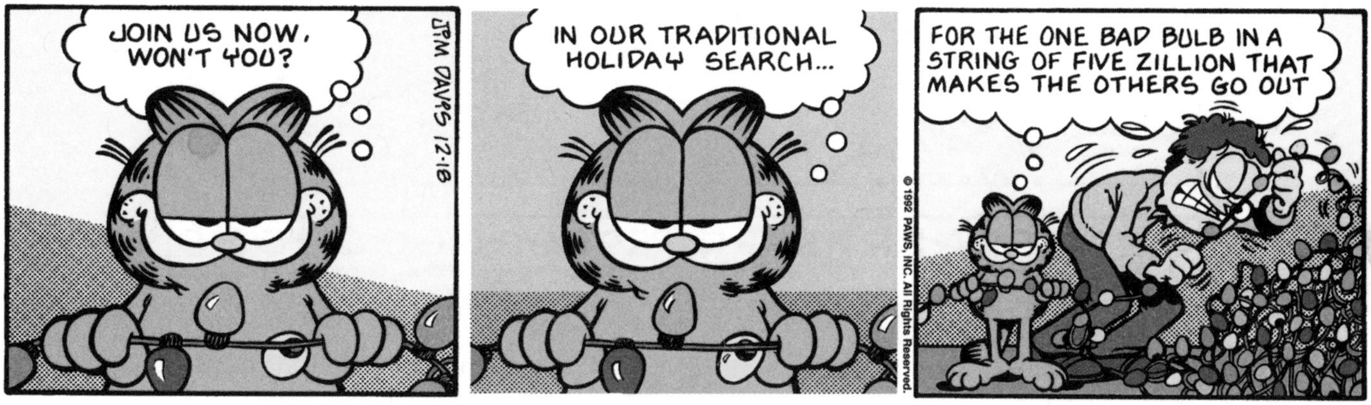
JOIN US NOW, WON'T YOU?
JIM DAVIS 12-18
IN OUR TRADITIONAL HOLIDAY SEARCH...
© 1992 PAWS, INC. All Rights Reserved.
FOR THE ONE BAD BULB IN A STRING OF FIVE ZILLION THAT MAKES THE OTHERS GO OUT

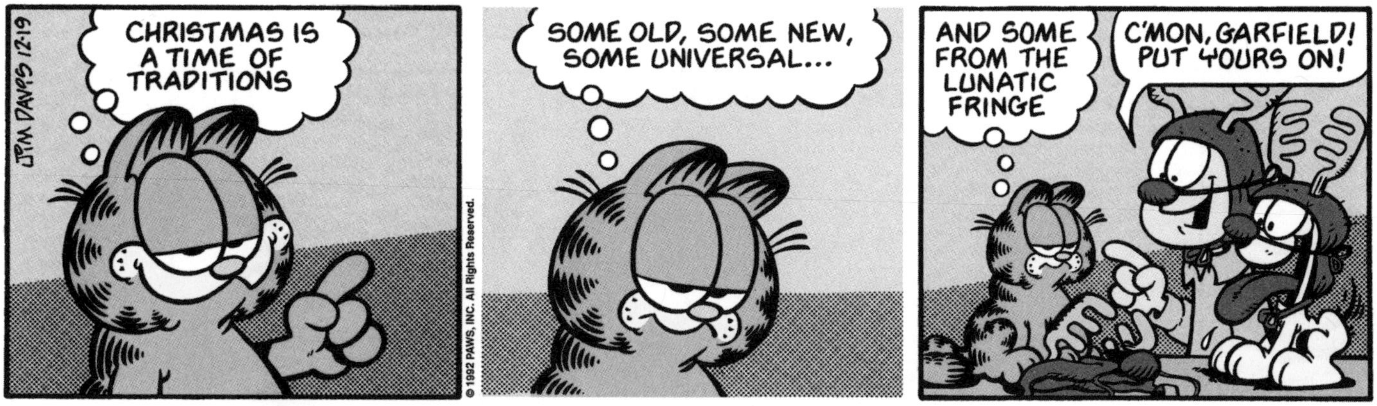
JIM DAVIS 12-19
CHRISTMAS IS A TIME OF TRADITIONS
© 1992 PAWS, INC. All Rights Reserved.
SOME OLD, SOME NEW, SOME UNIVERSAL...
AND SOME FROM THE LUNATIC FRINGE
C'MON, GARFIELD! PUT YOURS ON!

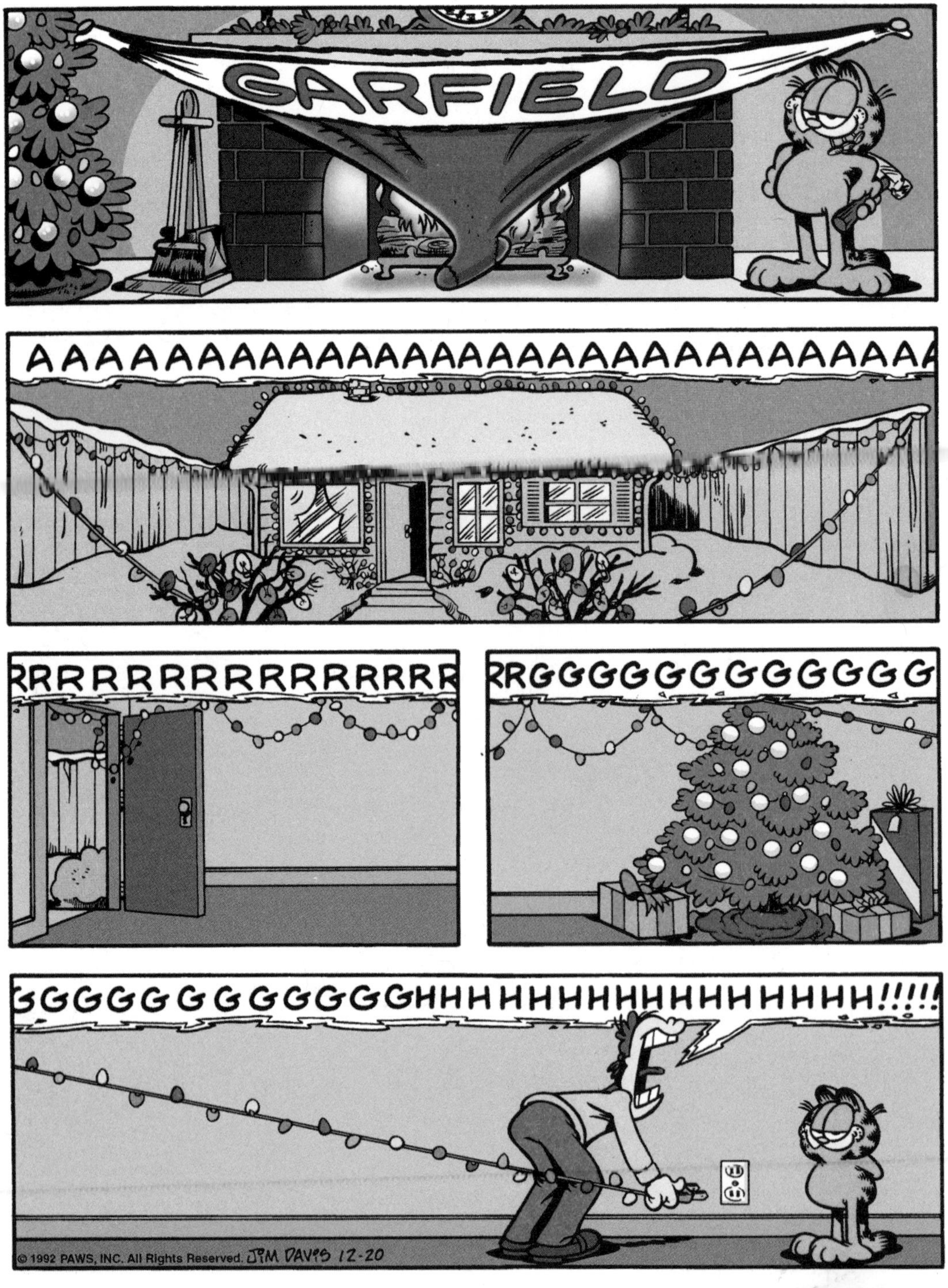
GARFIELD
AAAAAAAAAAAAAAAAAAAAAAAAAAAAA
RRRRRRRRRRRRRRRR
RRGGGGGGGGGGGG
GGGGGGGGGGGGHHHHHHHHHHHHHHHH!!!!!
© 1992 PAWS, INC. All Rights Reserved. JIM DAVIS 12-20

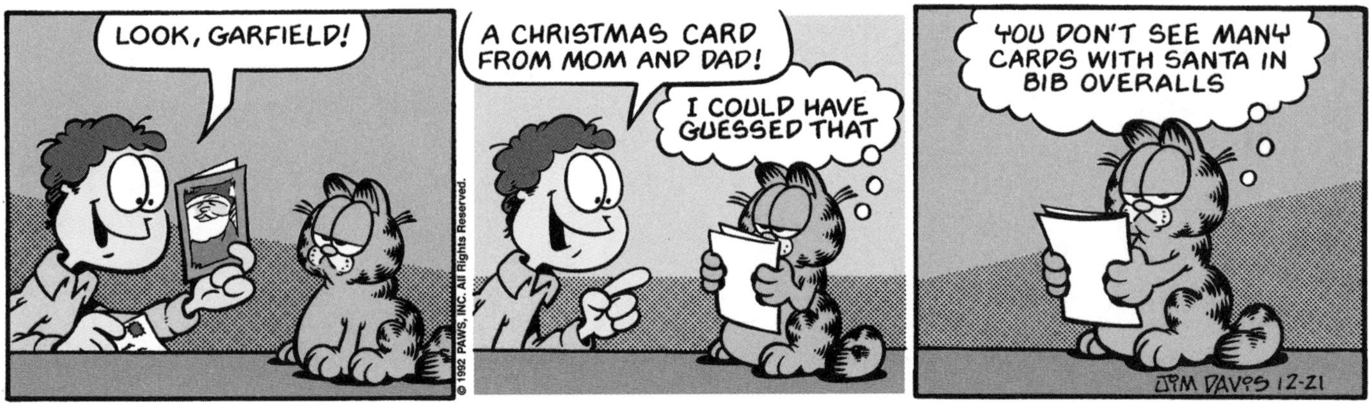
LOOK, GARFIELD!
© 1992 PAWS, INC. All Rights Reserved.
A CHRISTMAS CARD FROM MOM AND DAD!
I COULD HAVE GUESSED THAT
YOU DON'T SEE MANY CARDS WITH SANTA IN BIB OVERALLS
JIM DAVIS 12-21

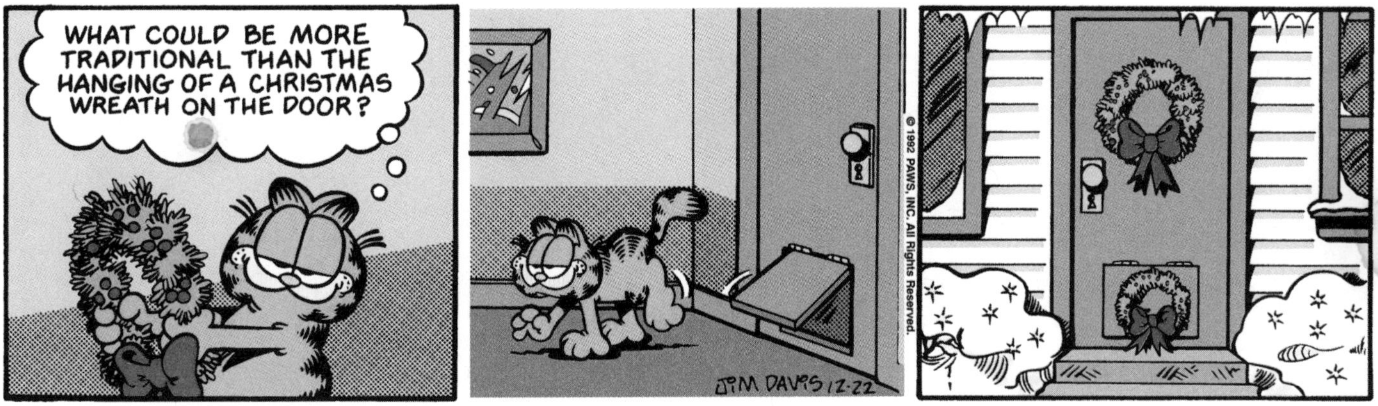
WHAT COULD BE MORE TRADITIONAL THAN THE HANGING OF A CHRISTMAS WREATH ON THE DOOR?
JIM DAVIS 12-22
© 1992 PAWS, INC. All Rights Reserved.

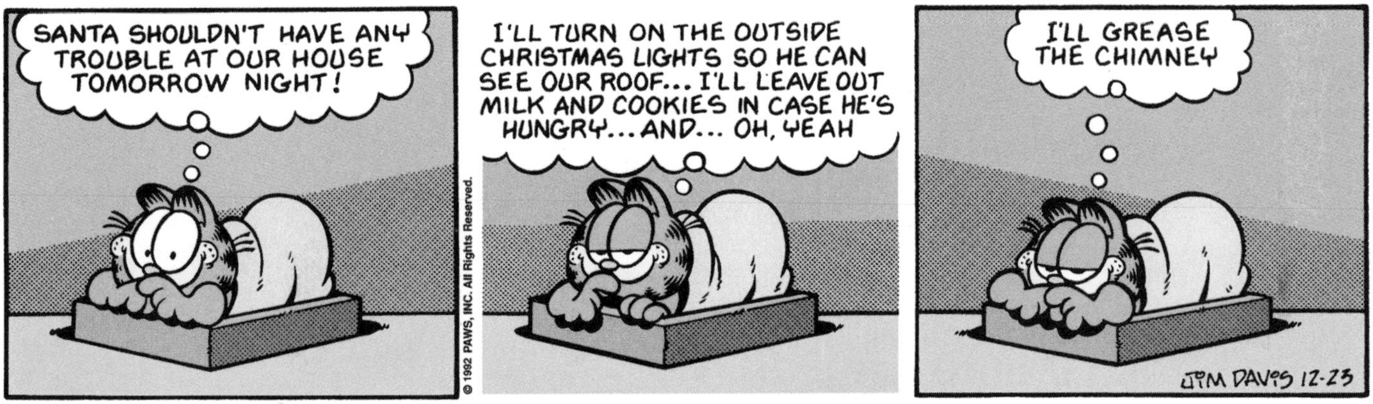
SANTA SHOULDN'T HAVE ANY TROUBLE AT OUR HOUSE TOMORROW NIGHT!
© 1992 PAWS, INC. All Rights Reserved.
I'LL TURN ON THE OUTSIDE CHRISTMAS LIGHTS SO HE CAN SEE OUR ROOF... I'LL LEAVE OUT MILK AND COOKIES IN CASE HE'S HUNGRY... AND... OH, YEAH
I'LL GREASE THE CHIMNEY
JIM DAVIS 12-23

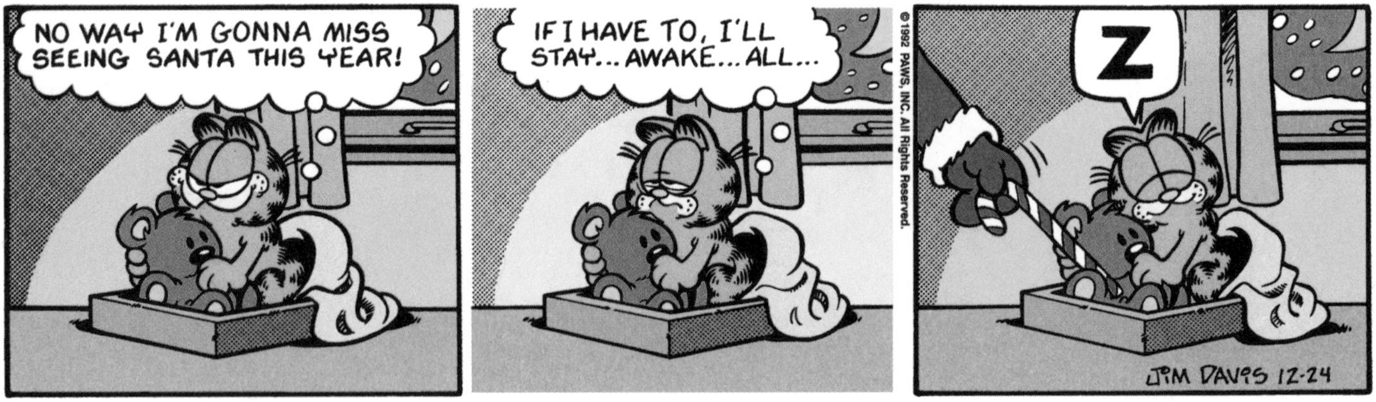
NO WAY I'M GONNA MISS SEEING SANTA THIS YEAR!
IF I HAVE TO, I'LL STAY... AWAKE... ALL...
© 1992 PAWS, INC. All Rights Reserved.
Z
JIM DAVIS 12-24

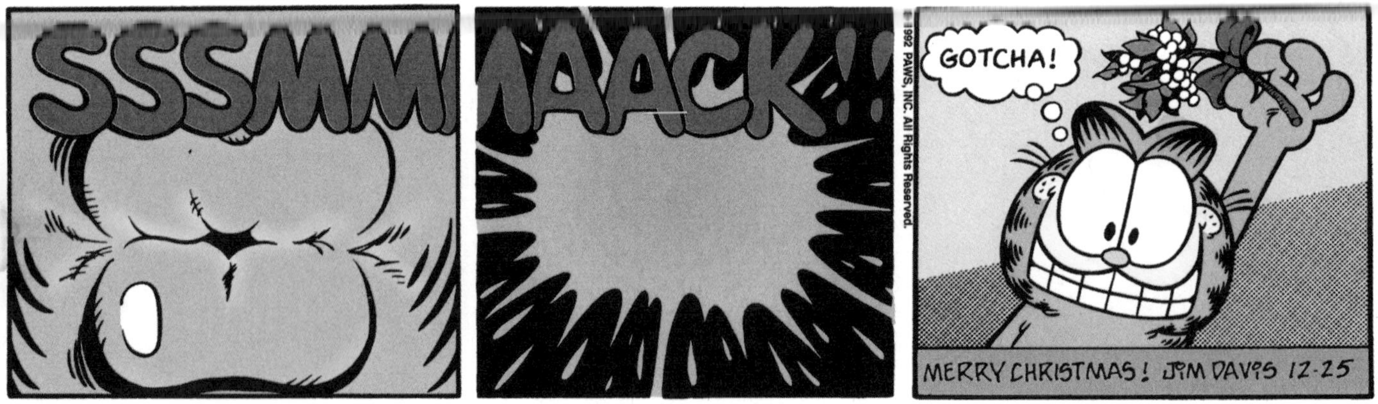
SSSMMMAACK!!
© 1992 PAWS, INC. All Rights Reserved.
GOTCHA!
MERRY CHRISTMAS! JIM DAVIS 12-25

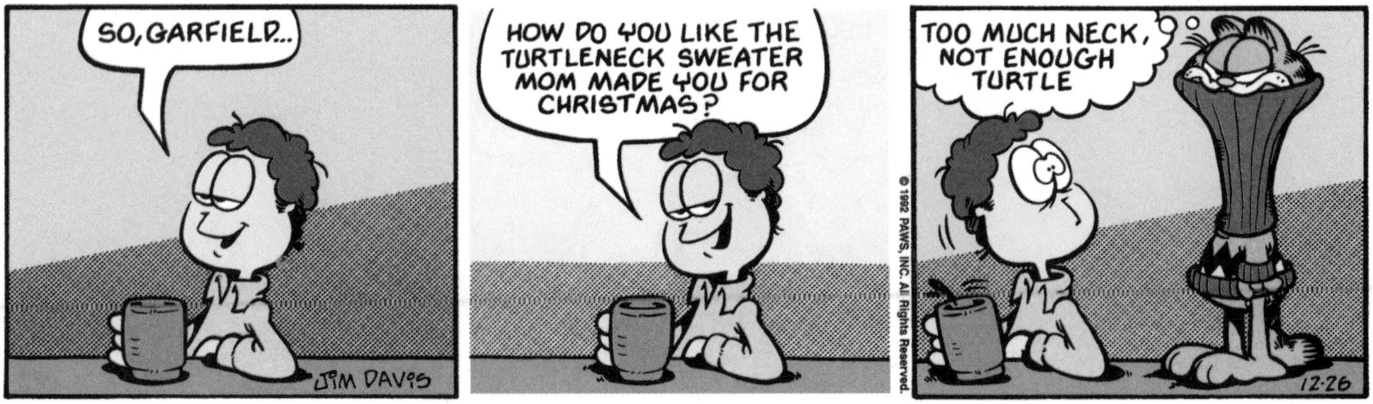
SO, GARFIELD...
JIM DAVIS
HOW DO YOU LIKE THE TURTLENECK SWEATER MOM MADE YOU FOR CHRISTMAS?
© 1992 PAWS, INC. All Rights Reserved.
TOO MUCH NECK, NOT ENOUGH TURTLE
12-26

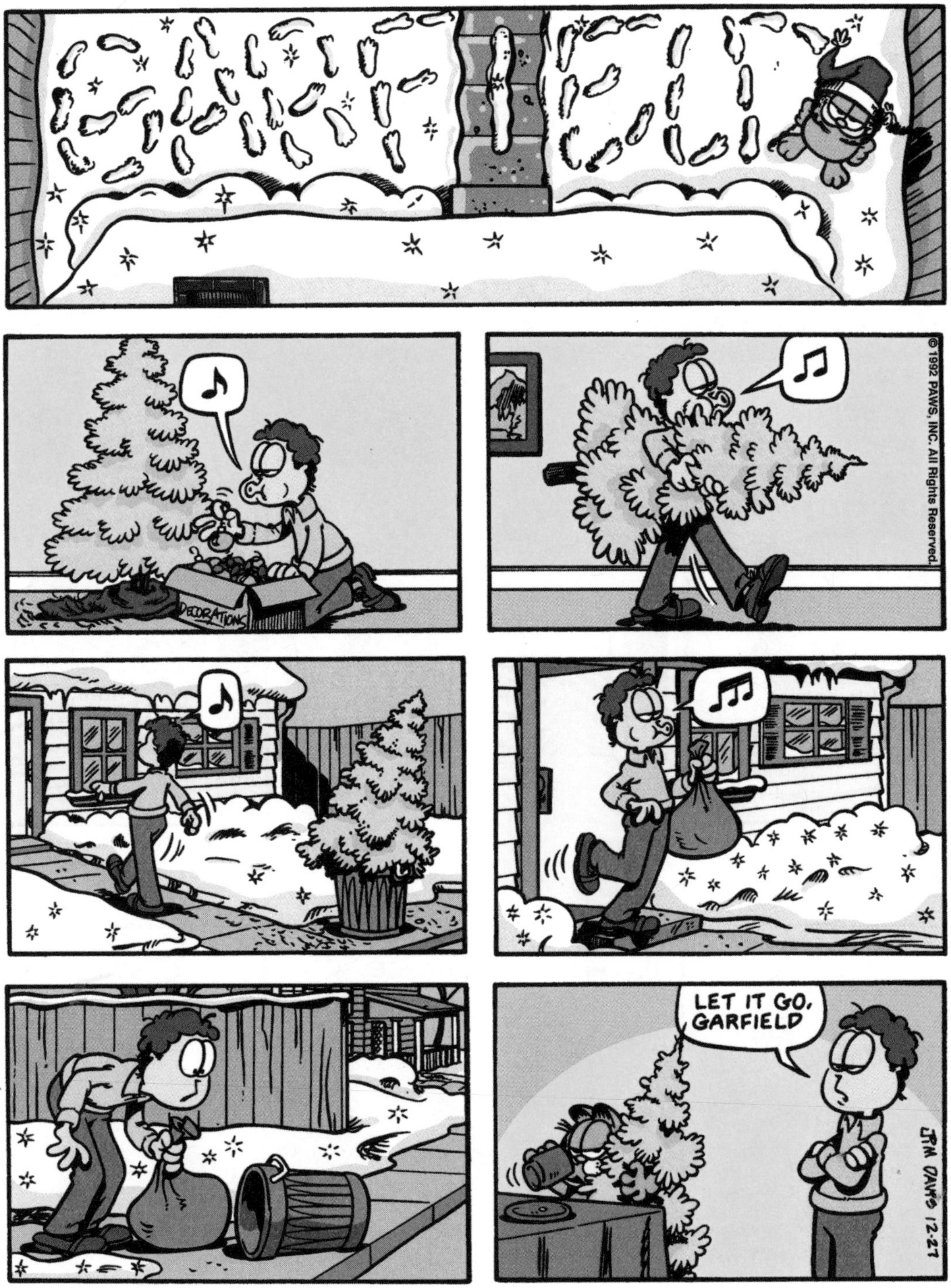
GARFIELD
© 1992 PAWS, INC. All Rights Reserved.
DECORATIONS
LET IT GO, GARFIELD
JIM DAVIS 12-27

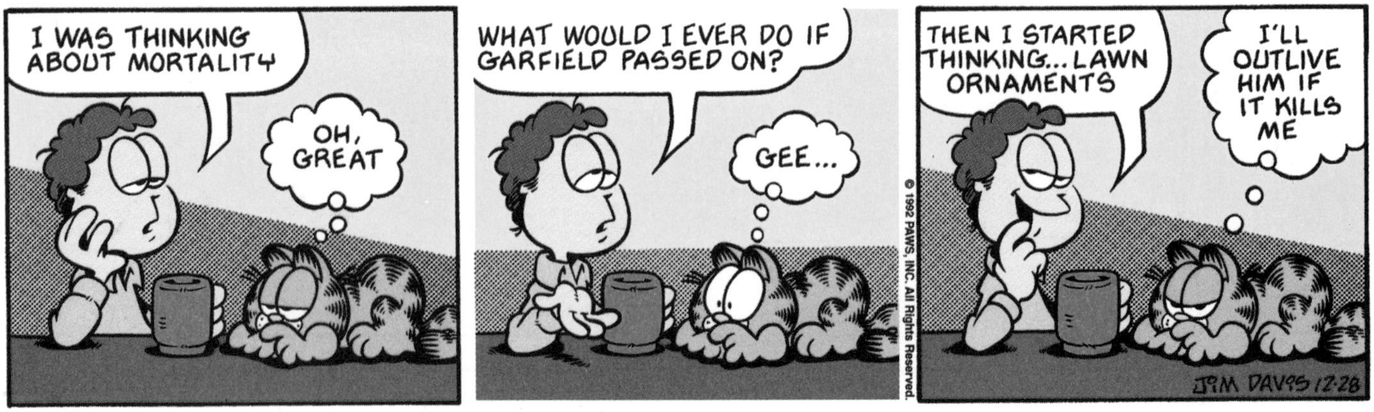
I WAS THINKING ABOUT MORTALITY
OH, GREAT
WHAT WOULD I EVER DO IF GARFIELD PASSED ON?
GEE...
THEN I STARTED THINKING... LAWN ORNAMENTS
I'LL OUTLIVE HIM IF IT KILLS ME
JIM DAVIS 12-28

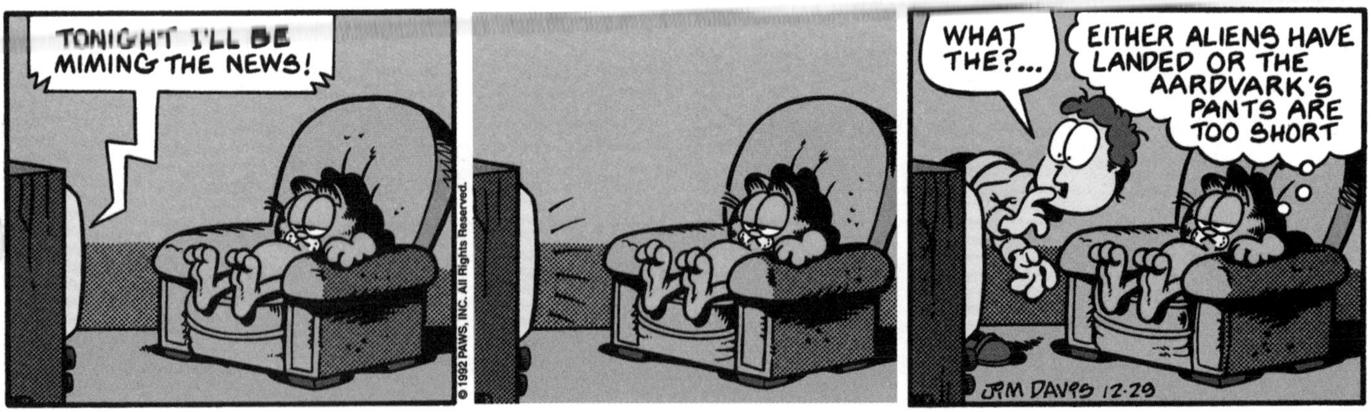
TONIGHT I'LL BE MIMING THE NEWS!
WHAT THE?...
EITHER ALIENS HAVE LANDED OR THE AARDVARK'S PANTS ARE TOO SHORT
JIM DAVIS 12-29

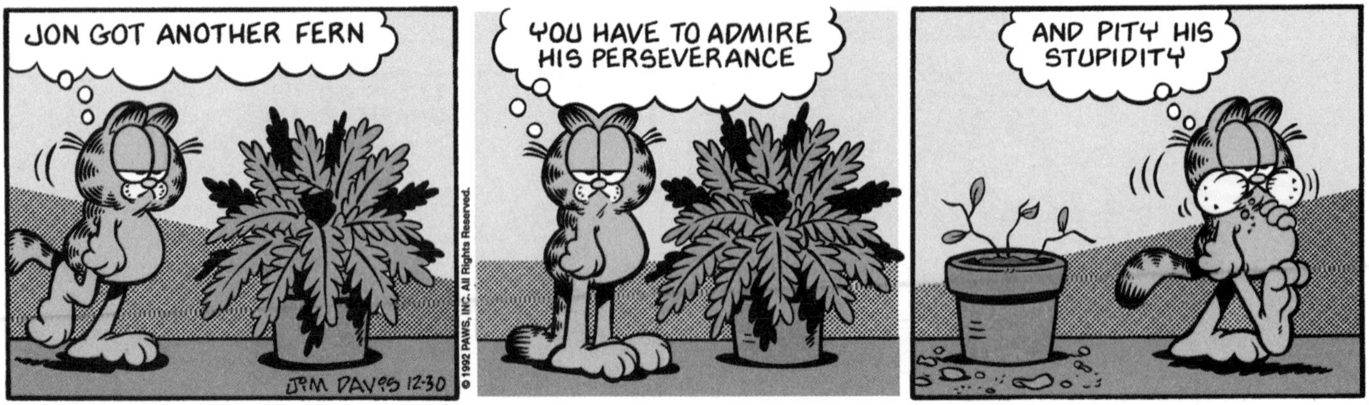
JON GOT ANOTHER FERN
YOU HAVE TO ADMIRE HIS PERSEVERANCE
AND PITY HIS STUPIDITY
JIM DAVIS 12-30

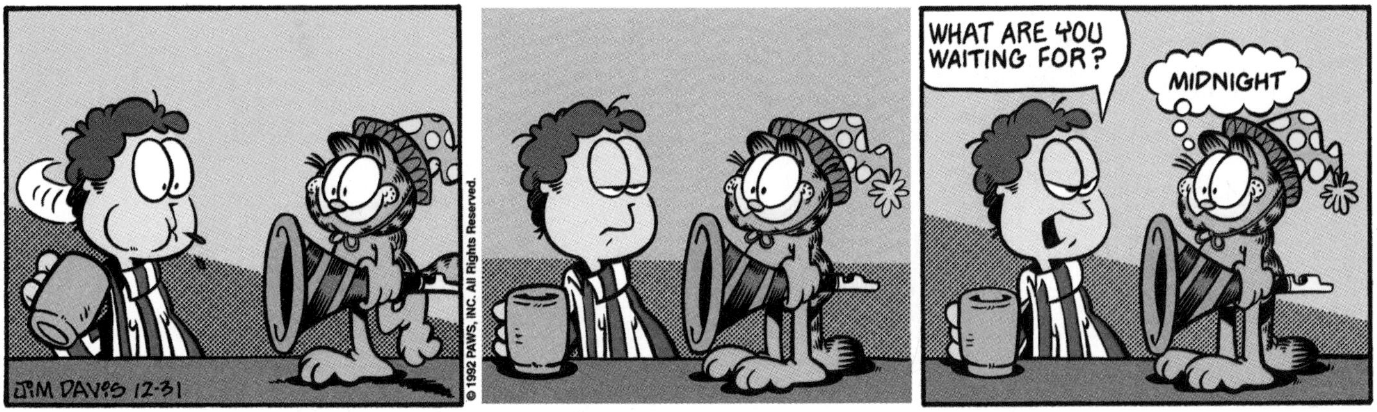
JIM DAVIS 12-31
© 1992 PAWS, INC. All Rights Reserved.
WHAT ARE YOU WAITING FOR?
MIDNIGHT

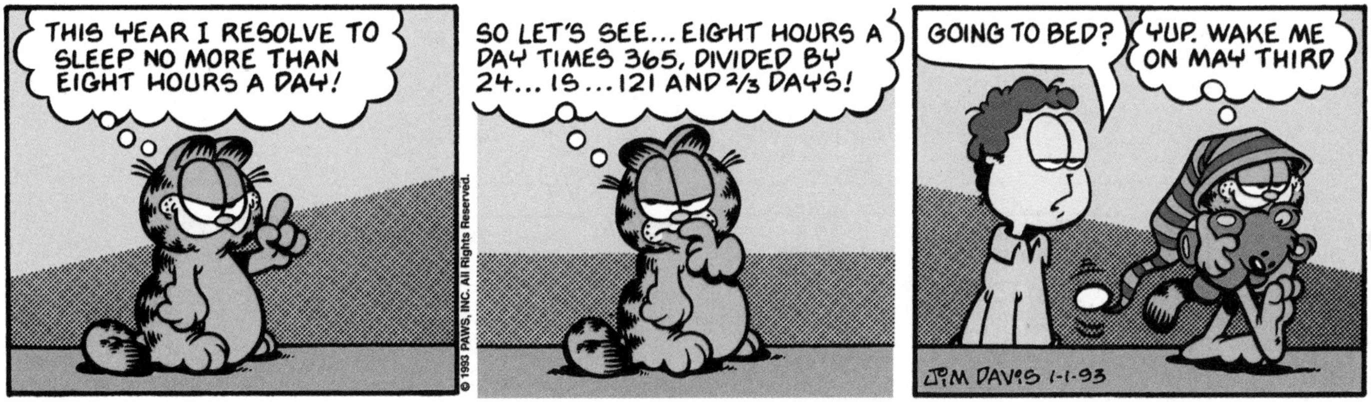
THIS YEAR I RESOLVE TO SLEEP NO MORE THAN EIGHT HOURS A DAY!
© 1993 PAWS, INC. All Rights Reserved.
SO LET'S SEE... EIGHT HOURS A DAY TIMES 365, DIVIDED BY 24... IS... 121 AND 2/3 DAYS!
GOING TO BED?
YUP. WAKE ME ON MAY THIRD
JIM DAVIS 1-1-93

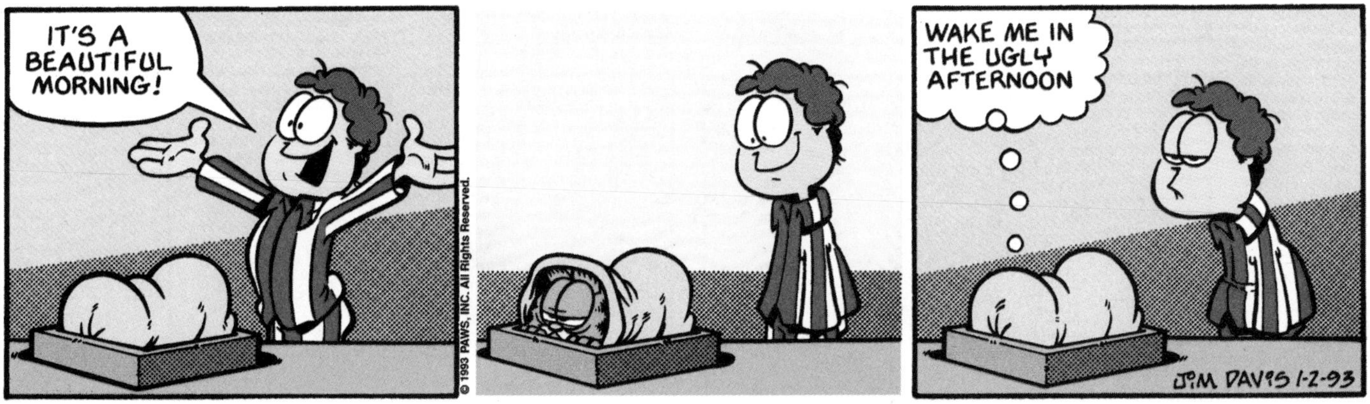
IT'S A BEAUTIFUL MORNING!
© 1993 PAWS, INC. All Rights Reserved.
WAKE ME IN THE UGLY AFTERNOON
JIM DAVIS 1-2-93

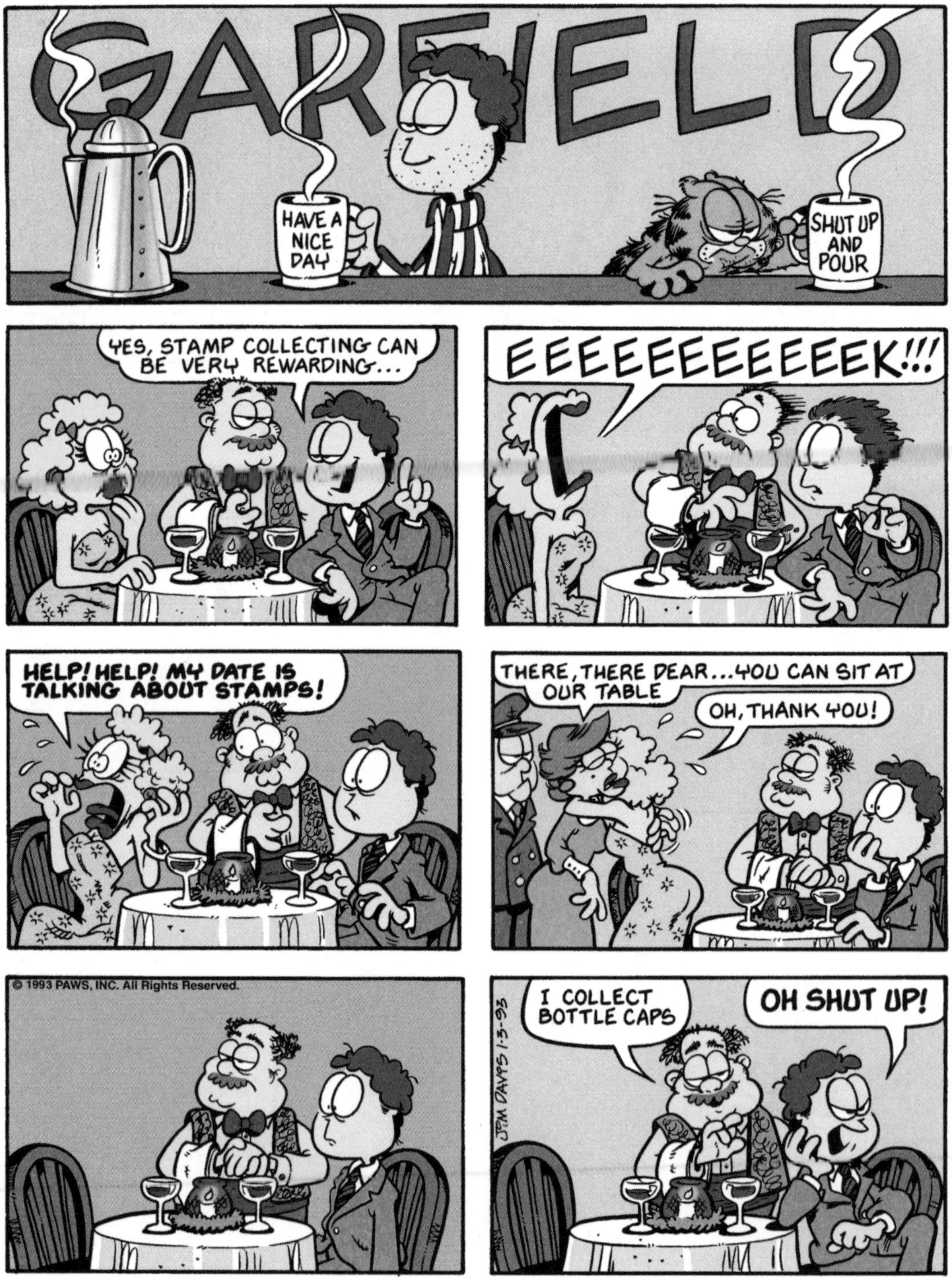
GARFIELD
HAVE A NICE DAY
SHUT UP AND POUR
YES, STAMP COLLECTING CAN BE VERY REWARDING...
EEEEEEEEEEEEK!!!
HELP! HELP! MY DATE IS TALKING ABOUT STAMPS!
THERE, THERE DEAR...YOU CAN SIT AT OUR TABLE
OH, THANK YOU!
© 1993 PAWS, INC. All Rights Reserved.
JPM DAVPS 1-3-93
I COLLECT BOTTLE CAPS
OH SHUT UP!

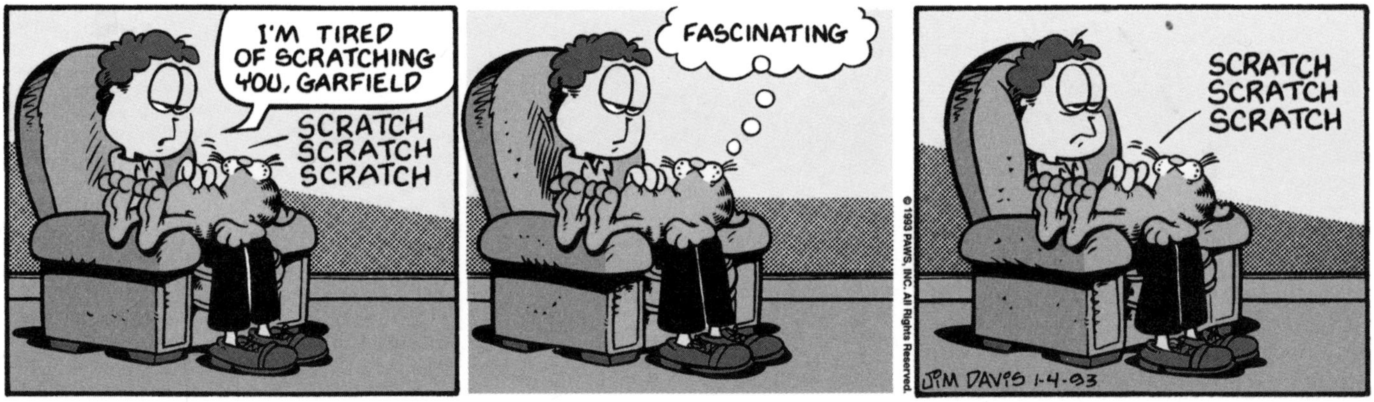
I'M TIRED OF SCRATCHING YOU, GARFIELD
SCRATCH SCRATCH SCRATCH
FASCINATING
© 1993 PAWS, INC. All Rights Reserved.
SCRATCH SCRATCH SCRATCH
JIM DAVIS 1-4-93

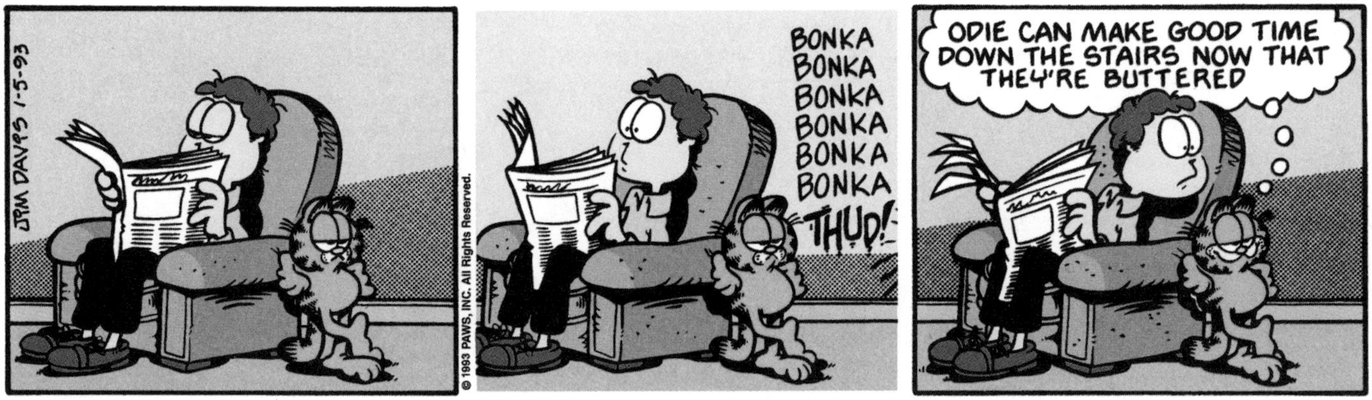
JIM DAVIS 1-5-93
© 1993 PAWS, INC. All Rights Reserved.
BONKA BONKA BONKA BONKA BONKA BONKA
THUD!
ODIE CAN MAKE GOOD TIME DOWN THE STAIRS NOW THAT THEY'RE BUTTERED

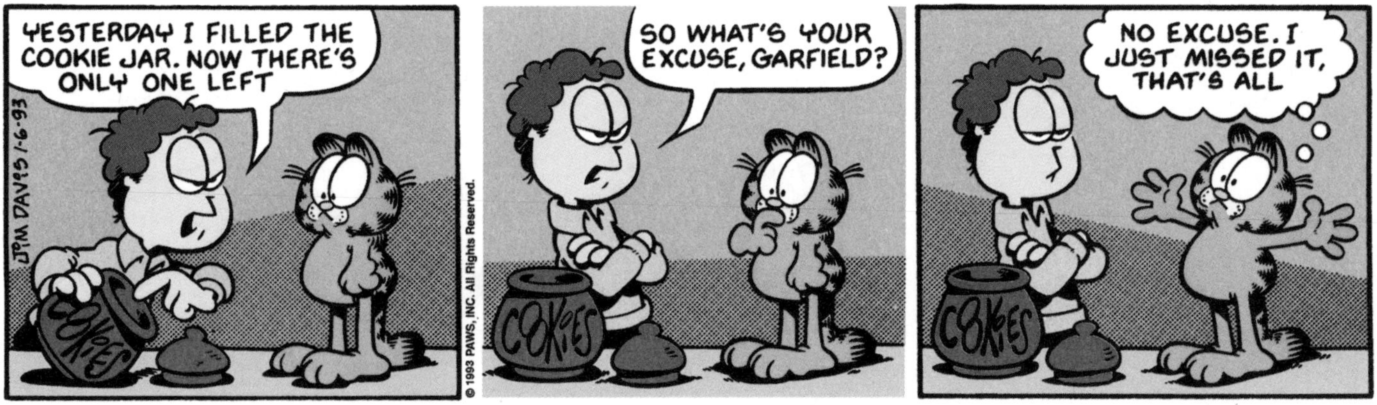
YESTERDAY I FILLED THE COOKIE JAR. NOW THERE'S ONLY ONE LEFT
JIM DAVIS 1-6-93
COOKIES
© 1993 PAWS, INC. All Rights Reserved.
SO WHAT'S YOUR EXCUSE, GARFIELD?
COOKIES
NO EXCUSE. I JUST MISSED IT, THAT'S ALL
COOKIES

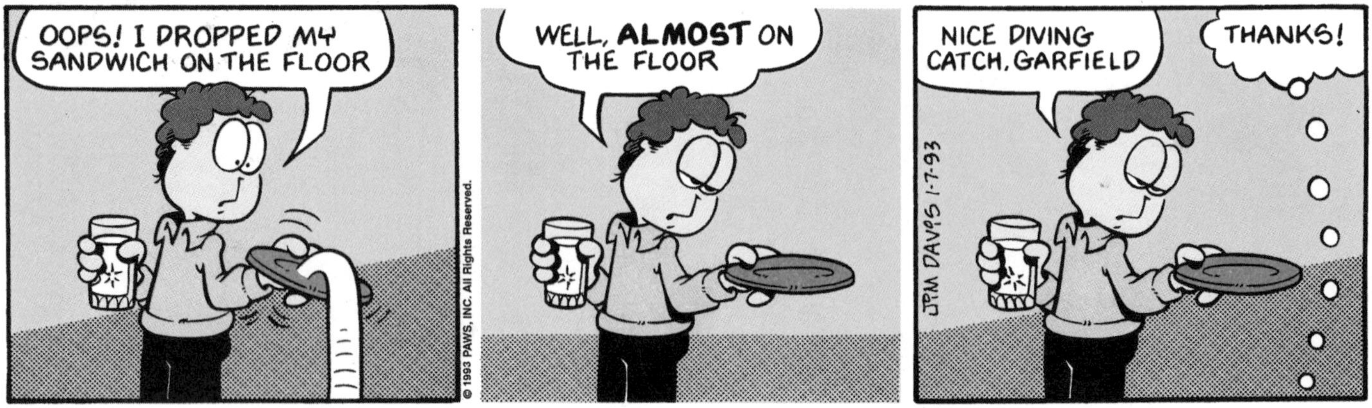
OOPS! I DROPPED MY SANDWICH ON THE FLOOR
© 1993 PAWS, INC. All Rights Reserved.
WELL, ALMOST ON THE FLOOR
NICE DIVING CATCH, GARFIELD
THANKS!
JIM DAVIS 1-7-93

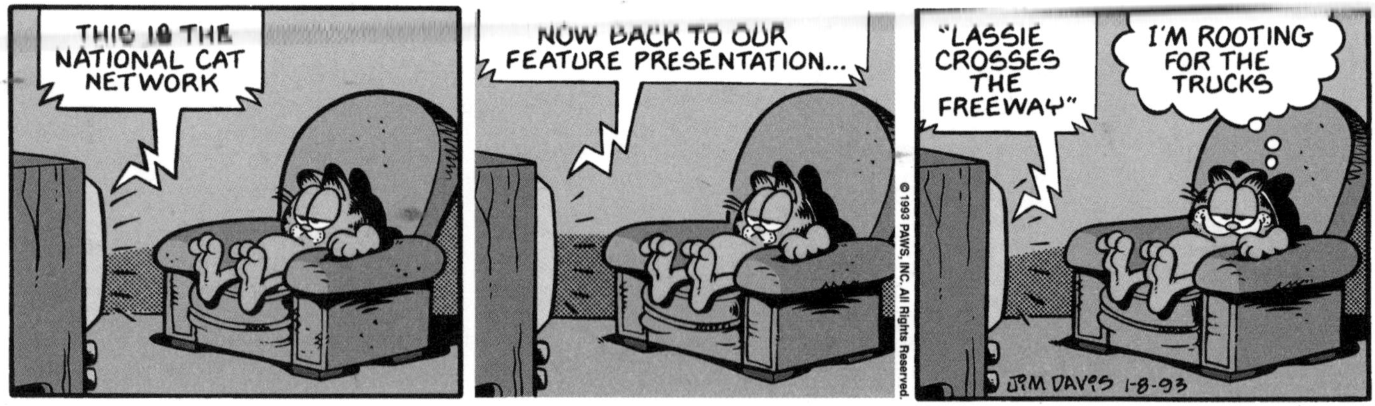
THIS IS THE NATIONAL CAT NETWORK
NOW BACK TO OUR FEATURE PRESENTATION...
© 1993 PAWS, INC. All Rights Reserved.
"LASSIE CROSSES THE FREEWAY"
I'M ROOTING FOR THE TRUCKS
JIM DAVIS 1-8-93

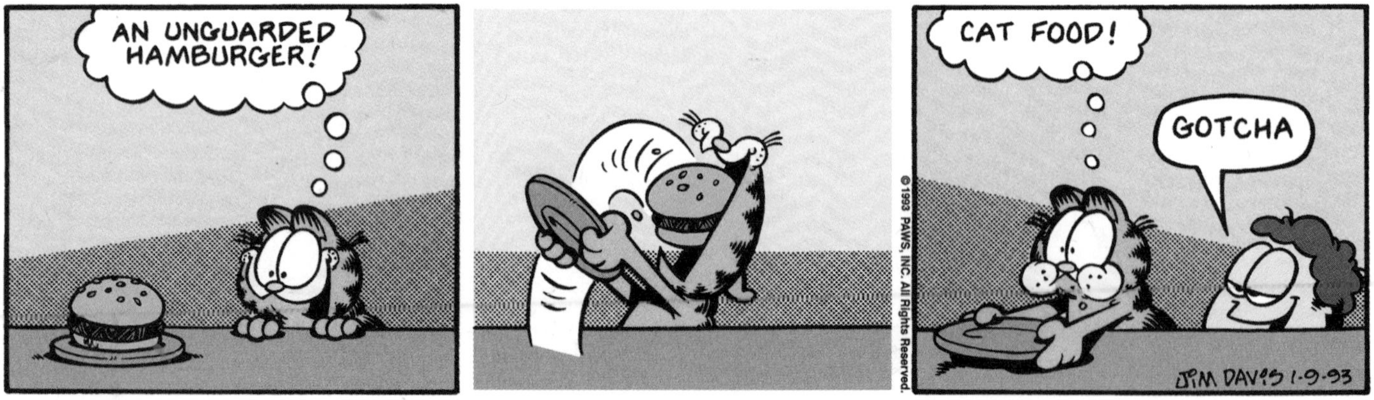
AN UNGUARDED HAMBURGER!
© 1993 PAWS, INC. All Rights Reserved.
CAT FOOD!
GOTCHA
JIM DAVIS 1-9-93

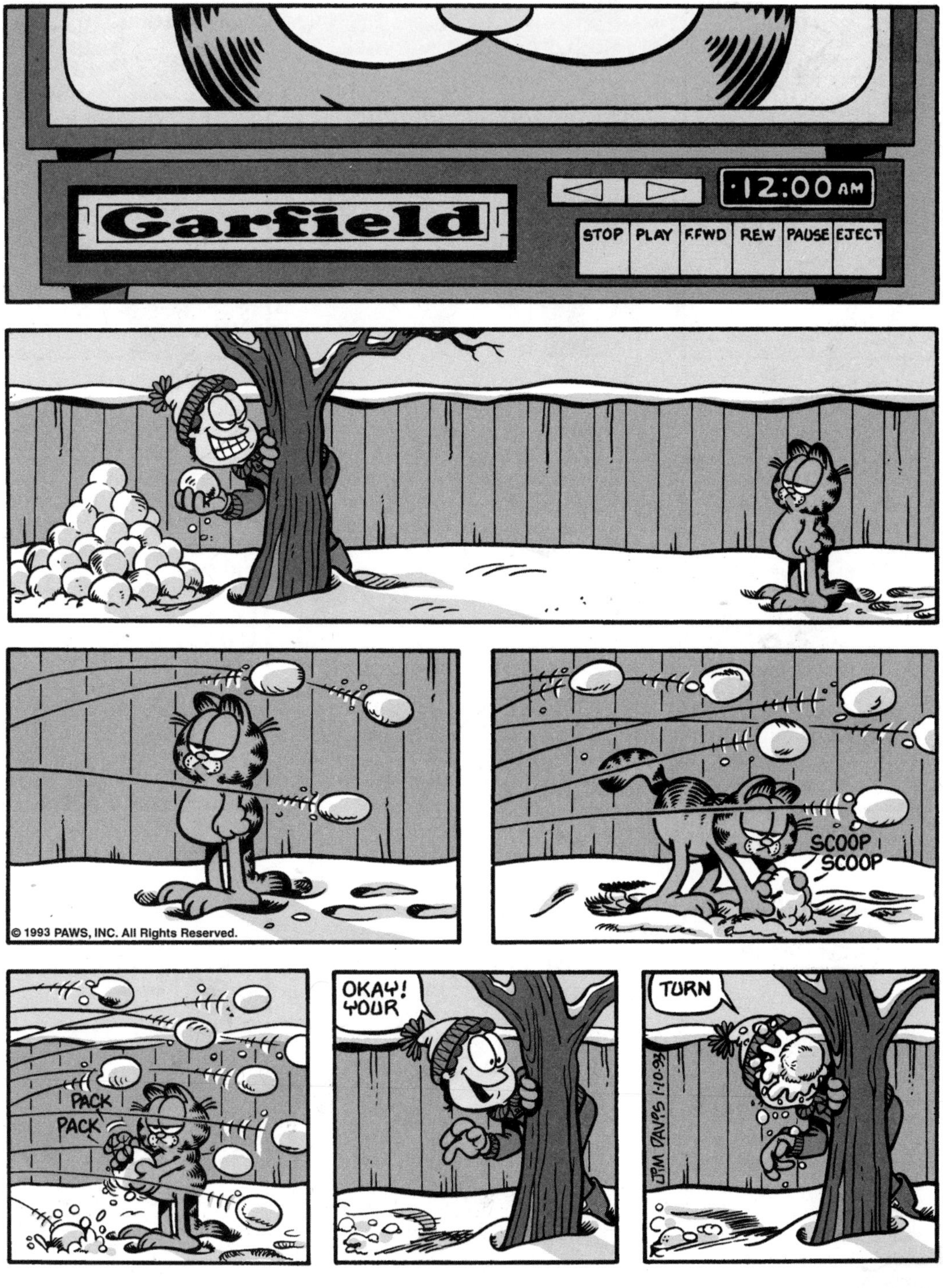
Garfield
·12:00 AM
STOP
PLAY
F.FWD
REW
PAUSE
EJECT
© 1993 PAWS, INC. All Rights Reserved.
SCOOP
SCOOP
PACK
PACK
OKAY! YOUR
JIM DAVIS 1-10-93
TURN

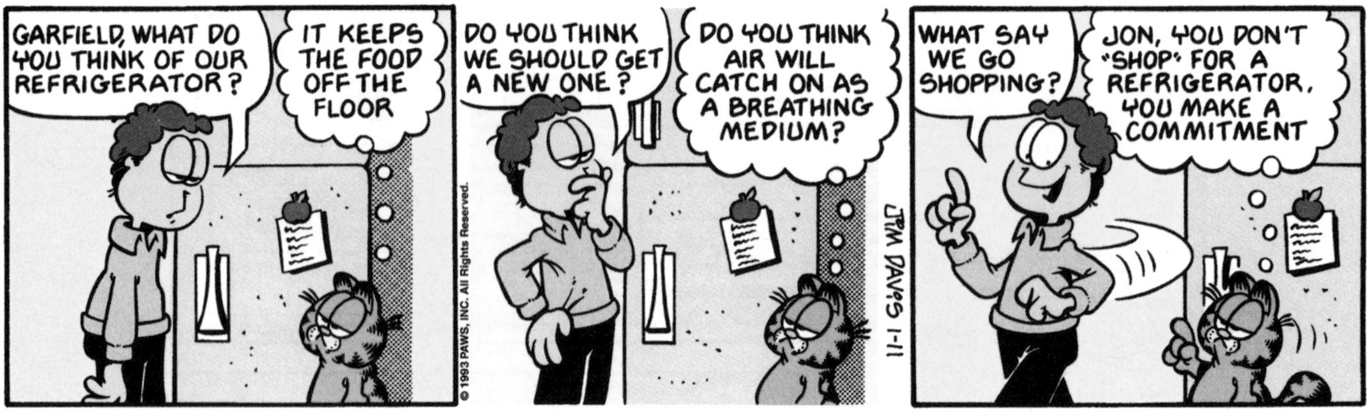
GARFIELD, WHAT DO YOU THINK OF OUR REFRIGERATOR?
IT KEEPS THE FOOD OFF THE FLOOR
DO YOU THINK WE SHOULD GET A NEW ONE?
DO YOU THINK AIR WILL CATCH ON AS A BREATHING MEDIUM?
WHAT SAY WE GO SHOPPING?
JON, YOU DON'T "SHOP" FOR A REFRIGERATOR, YOU MAKE A COMMITMENT
© 1993 PAWS, INC. All Rights Reserved.
JIM DAVIS 1-11

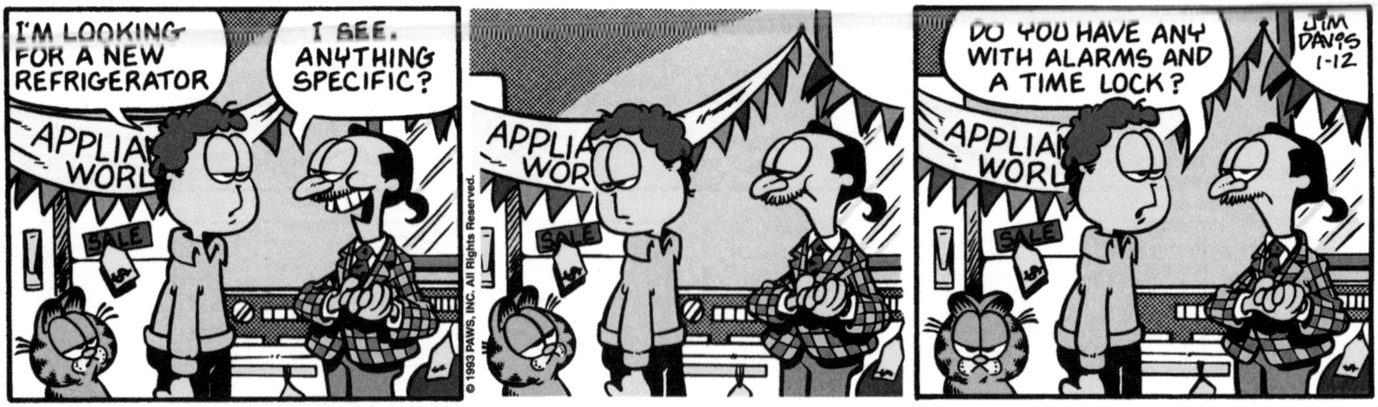
I'M LOOKING FOR A NEW REFRIGERATOR
I SEE. ANYTHING SPECIFIC?
DO YOU HAVE ANY WITH ALARMS AND A TIME LOCK?
© 1993 PAWS, INC. All Rights Reserved.
JIM DAVIS 1-12

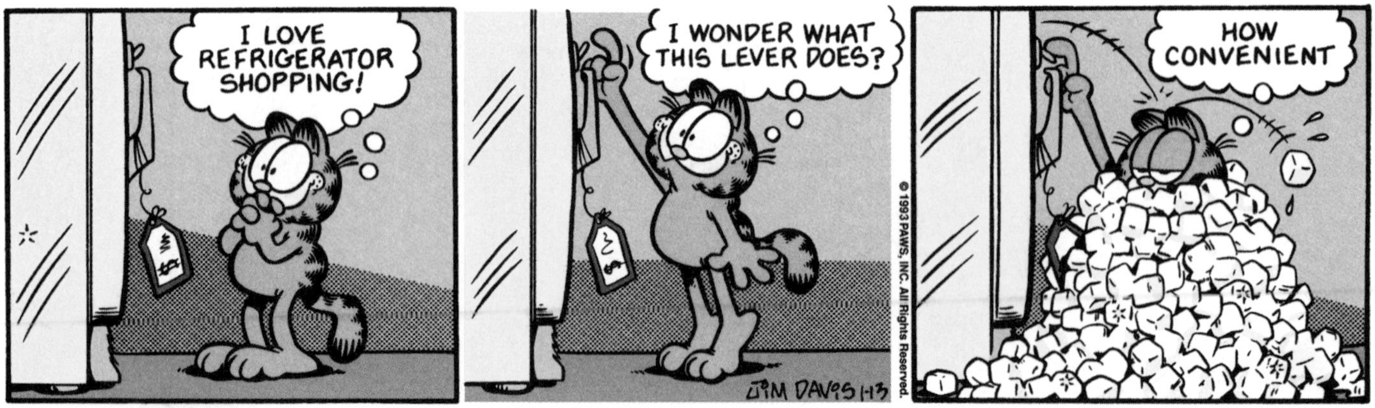
I LOVE REFRIGERATOR SHOPPING!
I WONDER WHAT THIS LEVER DOES?
HOW CONVENIENT
JIM DAVIS 1-13
© 1993 PAWS, INC. All Rights Reserved.

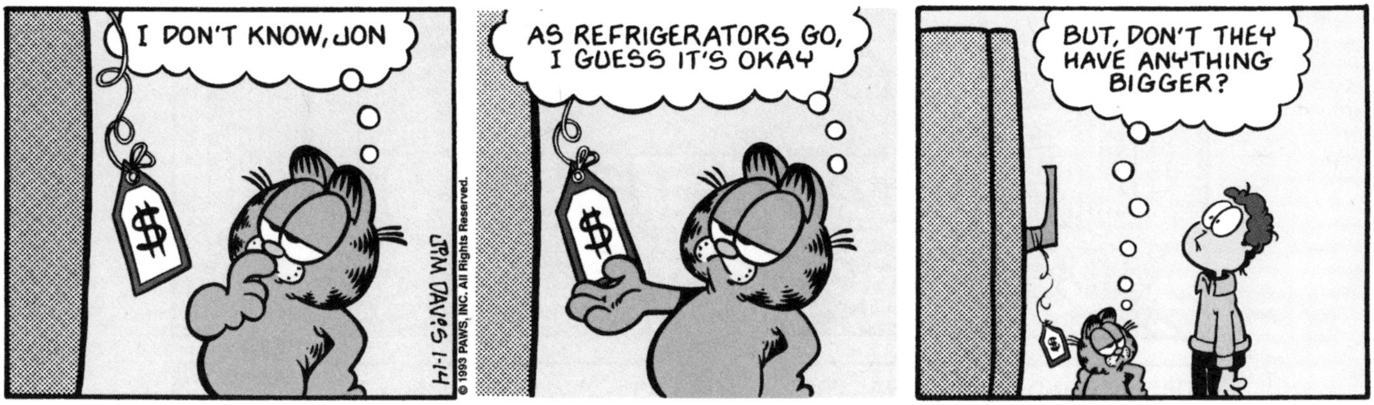
I DON'T KNOW, JON
JIM DAVIS 1-14
© 1993 PAWS, INC. All Rights Reserved.
AS REFRIGERATORS GO, I GUESS IT'S OKAY
BUT, DON'T THEY HAVE ANYTHING BIGGER?

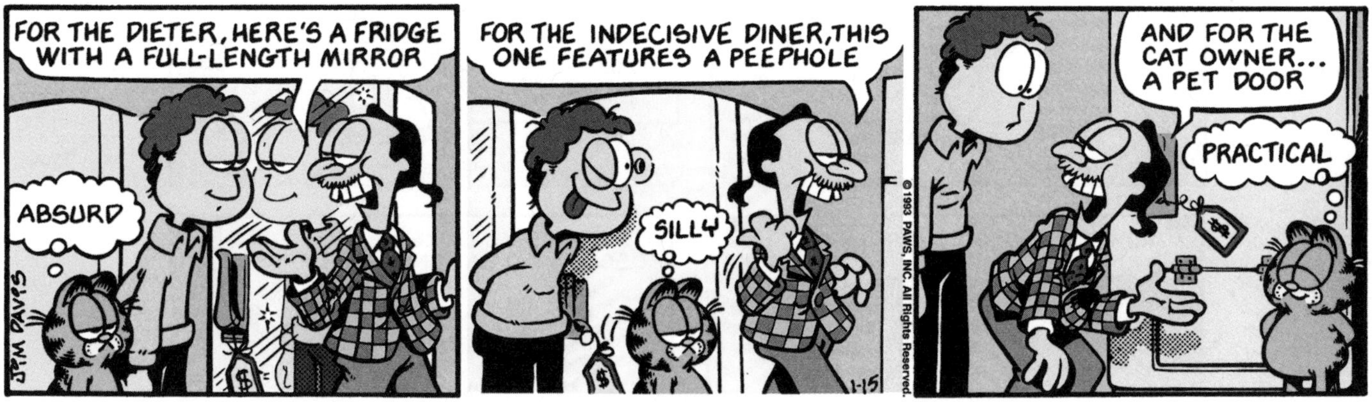
FOR THE DIETER, HERE'S A FRIDGE WITH A FULL-LENGTH MIRROR
ABSURD
JIM DAVIS
FOR THE INDECISIVE DINER, THIS ONE FEATURES A PEEPHOLE
SILLY
1-15
© 1993 PAWS, INC. All Rights Reserved.
AND FOR THE CAT OWNER... A PET DOOR
PRACTICAL

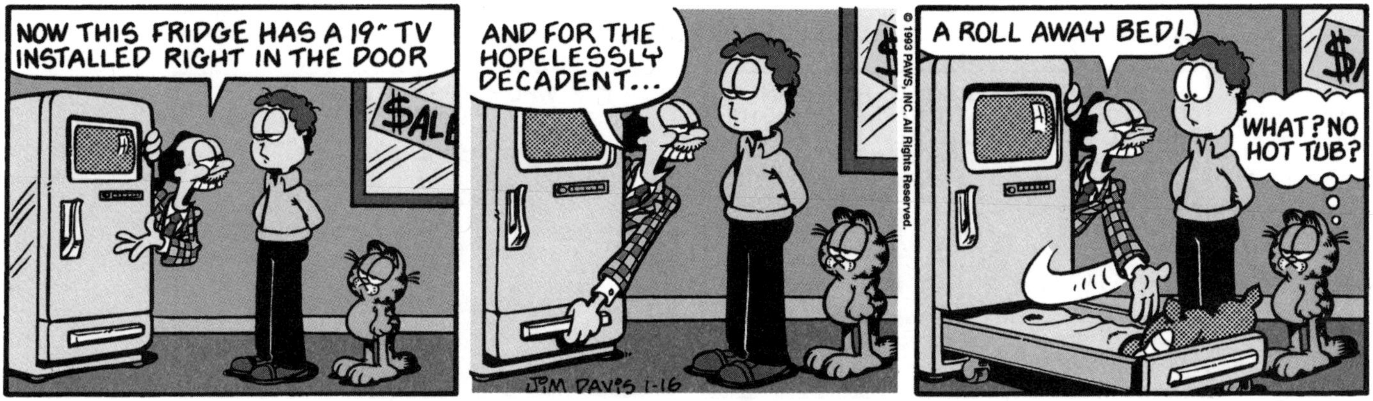
NOW THIS FRIDGE HAS A 19" TV INSTALLED RIGHT IN THE DOOR
SALE
AND FOR THE HOPELESSLY DECADENT...
JIM DAVIS 1-16
© 1993 PAWS, INC. All Rights Reserved.
A ROLL AWAY BED!
WHAT? NO HOT TUB?

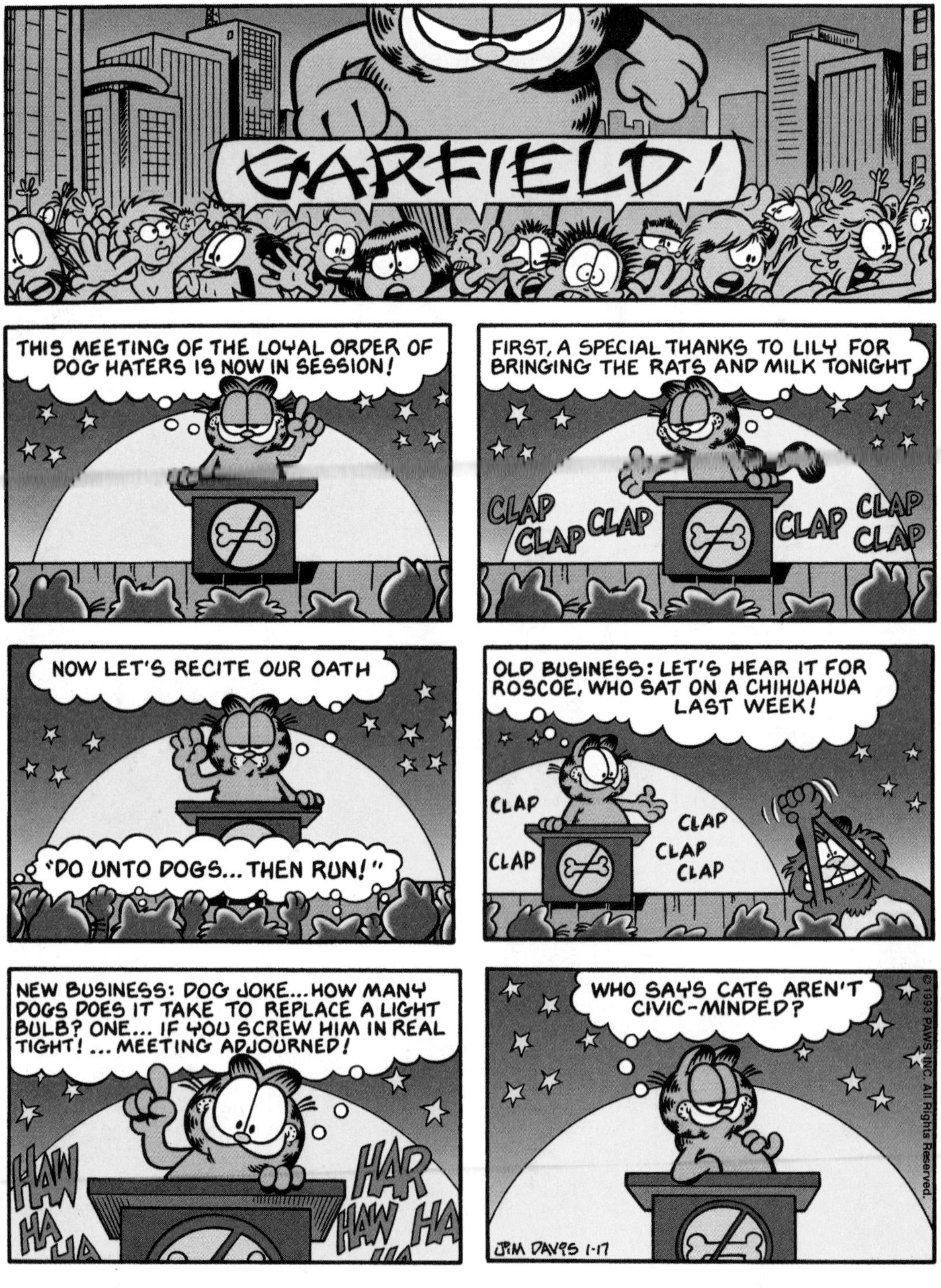
GARFIELD!
THIS MEETING OF THE LOYAL ORDER OF DOG HATERS IS NOW IN SESSION!
FIRST, A SPECIAL THANKS TO LILY FOR BRINGING THE RATS AND MILK TONIGHT
CLAP CLAP CLAP CLAP CLAP CLAP
NOW LET'S RECITE OUR OATH
"DO UNTO DOGS... THEN RUN!"
OLD BUSINESS: LET'S HEAR IT FOR ROSCOE, WHO SAT ON A CHIHUAHUA LAST WEEK!
CLAP CLAP CLAP CLAP CLAP
NEW BUSINESS: DOG JOKE... HOW MANY DOGS DOES IT TAKE TO REPLACE A LIGHT BULB? ONE... IF YOU SCREW HIM IN REAL TIGHT! ... MEETING ADJOURNED!
HAW HA HAR HAW HA
WHO SAYS CATS AREN'T CIVIC-MINDED?
JIM DAVIS 1-17
© 1993 PAWS, INC. All Rights Reserved.

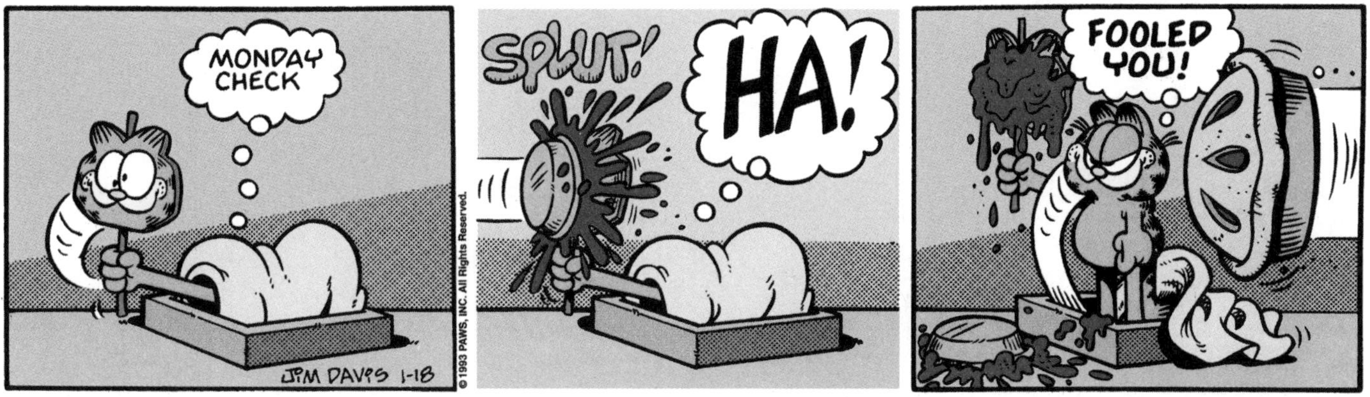
MONDAY CHECK
JIM DAVIS 1-18
© 1993 PAWS, INC. All Rights Reserved.
SPLUT!
HA!
FOOLED YOU!

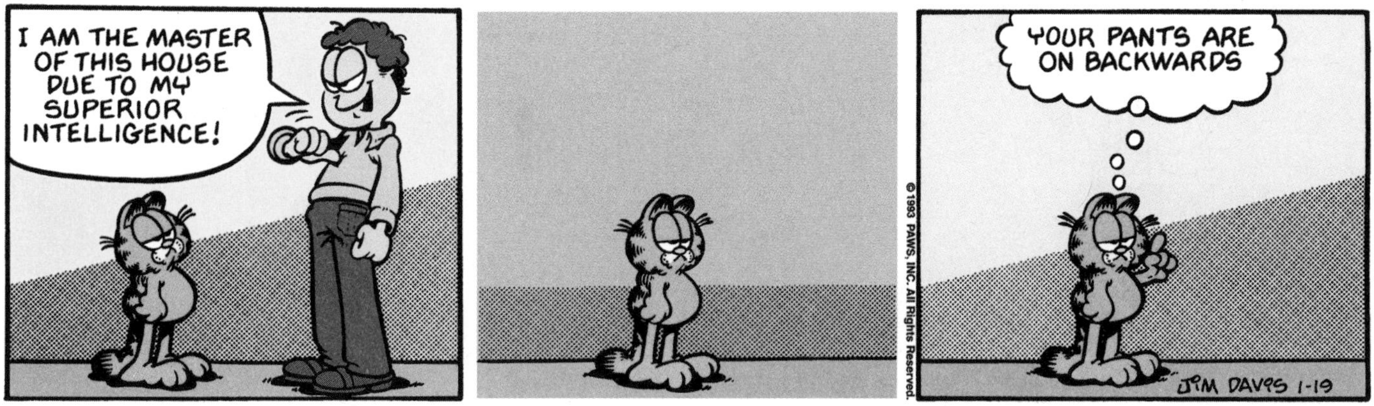
I AM THE MASTER OF THIS HOUSE DUE TO MY SUPERIOR INTELLIGENCE!
© 1993 PAWS, INC. All Rights Reserved.
YOUR PANTS ARE ON BACKWARDS
JIM DAVIS 1-19

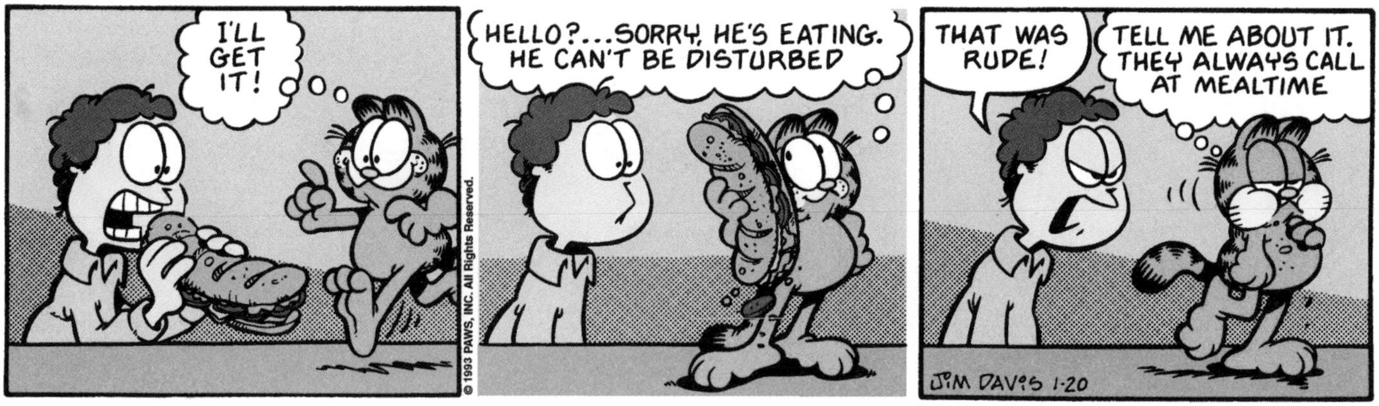
I'LL GET IT!
© 1993 PAWS, INC. All Rights Reserved.
HELLO?...SORRY, HE'S EATING. HE CAN'T BE DISTURBED
THAT WAS RUDE!
TELL ME ABOUT IT. THEY ALWAYS CALL AT MEALTIME
JIM DAVIS 1-20

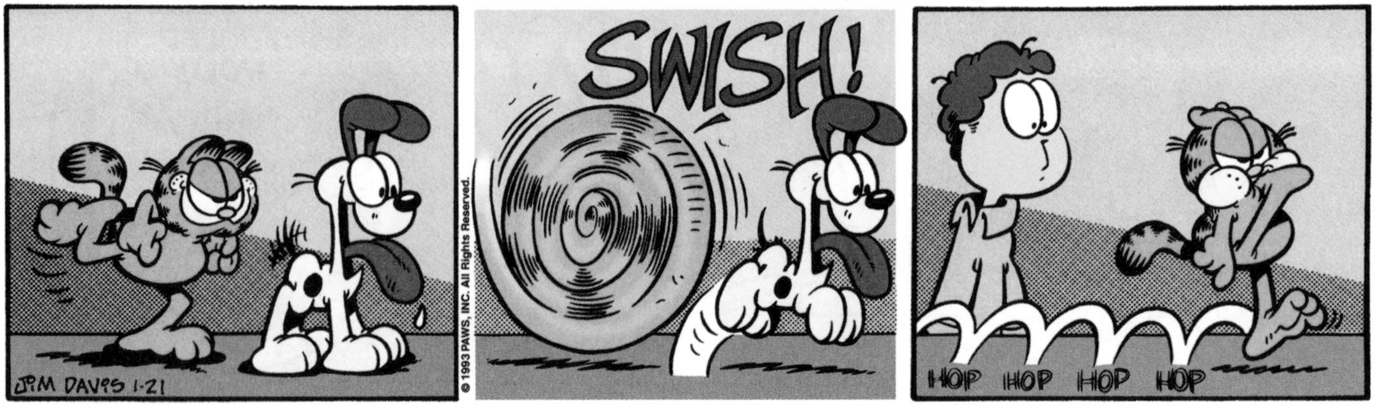
JIM DAVIS 1-21
© 1993 PAWS, INC. All Rights Reserved.
SWISH!
HOP HOP HOP HOP

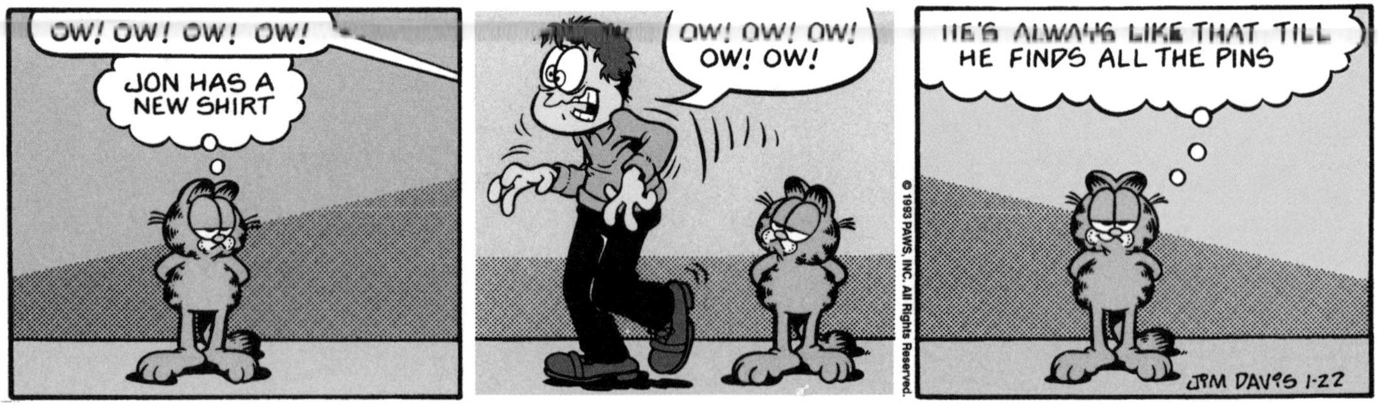
OW! OW! OW! OW!
JON HAS A NEW SHIRT
OW! OW! OW! OW! OW!
© 1993 PAWS, INC. All Rights Reserved.
HE'S ALWAYS LIKE THAT TILL HE FINDS ALL THE PINS
JIM DAVIS 1-22

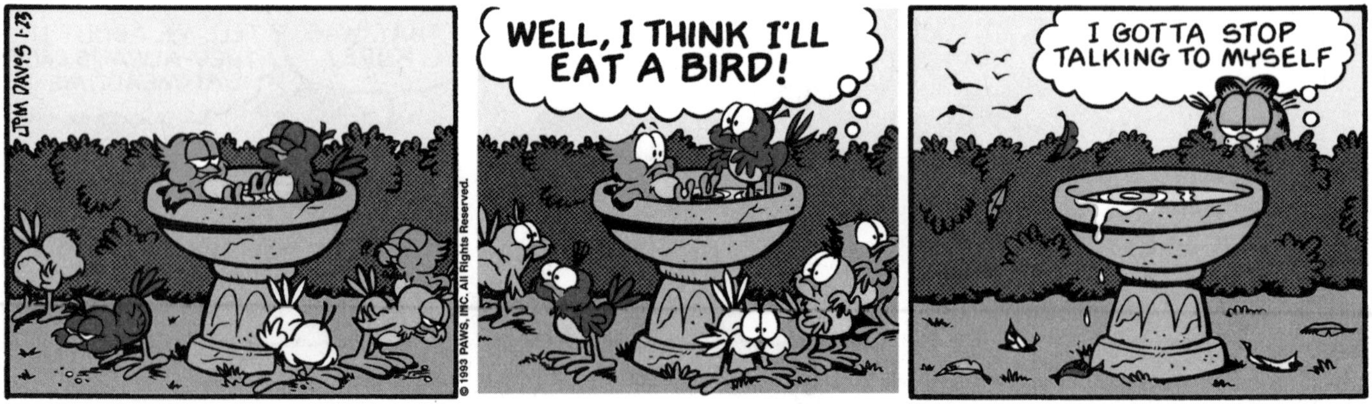
JIM DAVIS 1-23
© 1993 PAWS, INC. All Rights Reserved.
WELL, I THINK I'LL EAT A BIRD!
I GOTTA STOP TALKING TO MYSELF

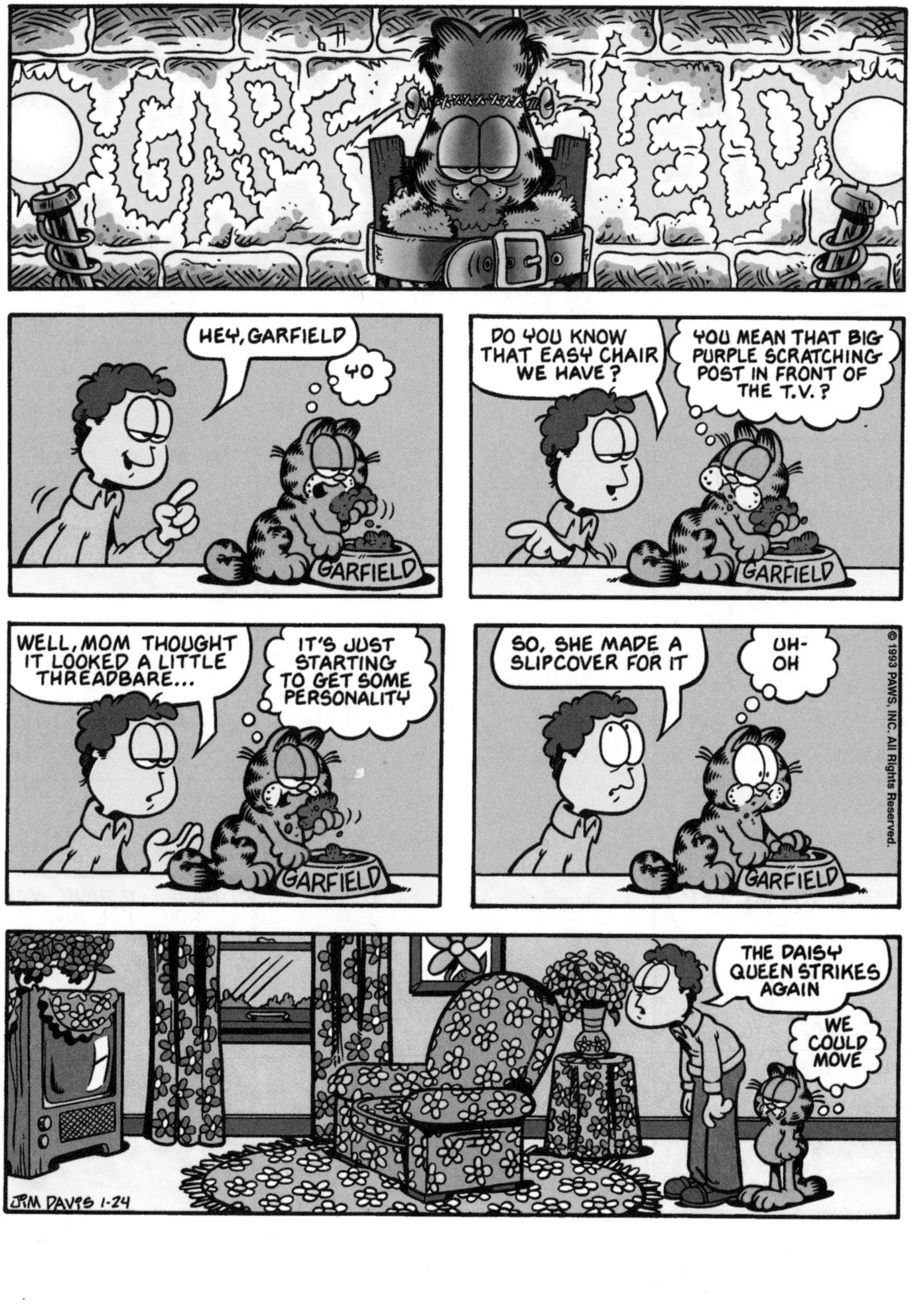
GARFIELD
HEY, GARFIELD
YO
DO YOU KNOW THAT EASY CHAIR WE HAVE?
YOU MEAN THAT BIG PURPLE SCRATCHING POST IN FRONT OF THE T.V.?
GARFIELD
GARFIELD
WELL, MOM THOUGHT IT LOOKED A LITTLE THREADBARE...
IT'S JUST STARTING TO GET SOME PERSONALITY
SO, SHE MADE A SLIPCOVER FOR IT
UH-OH
GARFIELD
GARFIELD
© 1993 PAWS, INC. All Rights Reserved.
THE DAISY QUEEN STRIKES AGAIN
WE COULD MOVE
JIM DAVIS 1-24

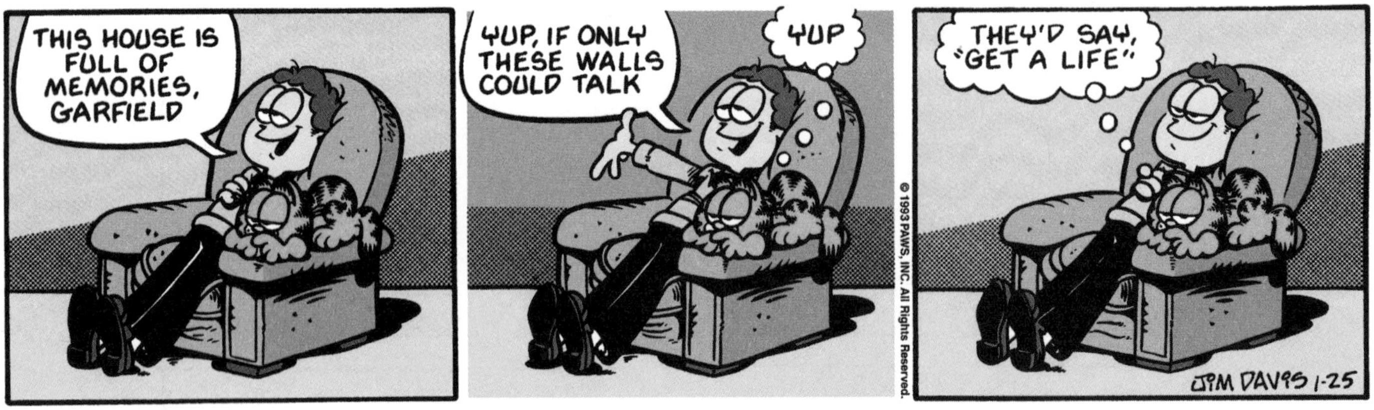
THIS HOUSE IS FULL OF MEMORIES, GARFIELD
YUP, IF ONLY THESE WALLS COULD TALK
YUP
THEY'D SAY, "GET A LIFE"
© 1993 PAWS, INC. All Rights Reserved.
JIM DAVIS 1-25

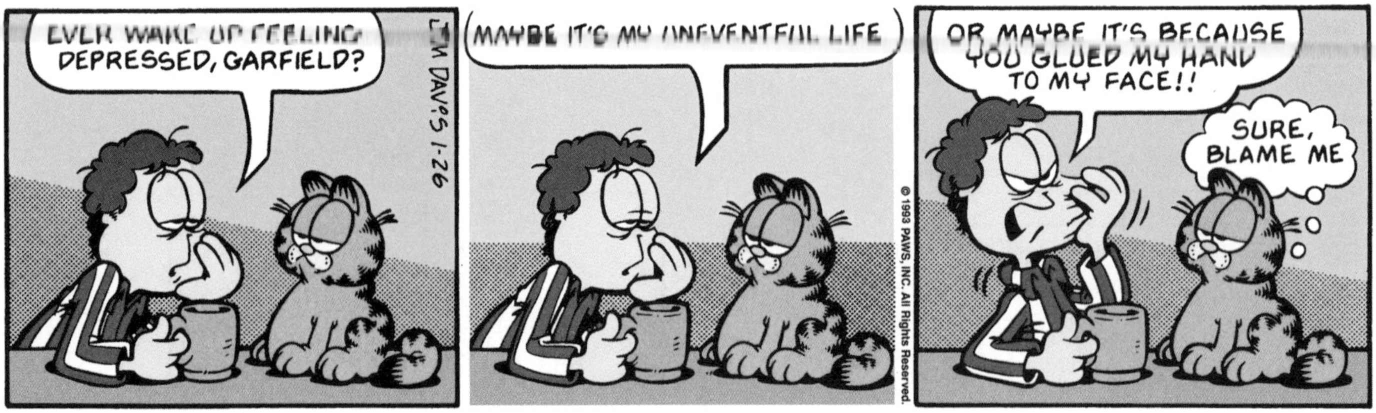
EVER WAKE UP FEELING DEPRESSED, GARFIELD?
JIM DAVIS 1-26
MAYBE IT'S MY UNEVENTFUL LIFE
OR MAYBE IT'S BECAUSE YOU GLUED MY HAND TO MY FACE!!
SURE, BLAME ME
© 1993 PAWS, INC. All Rights Reserved.

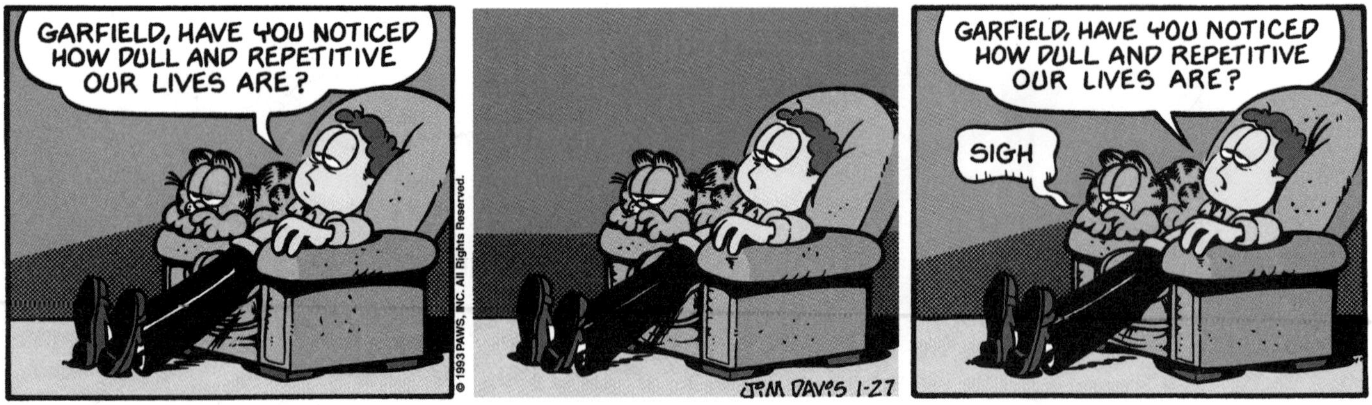
GARFIELD, HAVE YOU NOTICED HOW DULL AND REPETITIVE OUR LIVES ARE?
© 1993 PAWS, INC. All Rights Reserved.
JIM DAVIS 1-27
GARFIELD, HAVE YOU NOTICED HOW DULL AND REPETITIVE OUR LIVES ARE?
SIGH

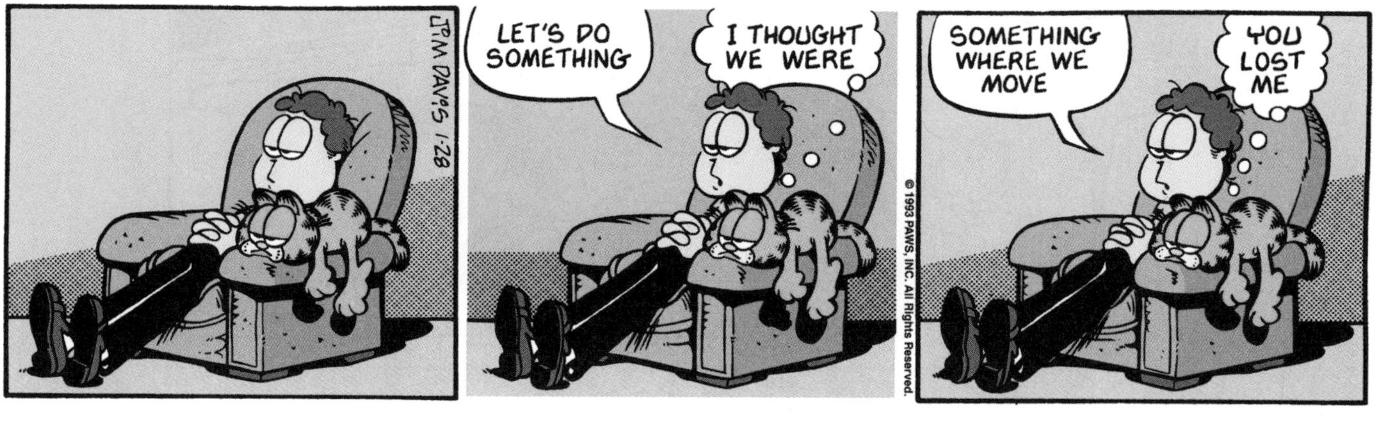
JIM DAVIS 1-28
LET'S DO SOMETHING
I THOUGHT WE WERE
© 1993 PAWS, INC. All Rights Reserved.
SOMETHING WHERE WE MOVE
YOU LOST ME

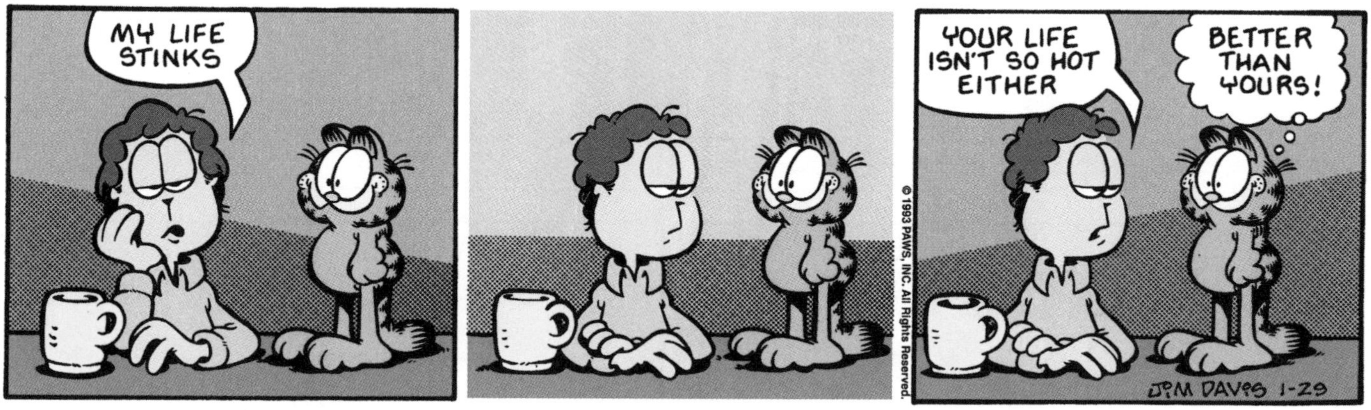
MY LIFE STINKS
© 1993 PAWS, INC. All Rights Reserved.
YOUR LIFE ISN'T SO HOT EITHER
BETTER THAN YOURS!
JIM DAVIS 1-29

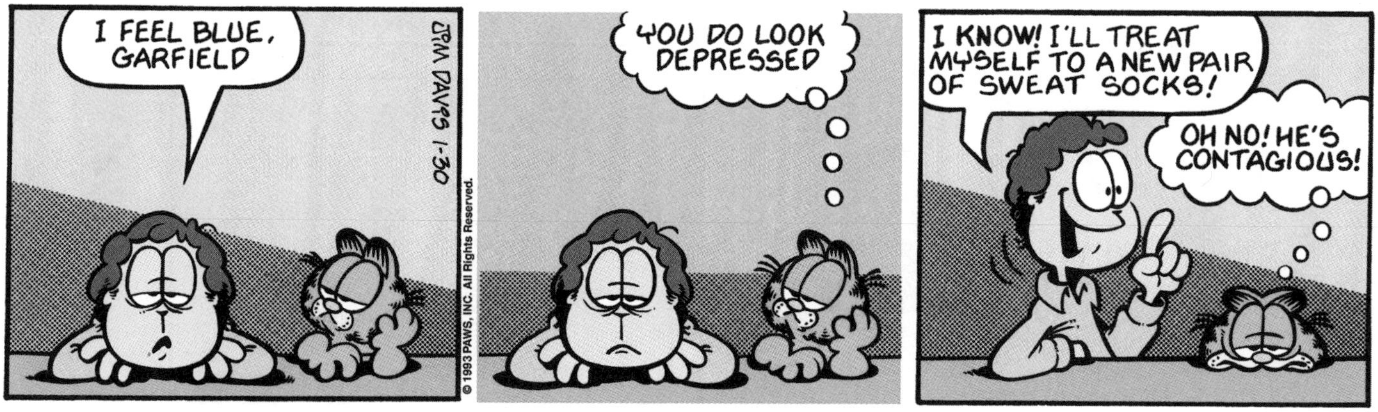
I FEEL BLUE, GARFIELD
JIM DAVIS 1-30
© 1993 PAWS, INC. All Rights Reserved.
YOU DO LOOK DEPRESSED
I KNOW! I'LL TREAT MYSELF TO A NEW PAIR OF SWEAT SOCKS!
OH NO! HE'S CONTAGIOUS!

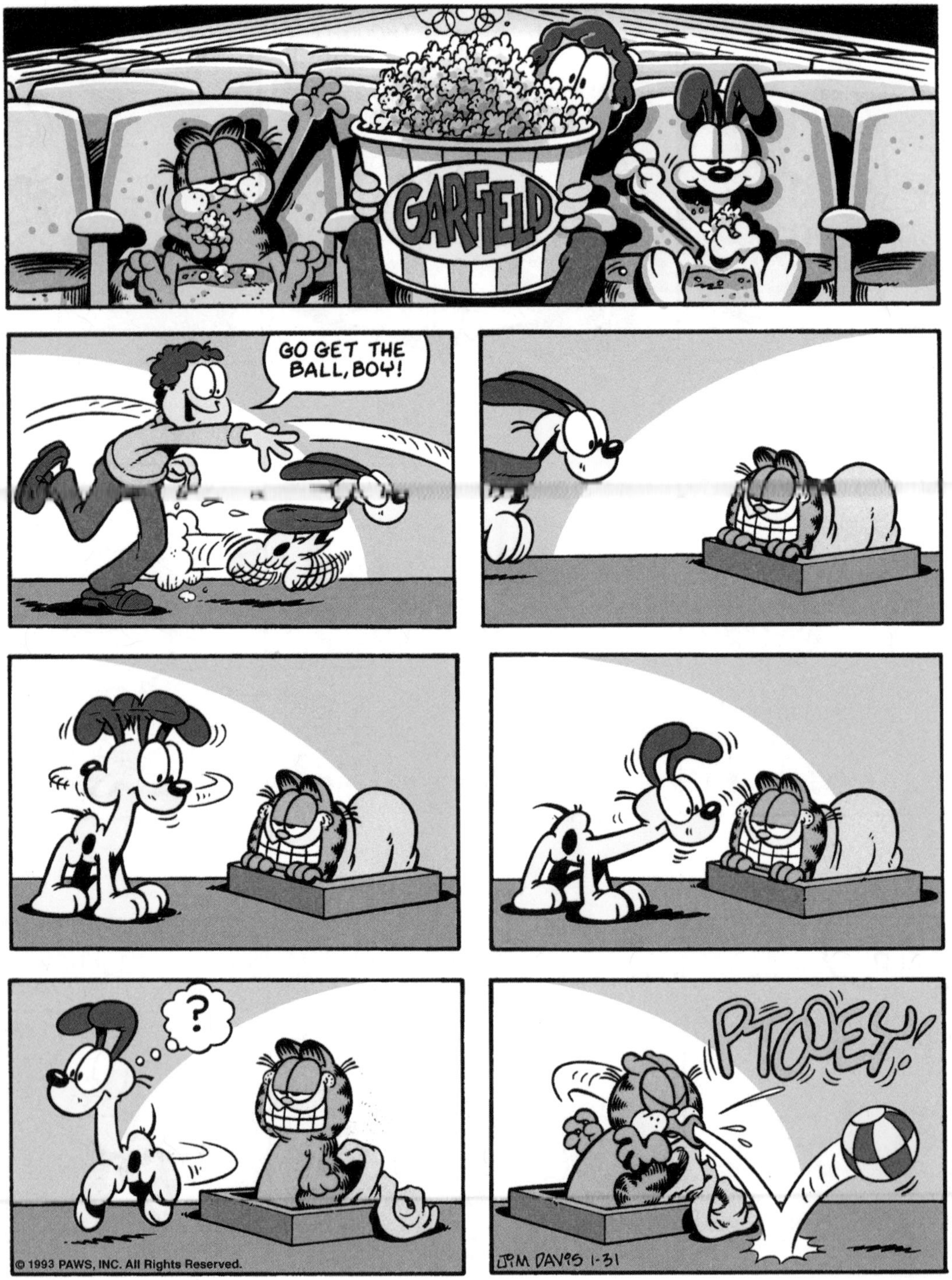
GARFIELD
GO GET THE BALL, BOY!
?
PTOOEY!
JIM DAVIS 1-31

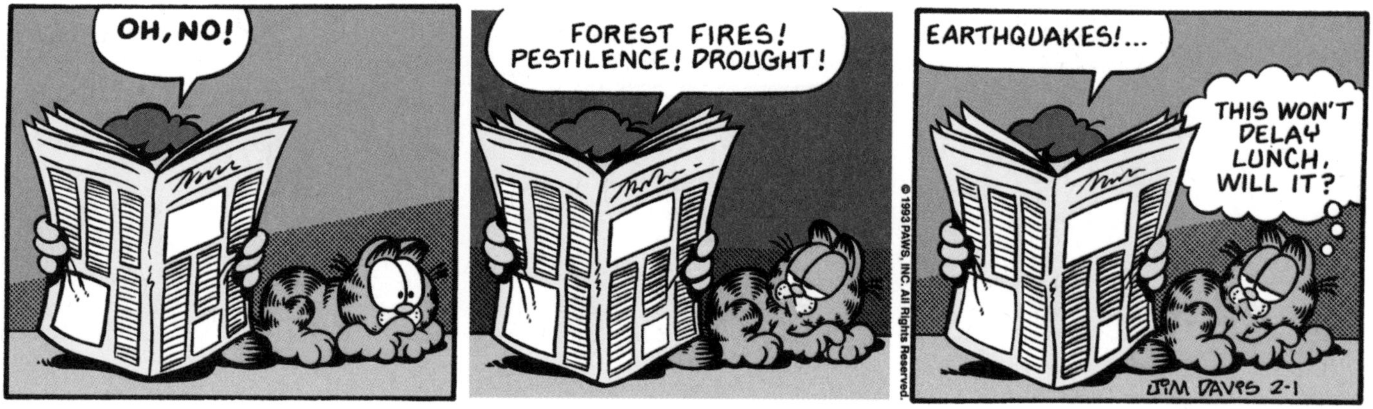
OH, NO!
FOREST FIRES! PESTILENCE! DROUGHT!
© 1993 PAWS, INC. All Rights Reserved.
EARTHQUAKES!...
THIS WON'T DELAY LUNCH, WILL IT?
JIM DAVIS 2-1

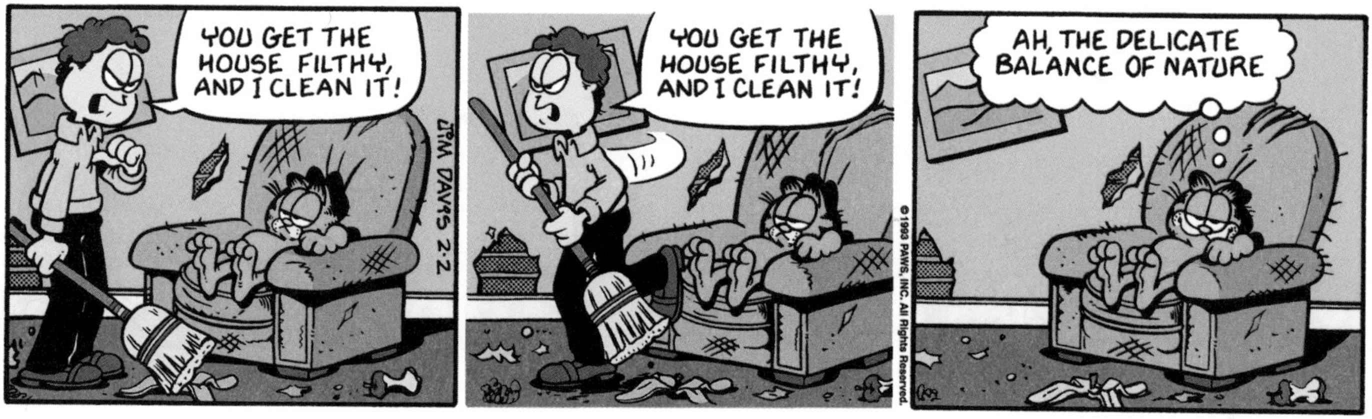
YOU GET THE HOUSE FILTHY, AND I CLEAN IT!
JIM DAVIS 2-2
YOU GET THE HOUSE FILTHY, AND I CLEAN IT!
© 1993 PAWS, INC. All Rights Reserved.
AH, THE DELICATE BALANCE OF NATURE

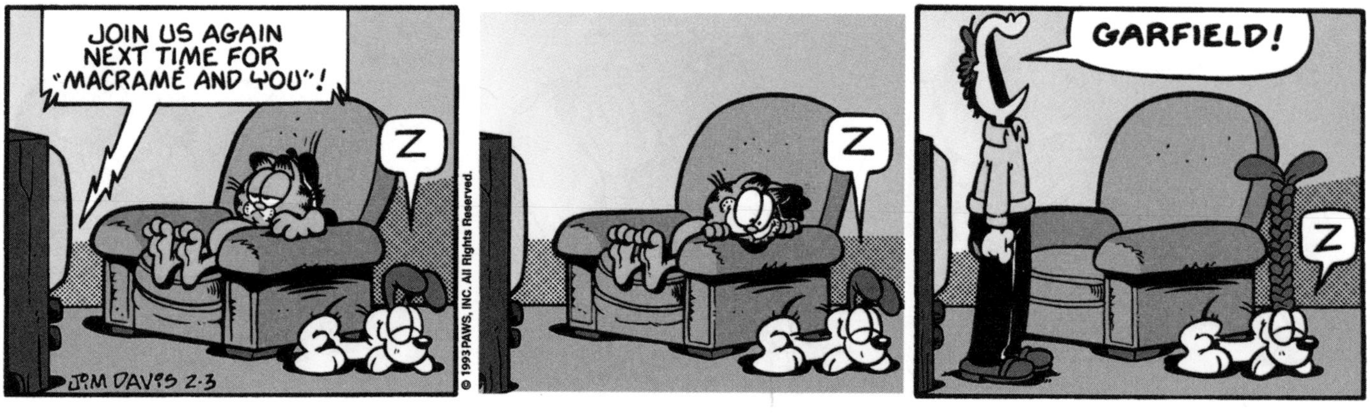
JOIN US AGAIN NEXT TIME FOR "MACRAMÉ AND YOU"!
Z
JIM DAVIS 2-3
© 1993 PAWS, INC. All Rights Reserved.
Z
GARFIELD!
Z

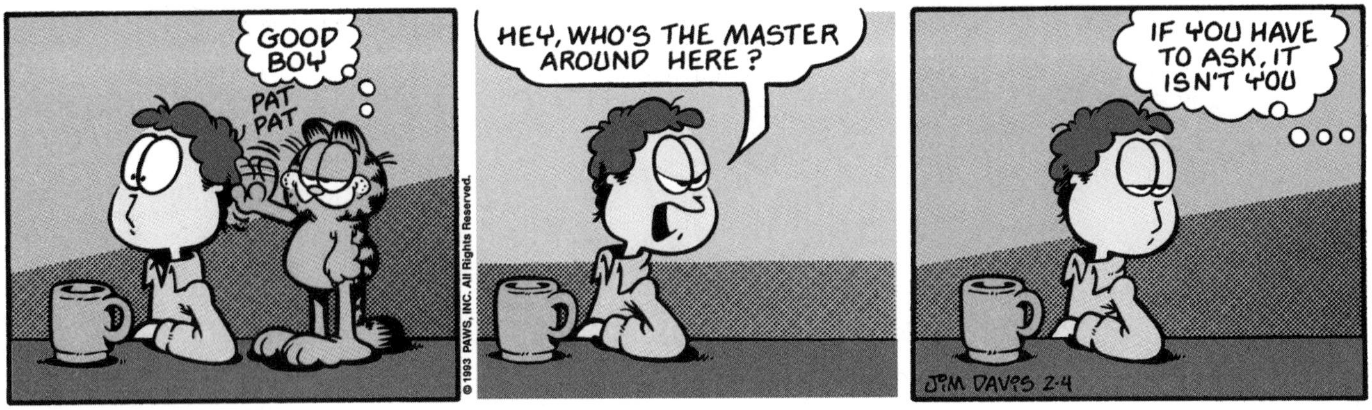
GOOD BOY
PAT PAT
HEY, WHO'S THE MASTER AROUND HERE?
IF YOU HAVE TO ASK, IT ISN'T YOU
JIM DAVIS 2-4

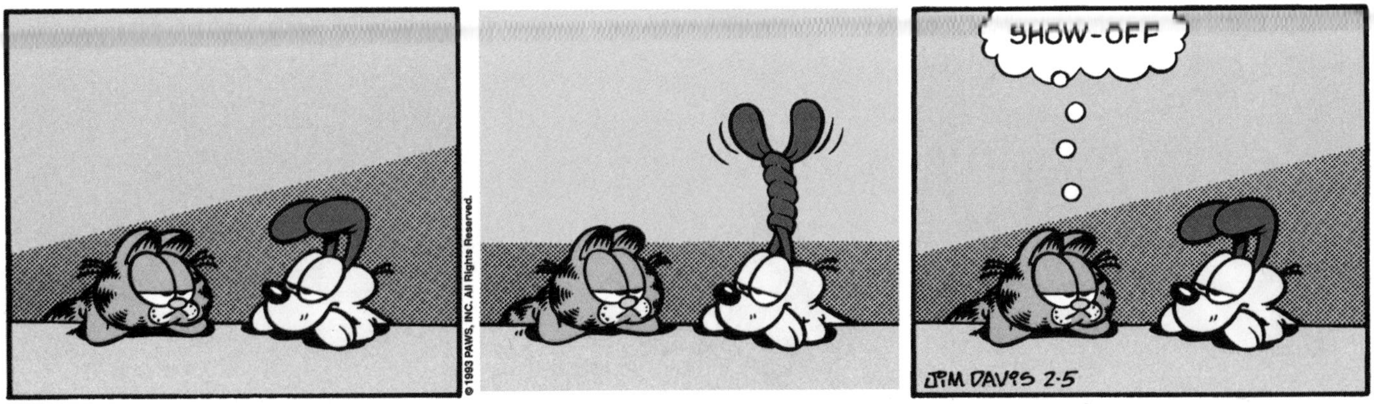
SHOW-OFF
JIM DAVIS 2-5

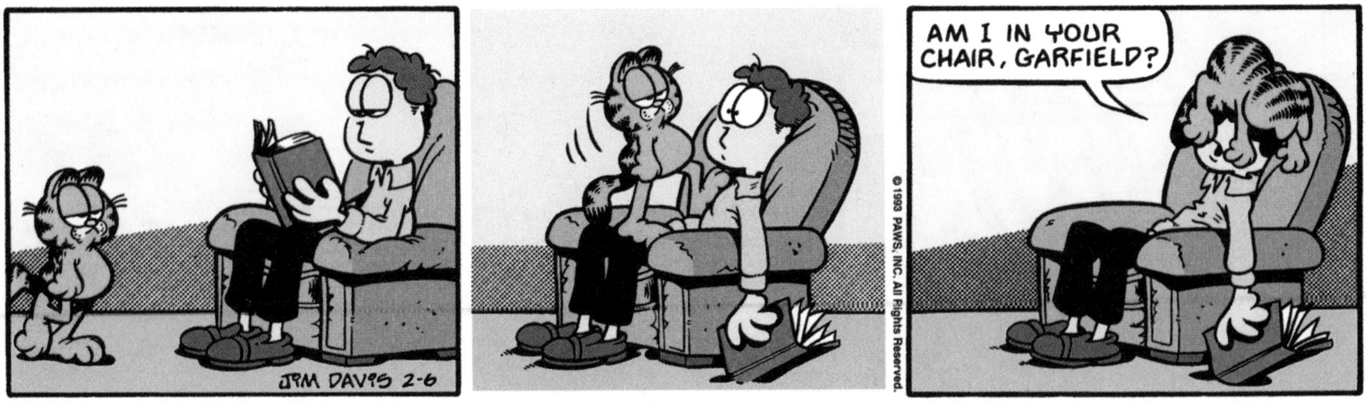
JIM DAVIS 2-6
AM I IN YOUR CHAIR, GARFIELD?

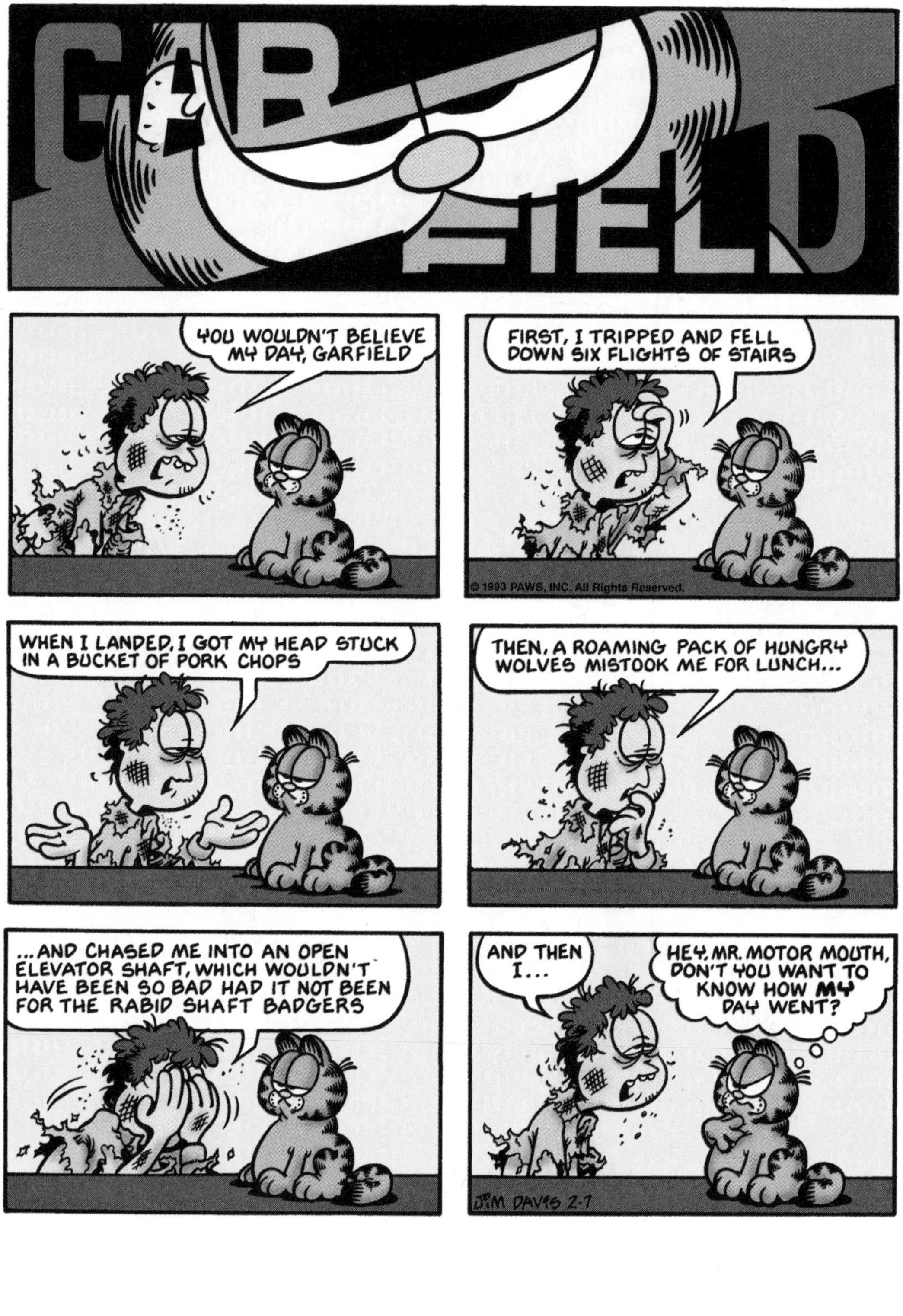
GARFIELD
YOU WOULDN'T BELIEVE MY DAY, GARFIELD
FIRST, I TRIPPED AND FELL DOWN SIX FLIGHTS OF STAIRS
© 1993 PAWS, INC. All Rights Reserved.
WHEN I LANDED, I GOT MY HEAD STUCK IN A BUCKET OF PORK CHOPS
THEN, A ROAMING PACK OF HUNGRY WOLVES MISTOOK ME FOR LUNCH...
...AND CHASED ME INTO AN OPEN ELEVATOR SHAFT, WHICH WOULDN'T HAVE BEEN SO BAD HAD IT NOT BEEN FOR THE RABID SHAFT BADGERS
AND THEN I...
HEY, MR. MOTOR MOUTH, DON'T YOU WANT TO KNOW HOW **MY** DAY WENT?
JIM DAVIS 2-7

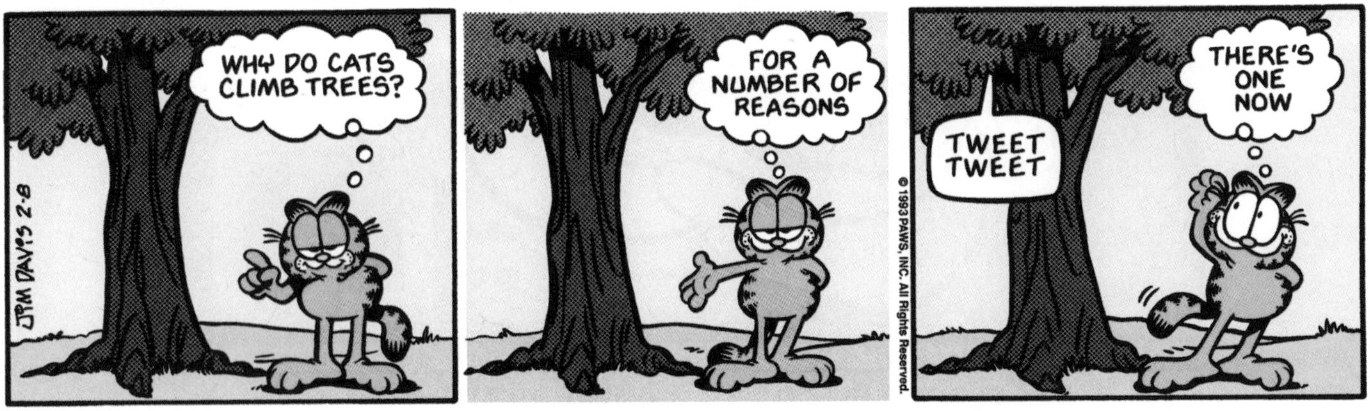
WHY DO CATS CLIMB TREES?
JIM DAVIS 2-8
FOR A NUMBER OF REASONS
© 1993 PAWS, INC. All Rights Reserved.
TWEET TWEET
THERE'S ONE NOW

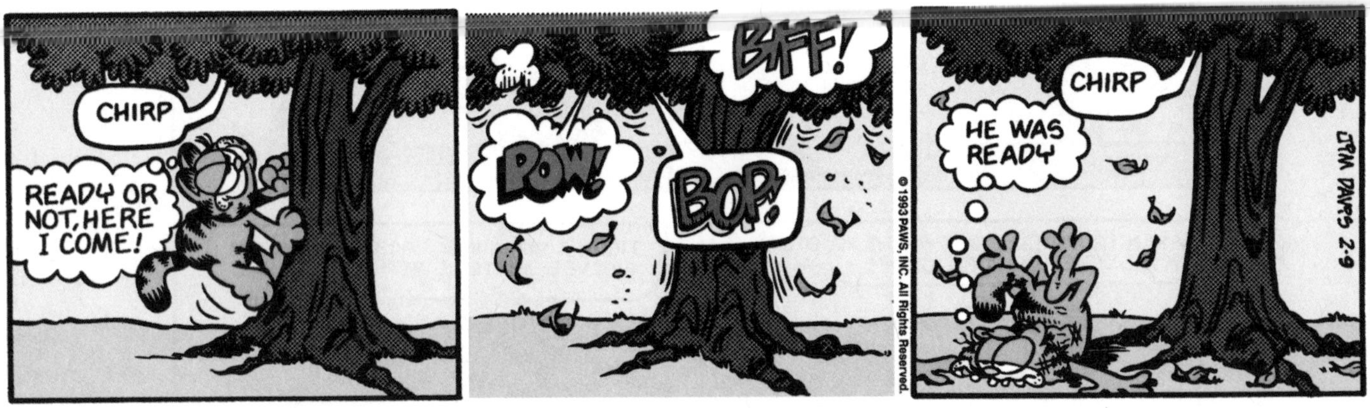
CHIRP
READY OR NOT, HERE I COME!
BAFF!
POW!
BOP!
© 1993 PAWS, INC. All Rights Reserved.
CHIRP
HE WAS READY
JIM DAVIS 2-9

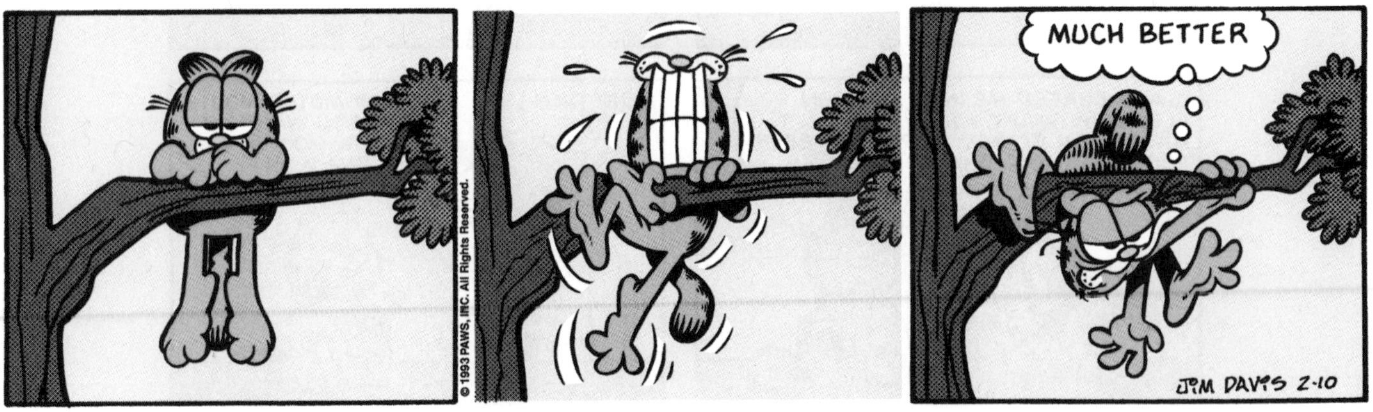
© 1993 PAWS, INC. All Rights Reserved.
MUCH BETTER
JIM DAVIS 2-10

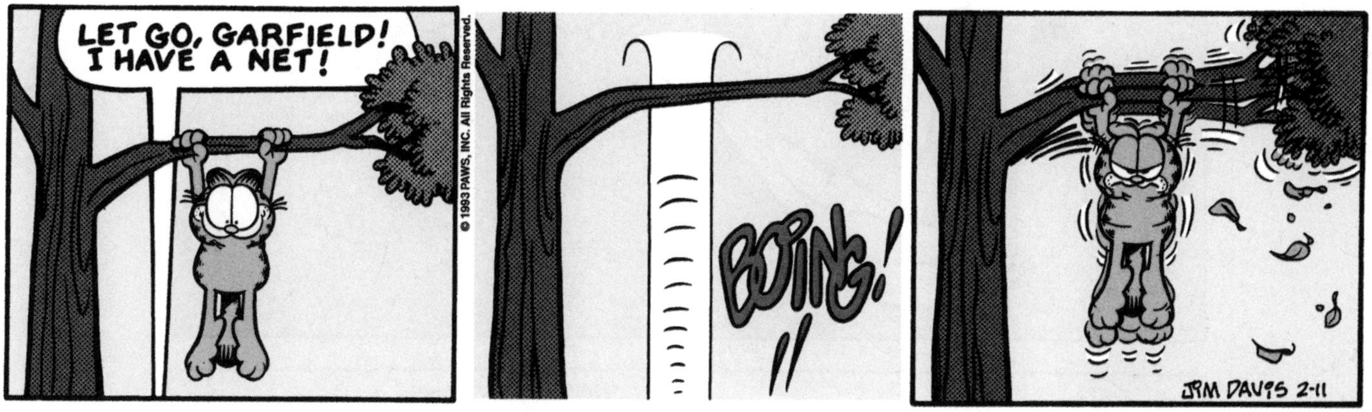
LET GO, GARFIELD! I HAVE A NET!
© 1993 PAWS, INC. All Rights Reserved.
BOING!
JIM DAVIS 2-11

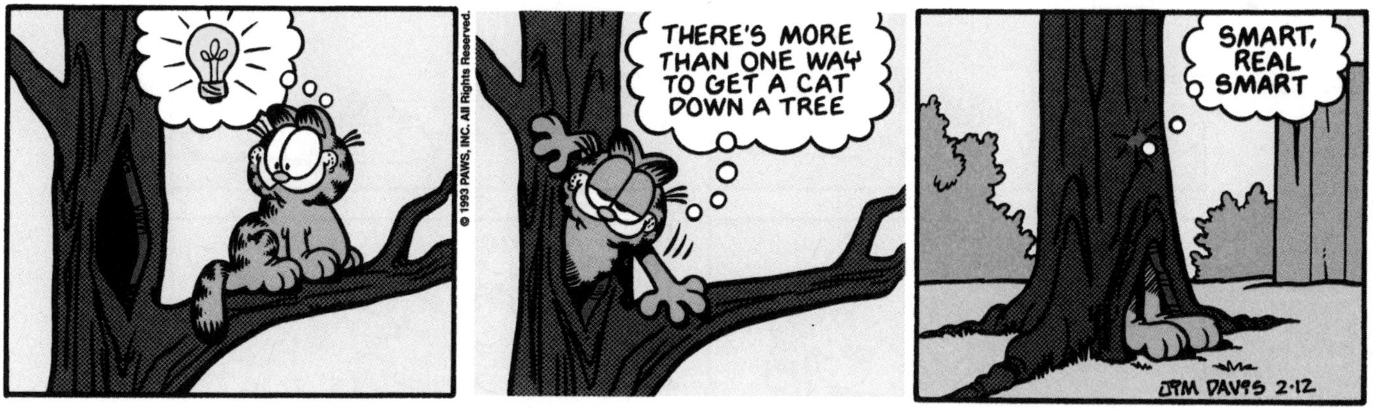
© 1993 PAWS, INC. All Rights Reserved.
THERE'S MORE THAN ONE WAY TO GET A CAT DOWN A TREE
SMART, REAL SMART
JIM DAVIS 2-12

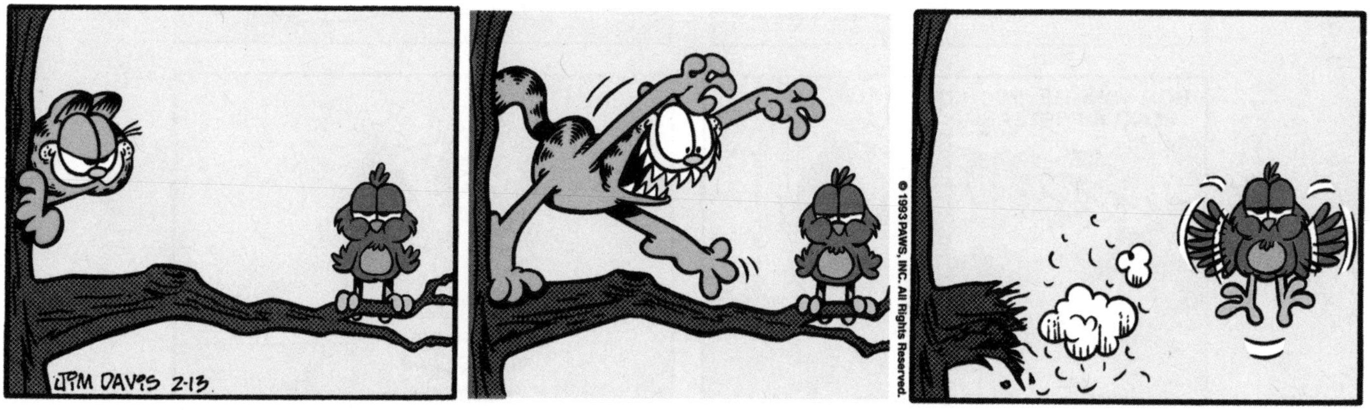
JIM DAVIS 2-13
© 1993 PAWS, INC. All Rights Reserved.

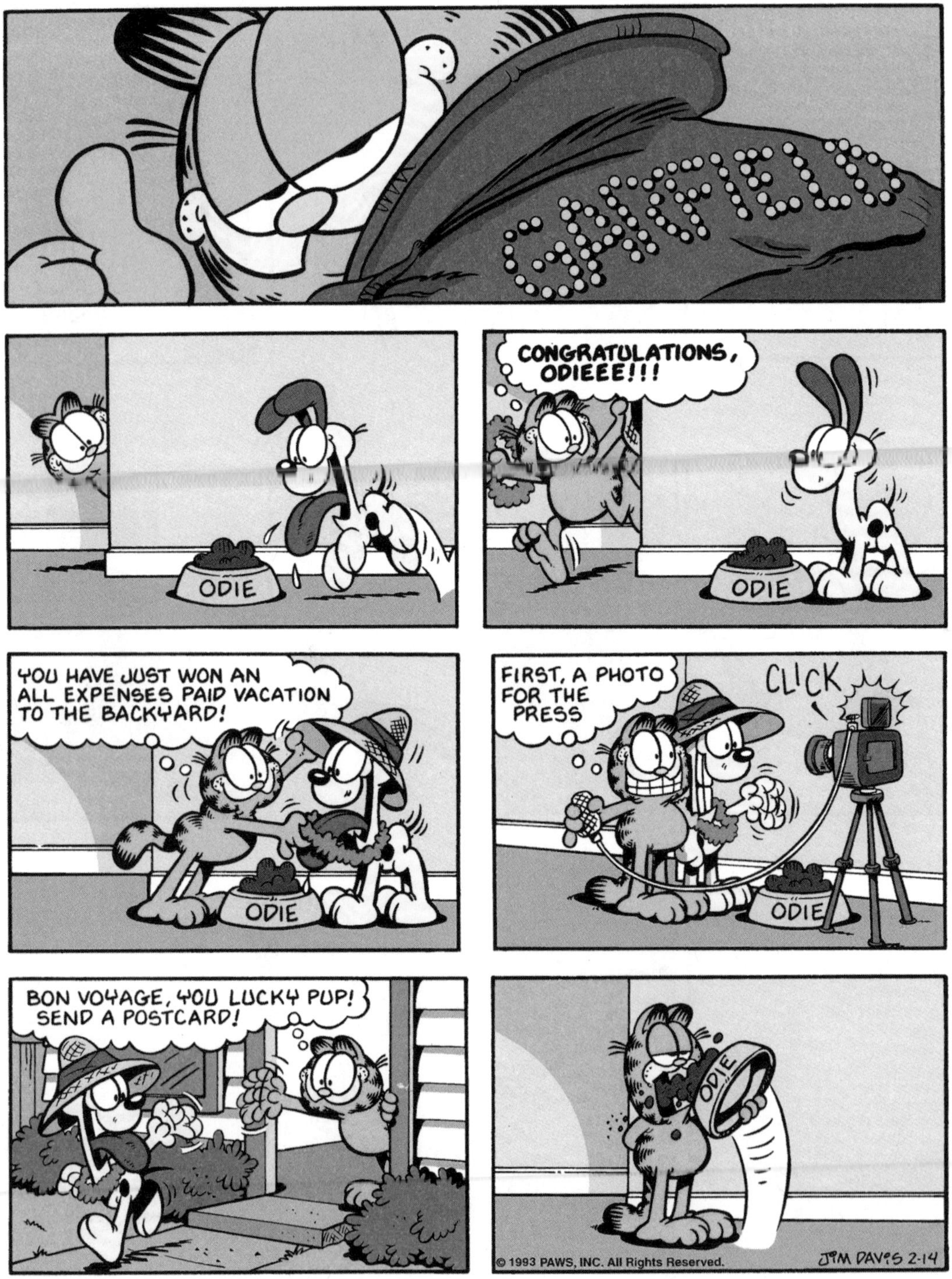
GARFIELD
CONGRATULATIONS, ODIEEE!!!
ODIE
YOU HAVE JUST WON AN ALL EXPENSES PAID VACATION TO THE BACKYARD!
FIRST, A PHOTO FOR THE PRESS
CLICK
BON VOYAGE, YOU LUCKY PUP! SEND A POSTCARD!
© 1993 PAWS, INC. All Rights Reserved.
JIM DAVIS 2-14

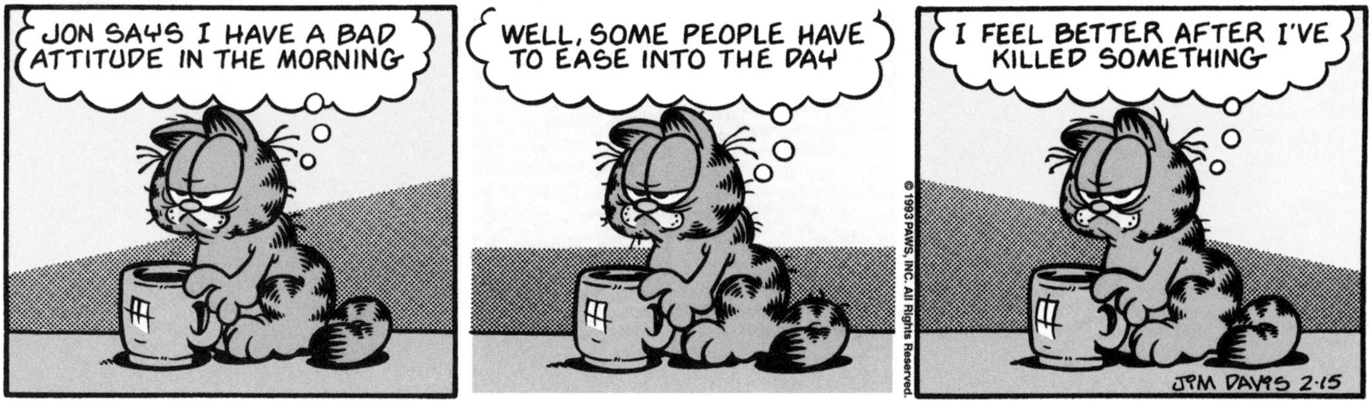
JON SAYS I HAVE A BAD ATTITUDE IN THE MORNING
WELL, SOME PEOPLE HAVE TO EASE INTO THE DAY
© 1993 PAWS, INC. All Rights Reserved.
I FEEL BETTER AFTER I'VE KILLED SOMETHING
JIM DAVIS 2-15

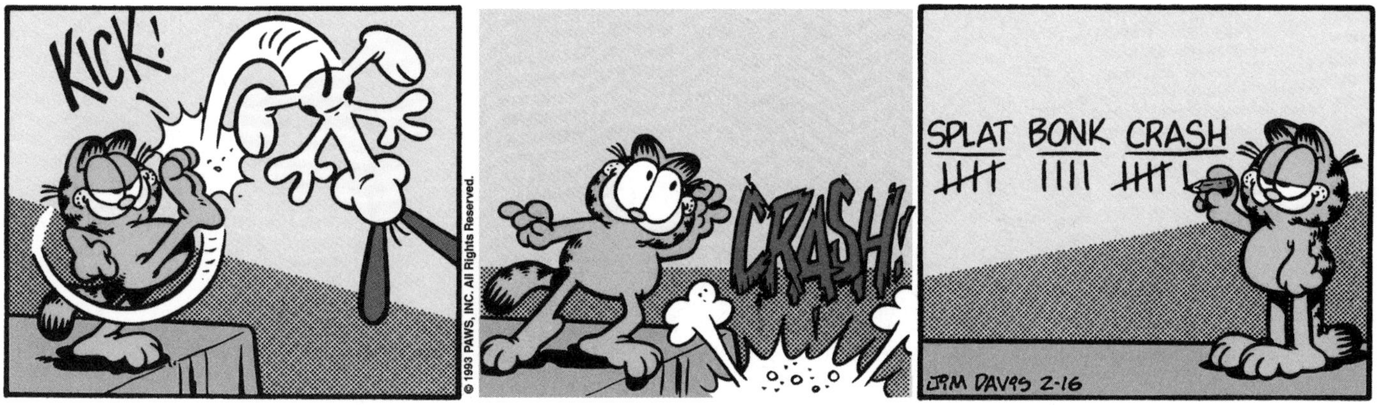
KICK!
© 1993 PAWS, INC. All Rights Reserved.
CRASH!
SPLAT BONK CRASH
JIM DAVIS 2-16

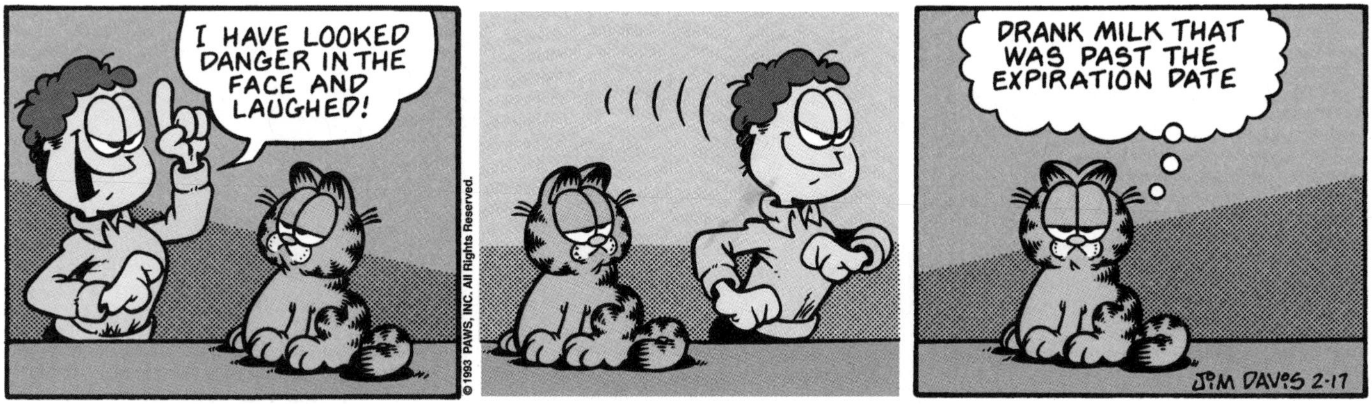
I HAVE LOOKED DANGER IN THE FACE AND LAUGHED!
© 1993 PAWS, INC. All Rights Reserved.
DRANK MILK THAT WAS PAST THE EXPIRATION DATE
JIM DAVIS 2-17

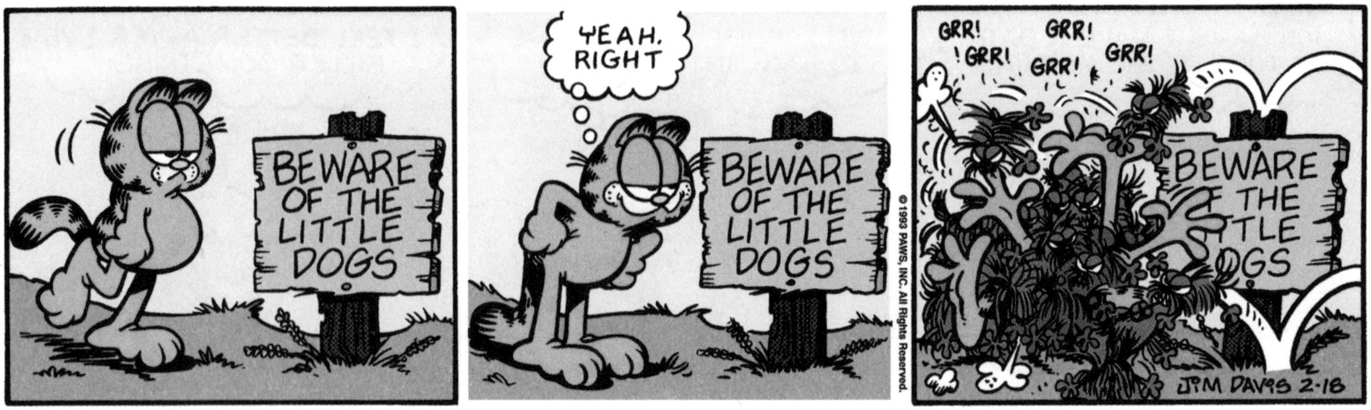
BEWARE OF THE LITTLE DOGS
YEAH, RIGHT
BEWARE OF THE LITTLE DOGS
© 1993 PAWS, INC. All Rights Reserved.
GRR! GRR! GRR! GRR! GRR!
BEWARE
JIM DAVIS 2-18

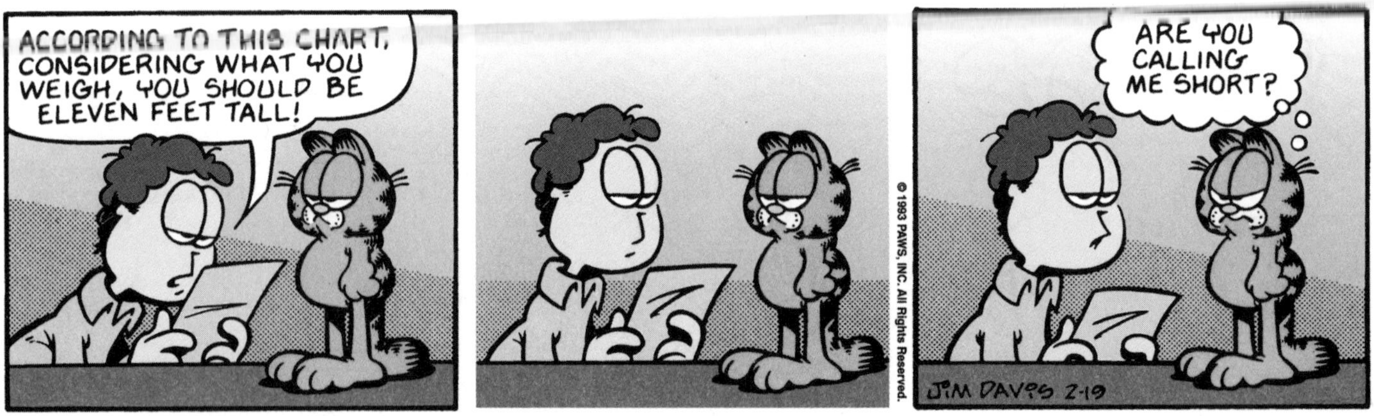
ACCORDING TO THIS CHART, CONSIDERING WHAT YOU WEIGH, YOU SHOULD BE ELEVEN FEET TALL!
© 1993 PAWS, INC. All Rights Reserved.
ARE YOU CALLING ME SHORT?
JIM DAVIS 2-19

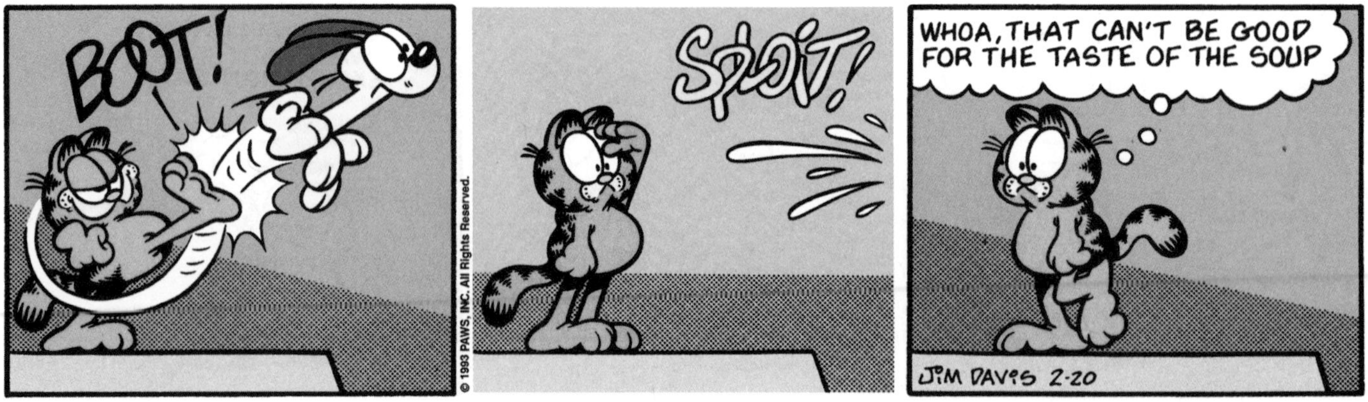
BOOT!
© 1993 PAWS, INC. All Rights Reserved.
SPLOIT!
WHOA, THAT CAN'T BE GOOD FOR THE TASTE OF THE SOUP
JIM DAVIS 2-20

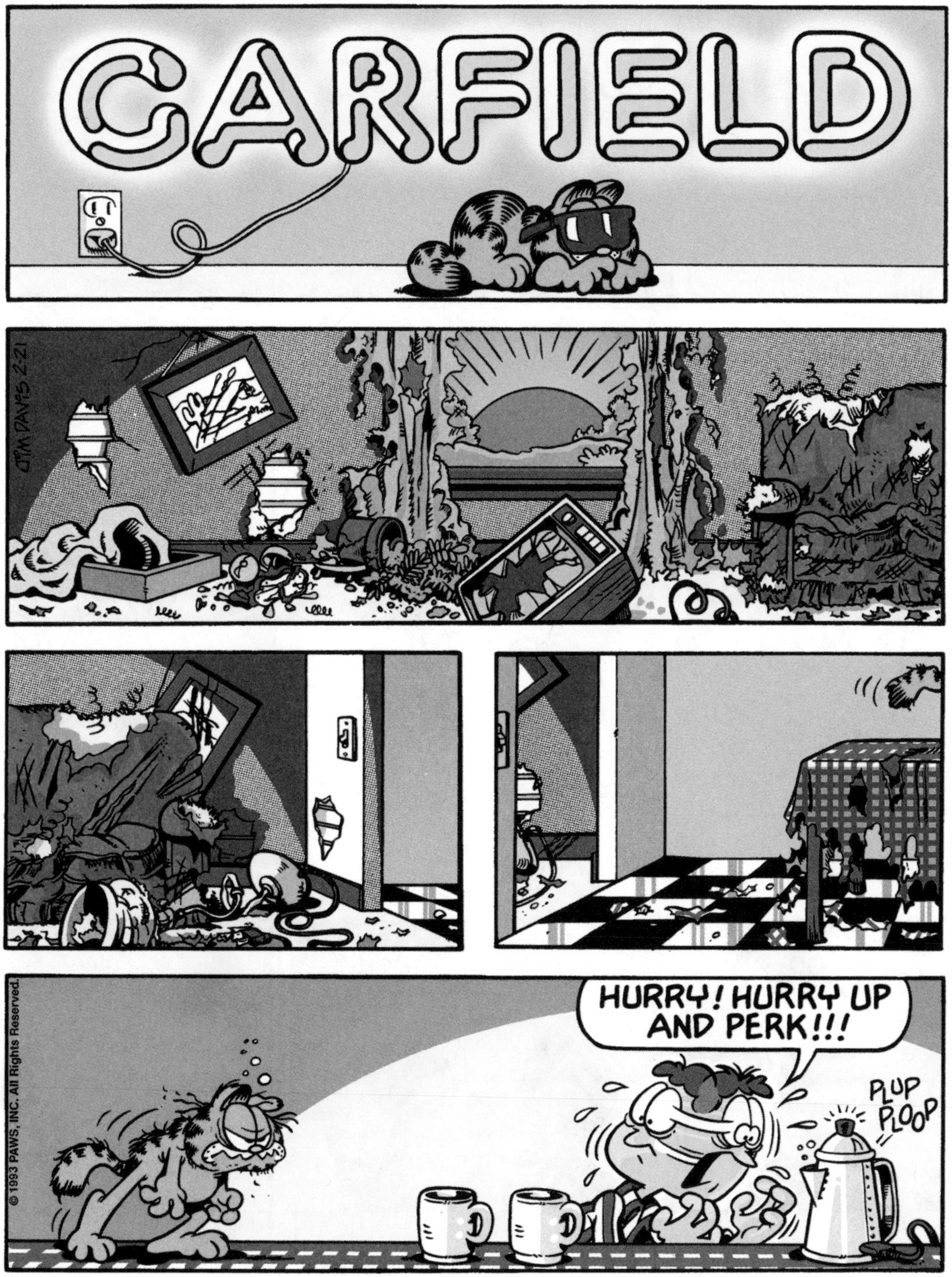
GARFIELD
JIM DAVIS 2-21
© 1993 PAWS, INC. All Rights Reserved.
HURRY! HURRY UP AND PERK!!!
PLUP
PLOOP

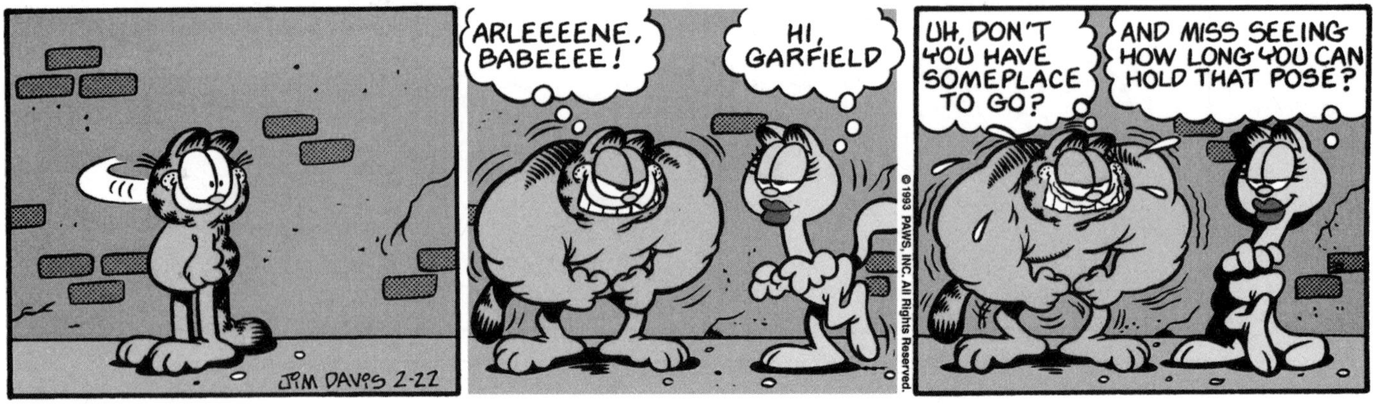
JIM DAVIS 2-22
ARLEEEENE, BABEEEE!
HI, GARFIELD
© 1993 PAWS, INC. All Rights Reserved.
UH, DON'T YOU HAVE SOMEPLACE TO GO?
AND MISS SEEING HOW LONG YOU CAN HOLD THAT POSE?

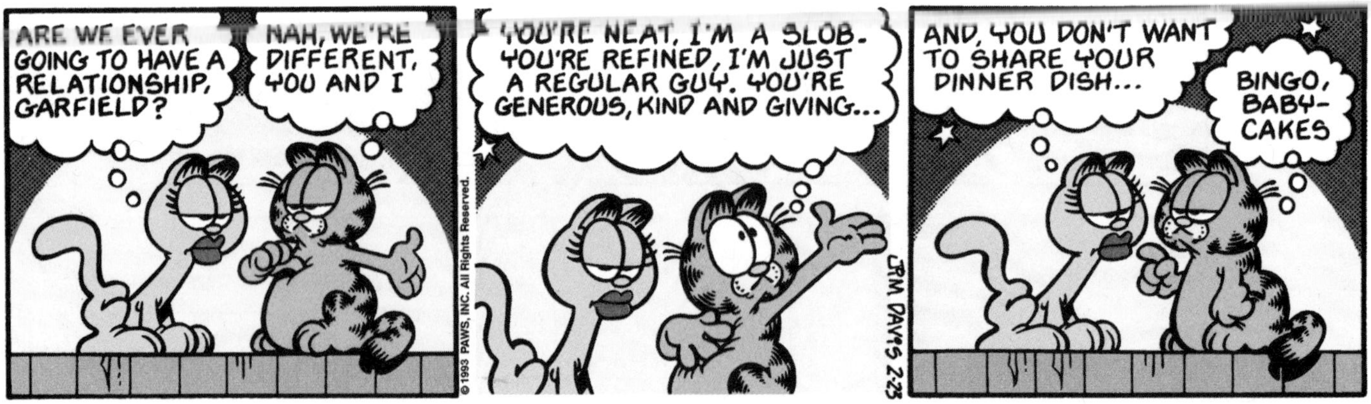
ARE WE EVER GOING TO HAVE A RELATIONSHIP, GARFIELD?
NAH, WE'RE DIFFERENT, YOU AND I
© 1993 PAWS, INC. All Rights Reserved.
YOU'RE NEAT, I'M A SLOB. YOU'RE REFINED, I'M JUST A REGULAR GUY. YOU'RE GENEROUS, KIND AND GIVING...
JIM DAVIS 2-23
AND, YOU DON'T WANT TO SHARE YOUR DINNER DISH...
BINGO, BABY-CAKES

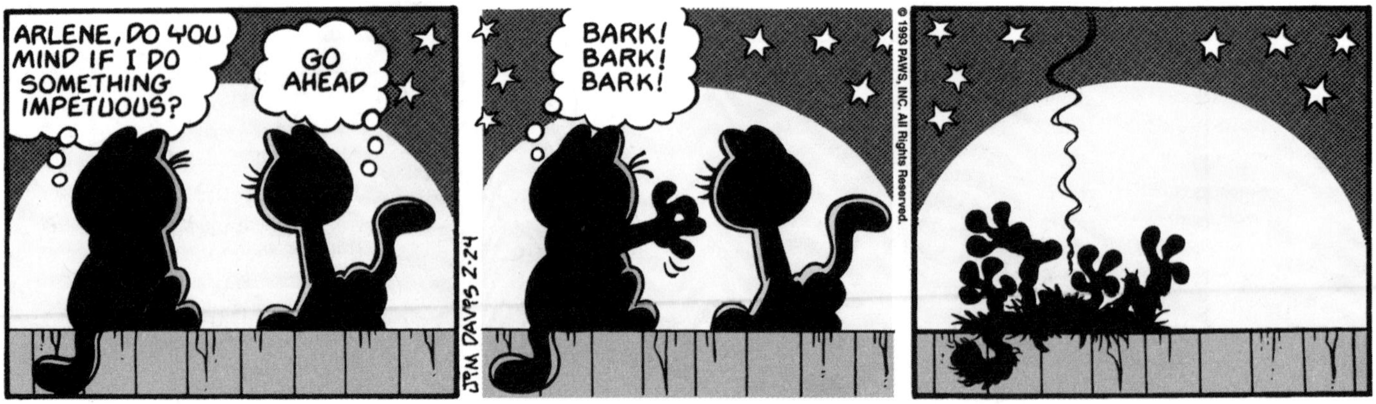
ARLENE, DO YOU MIND IF I DO SOMETHING IMPETUOUS?
GO AHEAD
JIM DAVIS 2-24
BARK! BARK! BARK!
© 1993 PAWS, INC. All Rights Reserved.

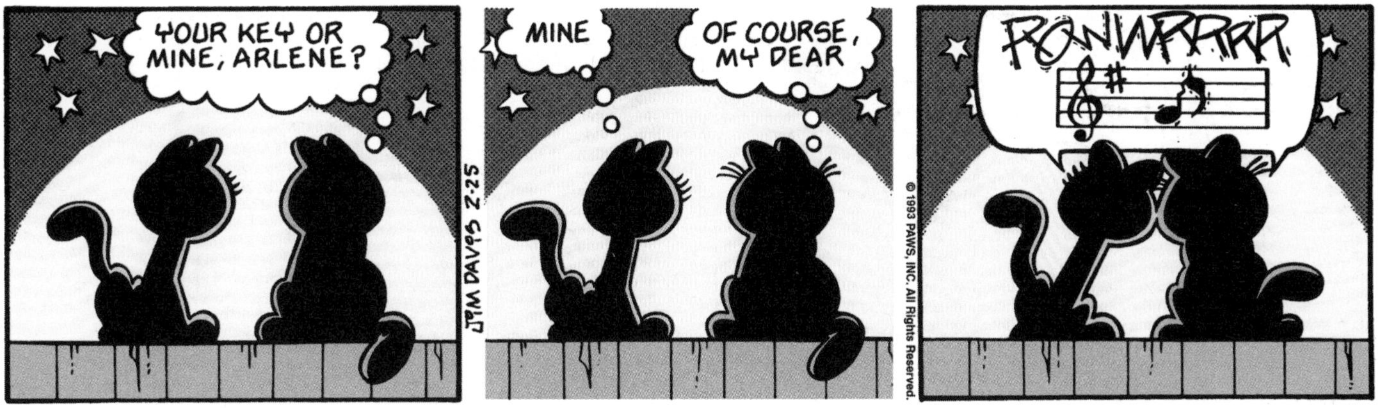
YOUR KEY OR MINE, ARLENE?
MINE
OF COURSE, MY DEAR
RONWRRRR
JIM DAVIS 2-25
© 1993 PAWS, INC. All Rights Reserved.

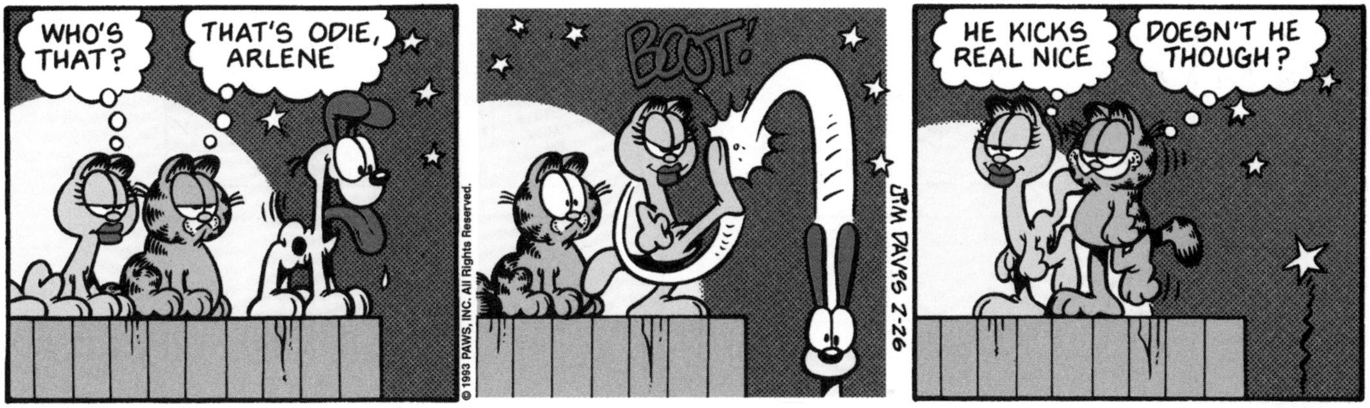
WHO'S THAT?
THAT'S ODIE, ARLENE
BOOT!
HE KICKS REAL NICE
DOESN'T HE THOUGH?
JIM DAVIS 2-26
© 1993 PAWS, INC. All Rights Reserved.

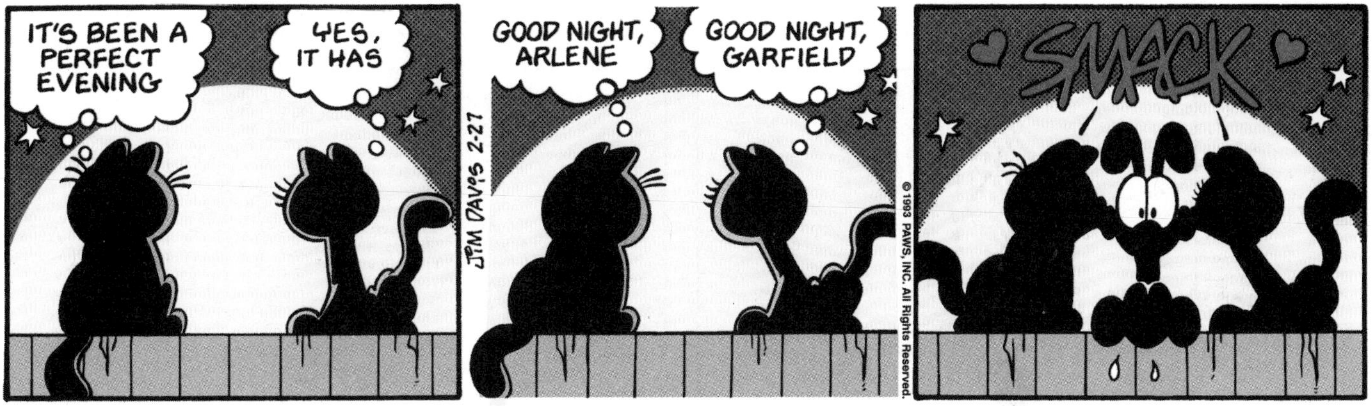
IT'S BEEN A PERFECT EVENING
YES, IT HAS
GOOD NIGHT, ARLENE
GOOD NIGHT, GARFIELD
SMACK
JIM DAVIS 2-27
© 1993 PAWS, INC. All Rights Reserved.

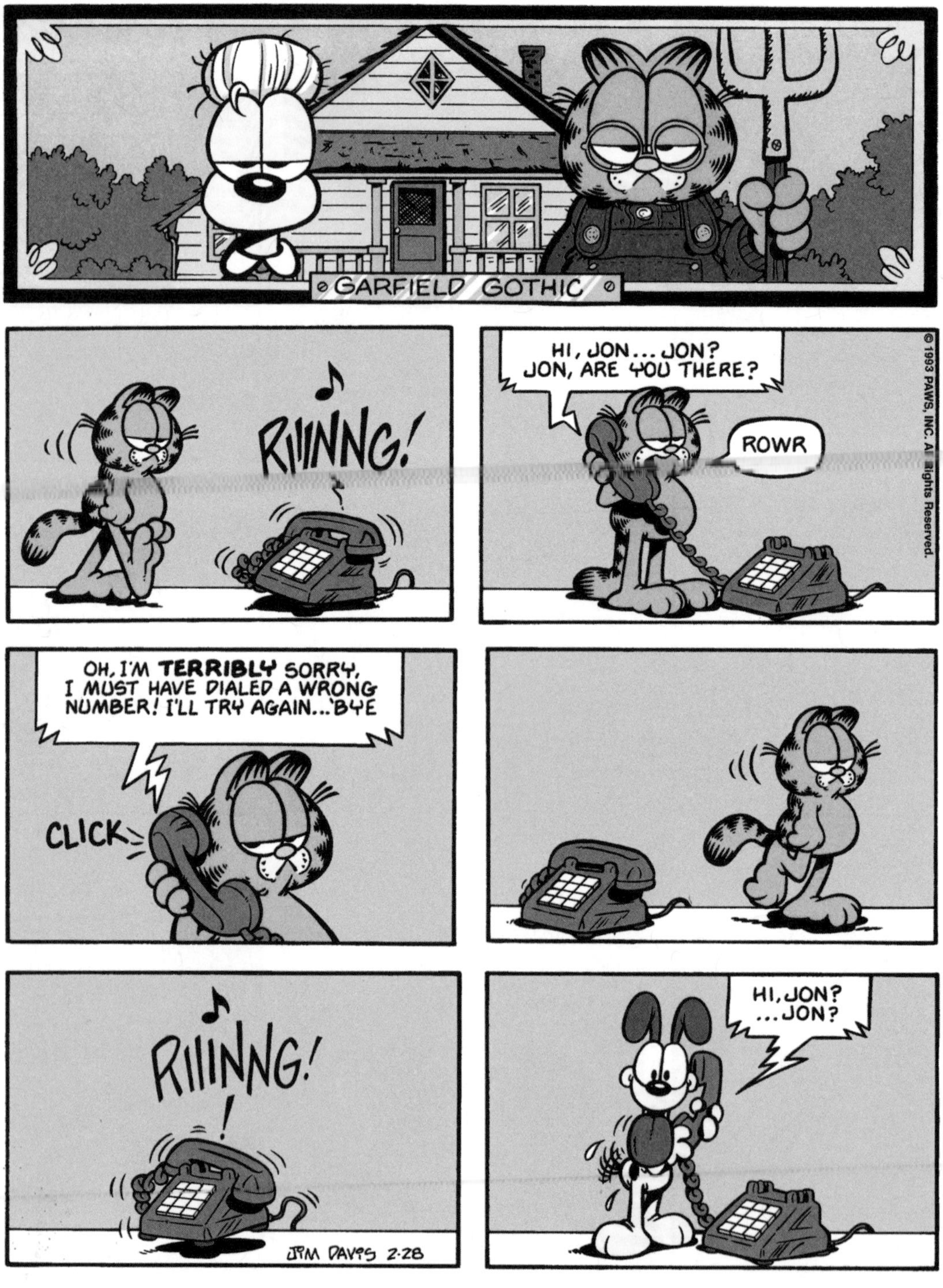
GARFIELD GOTHIC
© 1993 PAWS, INC. All Rights Reserved.
RIIINNG!
HI, JON... JON? JON, ARE YOU THERE?
ROWR
OH, I'M **TERRIBLY** SORRY, I MUST HAVE DIALED A WRONG NUMBER! I'LL TRY AGAIN...'BYE
CLICK
RIIINNG!
JIM DAVIS 2-28
HI, JON? ...JON?

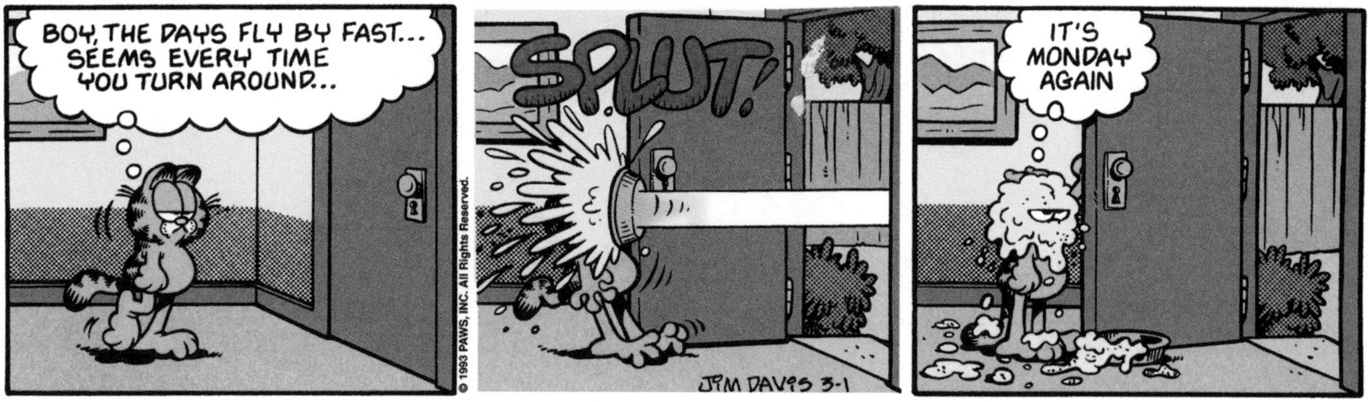
BOY, THE DAYS FLY BY FAST... SEEMS EVERY TIME YOU TURN AROUND...
© 1993 PAWS, INC. All Rights Reserved.
SPLUT!
JIM DAVIS 3-1
IT'S MONDAY AGAIN

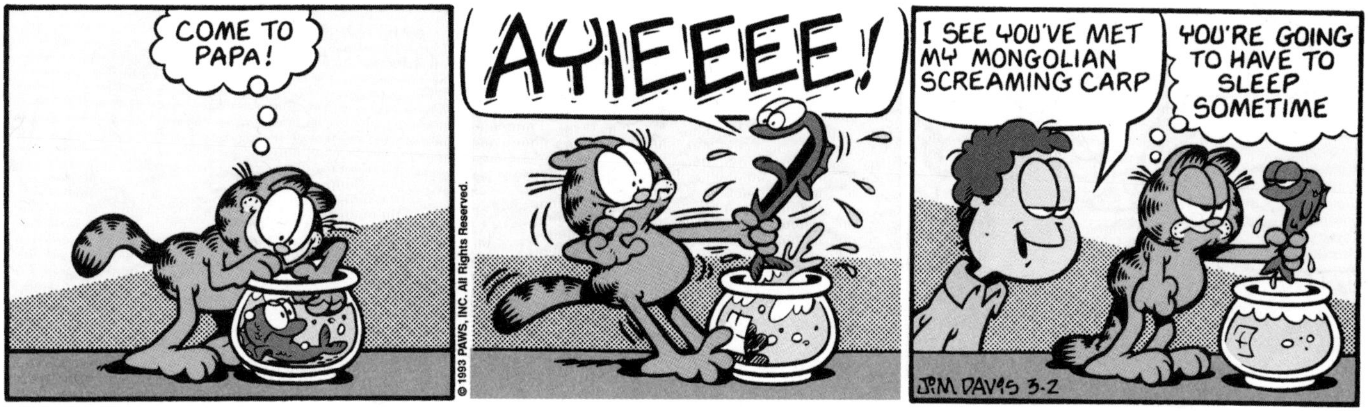
COME TO PAPA!
© 1993 PAWS, INC. All Rights Reserved.
AYIEEEEE!
I SEE YOU'VE MET MY MONGOLIAN SCREAMING CARP
YOU'RE GOING TO HAVE TO SLEEP SOMETIME
JIM DAVIS 3-2

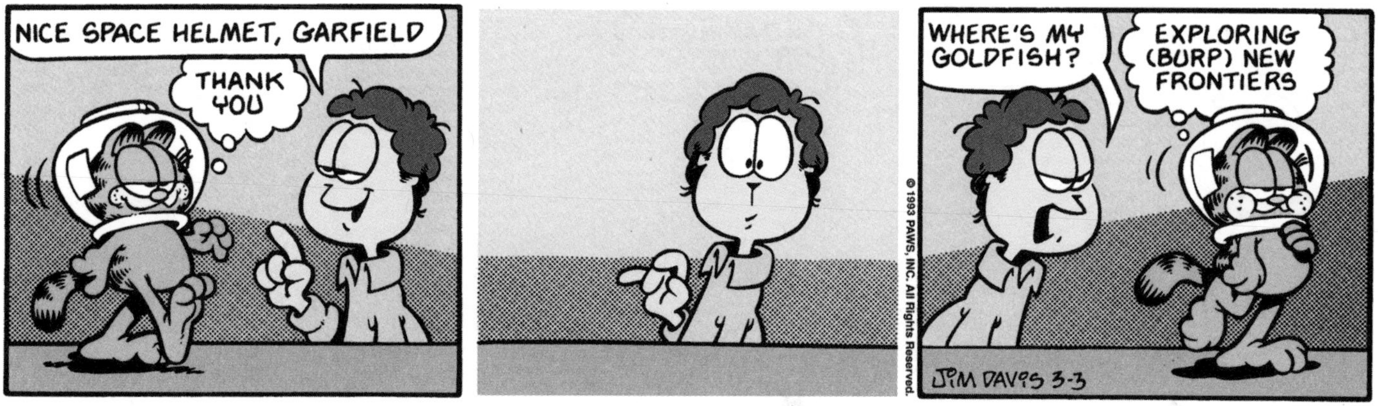
NICE SPACE HELMET, GARFIELD
THANK YOU
© 1993 PAWS, INC. All Rights Reserved.
WHERE'S MY GOLDFISH?
EXPLORING (BURP) NEW FRONTIERS
JIM DAVIS 3-3

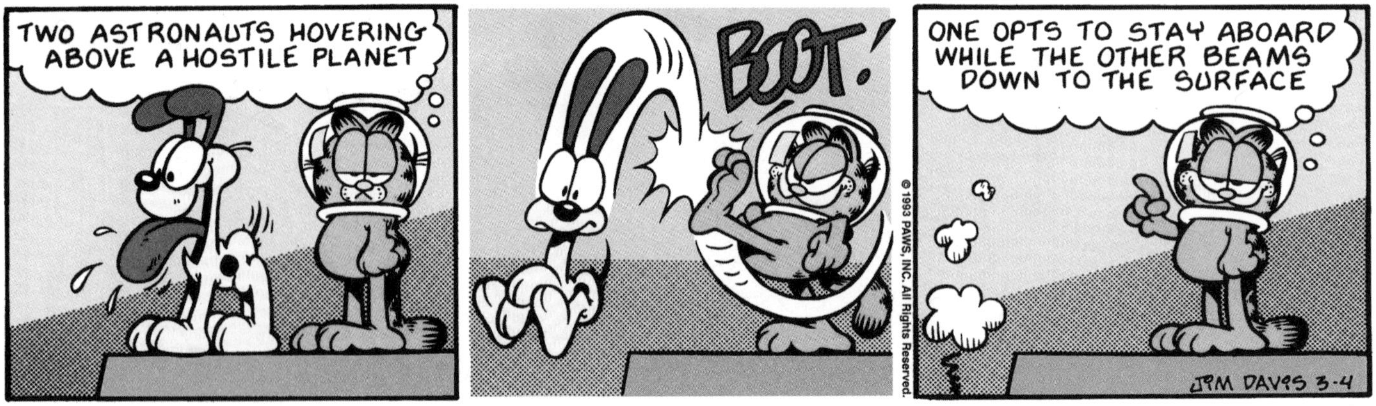
TWO ASTRONAUTS HOVERING ABOVE A HOSTILE PLANET
BOOT!
© 1993 PAWS, INC. All Rights Reserved.
ONE OPTS TO STAY ABOARD WHILE THE OTHER BEAMS DOWN TO THE SURFACE
JIM DAVIS 3-4

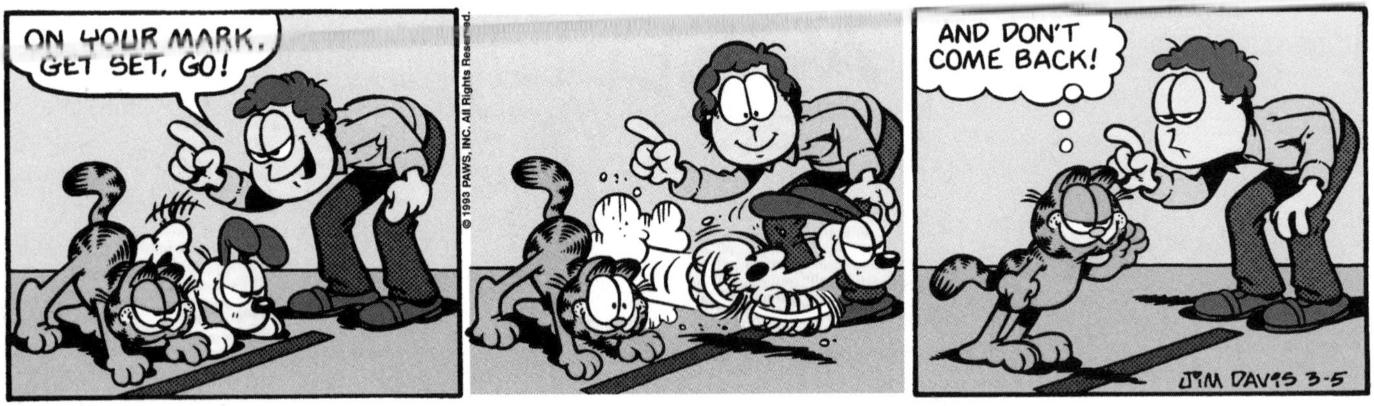
ON YOUR MARK. GET SET, GO!
© 1993 PAWS, INC. All Rights Reserved.
AND DON'T COME BACK!
JIM DAVIS 3-5

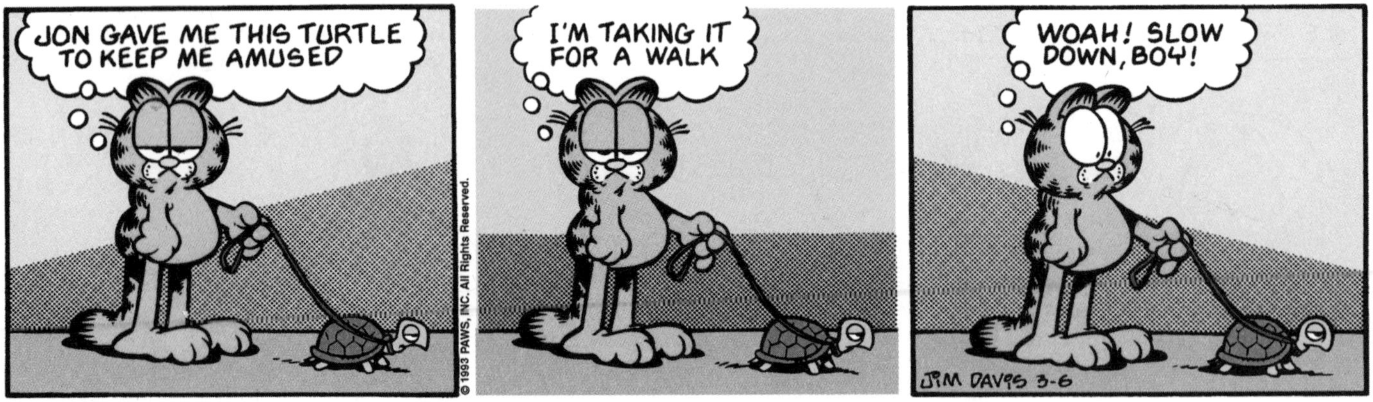
JON GAVE ME THIS TURTLE TO KEEP ME AMUSED
© 1993 PAWS, INC. All Rights Reserved.
I'M TAKING IT FOR A WALK
WOAH! SLOW DOWN, BOY!
JIM DAVIS 3-6

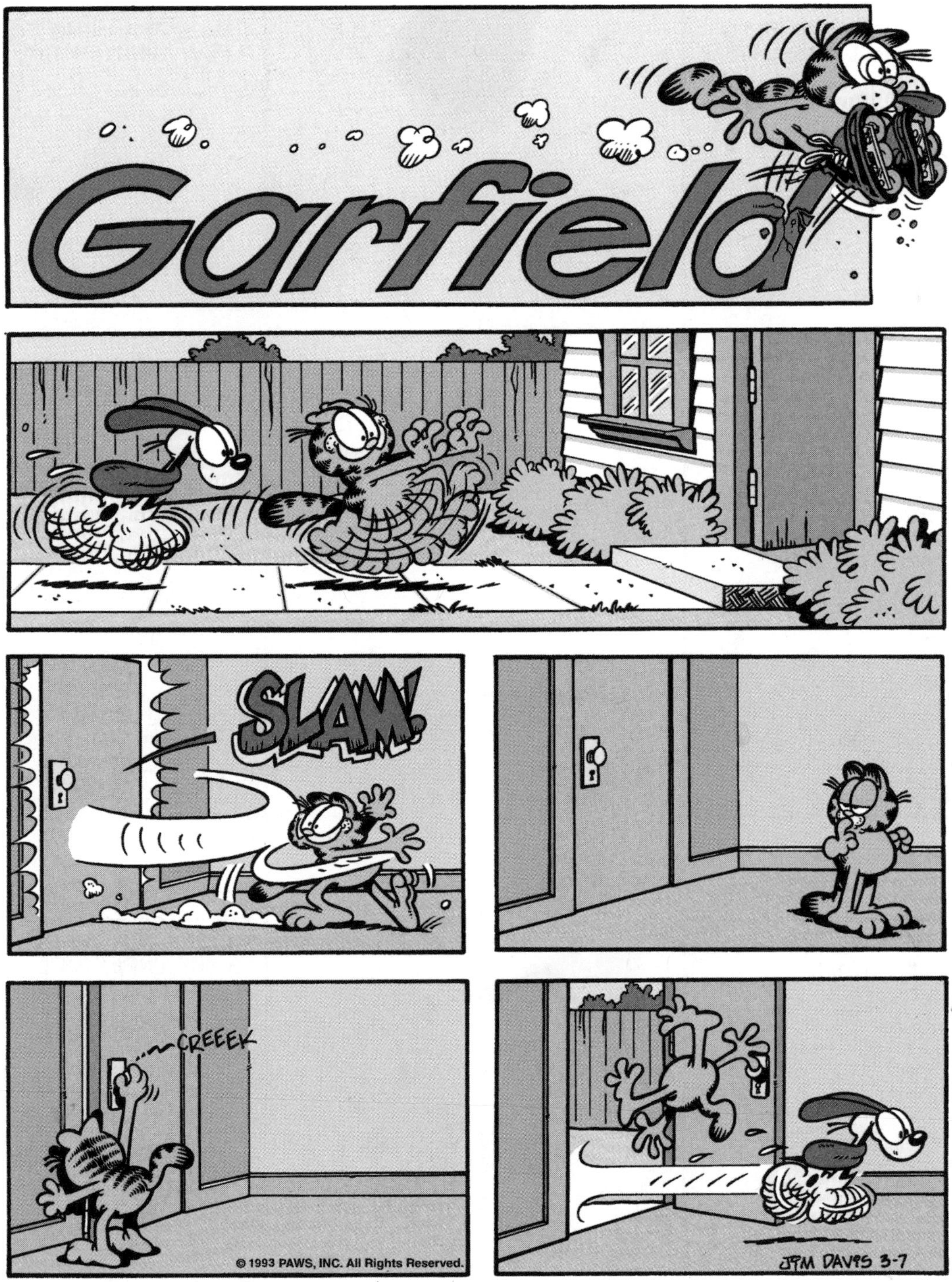
Garfield
SLAM!
CREEEK
© 1993 PAWS, INC. All Rights Reserved.
JIM DAVIS 3-7

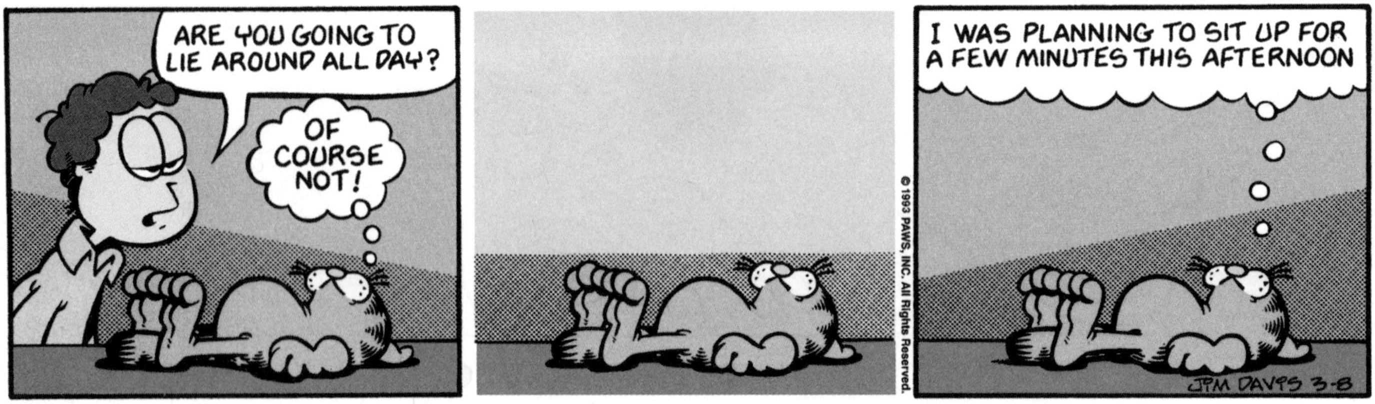
ARE YOU GOING TO LIE AROUND ALL DAY?
OF COURSE NOT!
I WAS PLANNING TO SIT UP FOR A FEW MINUTES THIS AFTERNOON
© 1993 PAWS, INC. All Rights Reserved.
JIM DAVIS 3-8

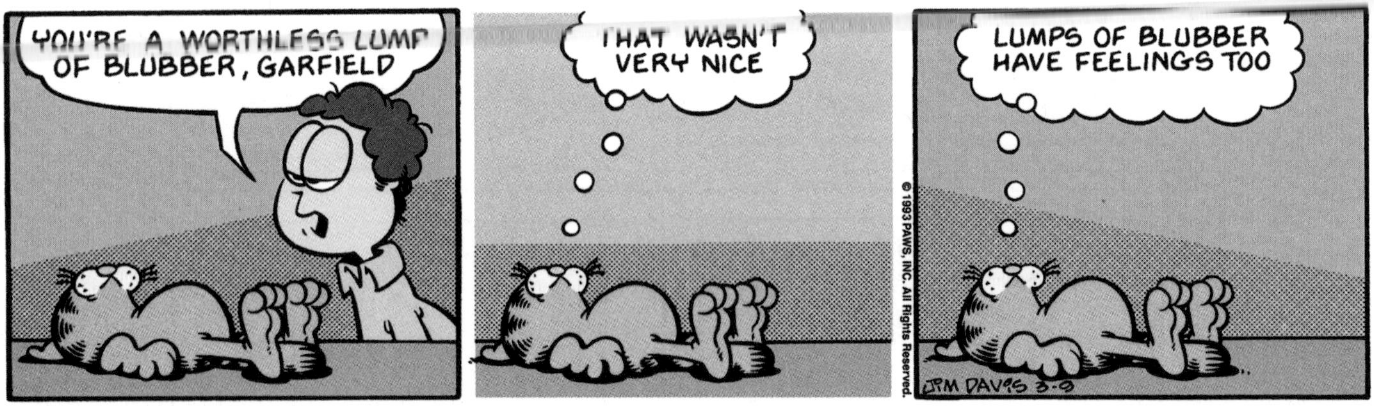
YOU'RE A WORTHLESS LUMP OF BLUBBER, GARFIELD
THAT WASN'T VERY NICE
LUMPS OF BLUBBER HAVE FEELINGS TOO
© 1993 PAWS, INC. All Rights Reserved.
JIM DAVIS 3-9

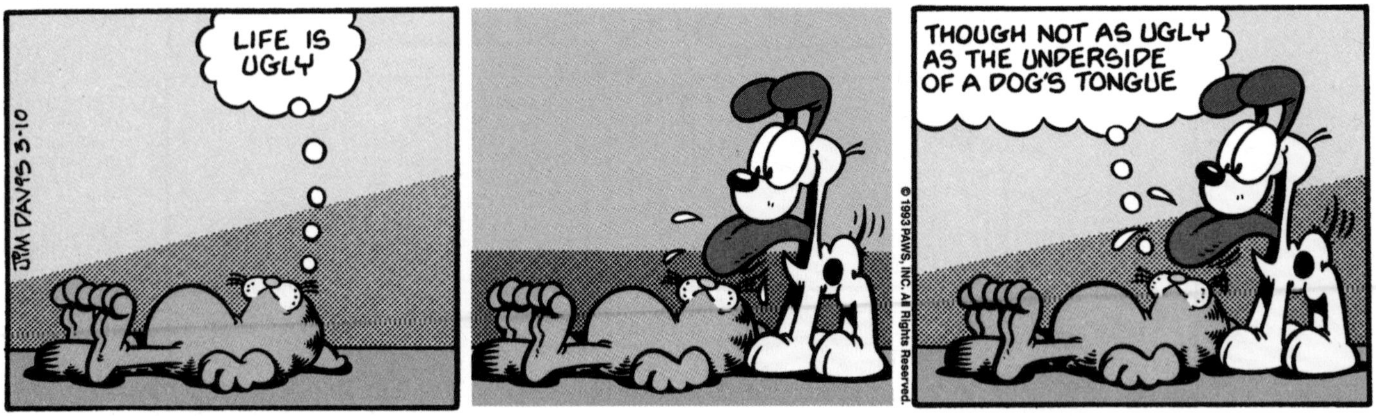
JIM DAVIS 3-10
LIFE IS UGLY
THOUGH NOT AS UGLY AS THE UNDERSIDE OF A DOG'S TONGUE
© 1993 PAWS, INC. All Rights Reserved.

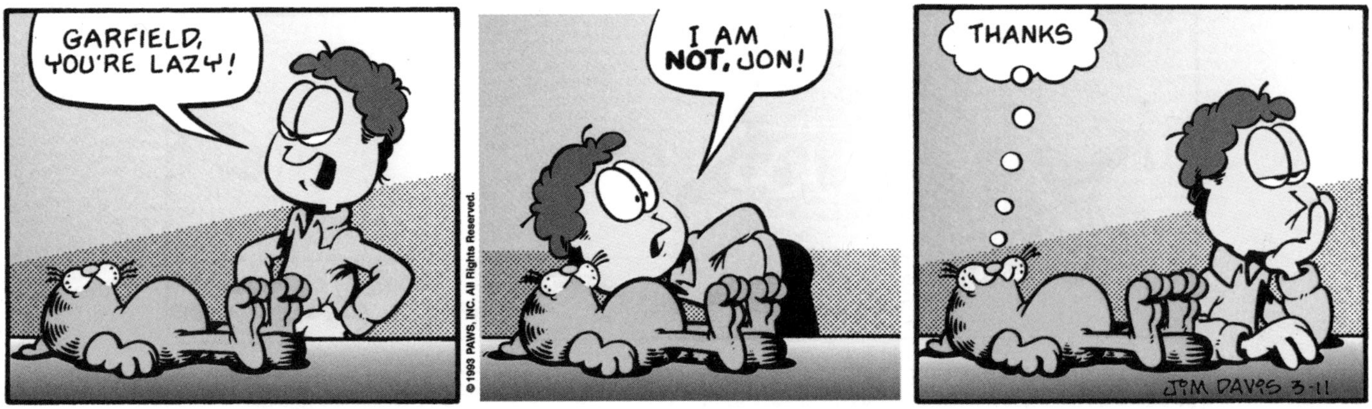
GARFIELD, YOU'RE LAZY!
I AM NOT, JON!
THANKS
© 1993 PAWS, INC. All Rights Reserved.
JIM DAVIS 3-11

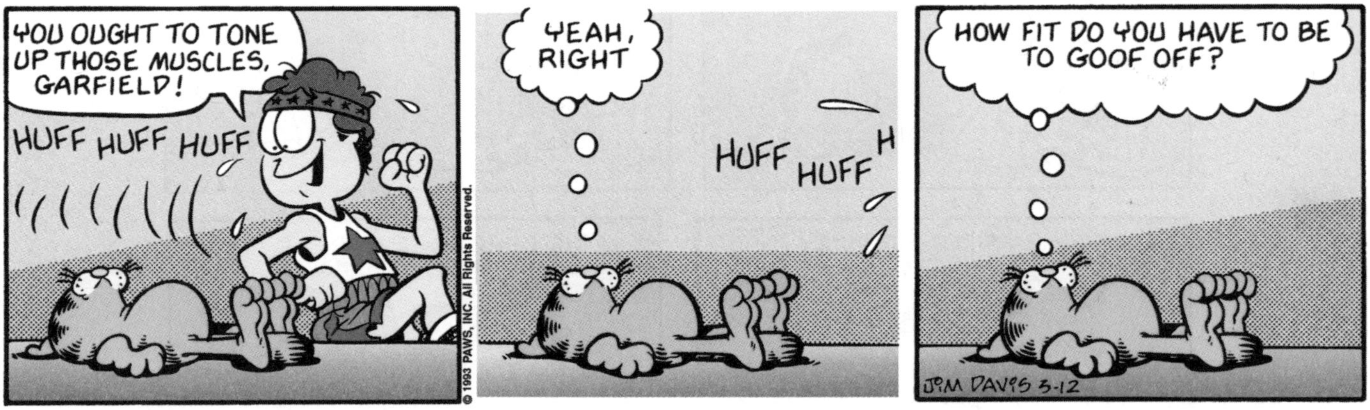
YOU OUGHT TO TONE UP THOSE MUSCLES, GARFIELD!
HUFF HUFF HUFF
YEAH, RIGHT
HUFF HUFF H
HOW FIT DO YOU HAVE TO BE TO GOOF OFF?
© 1993 PAWS, INC. All Rights Reserved.
JIM DAVIS 3-12

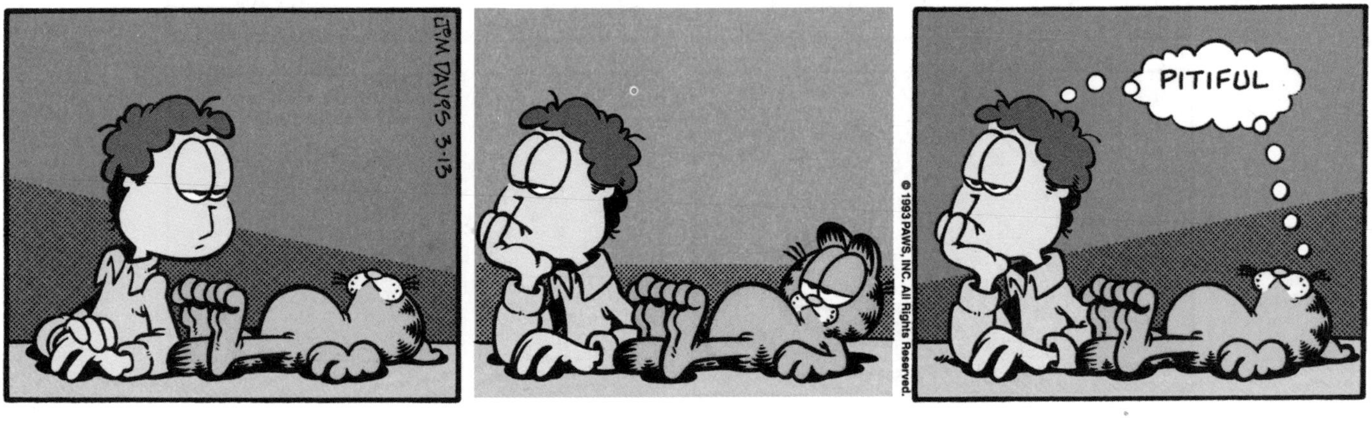
JIM DAVIS 3-13
PITIFUL
© 1993 PAWS, INC. All Rights Reserved.

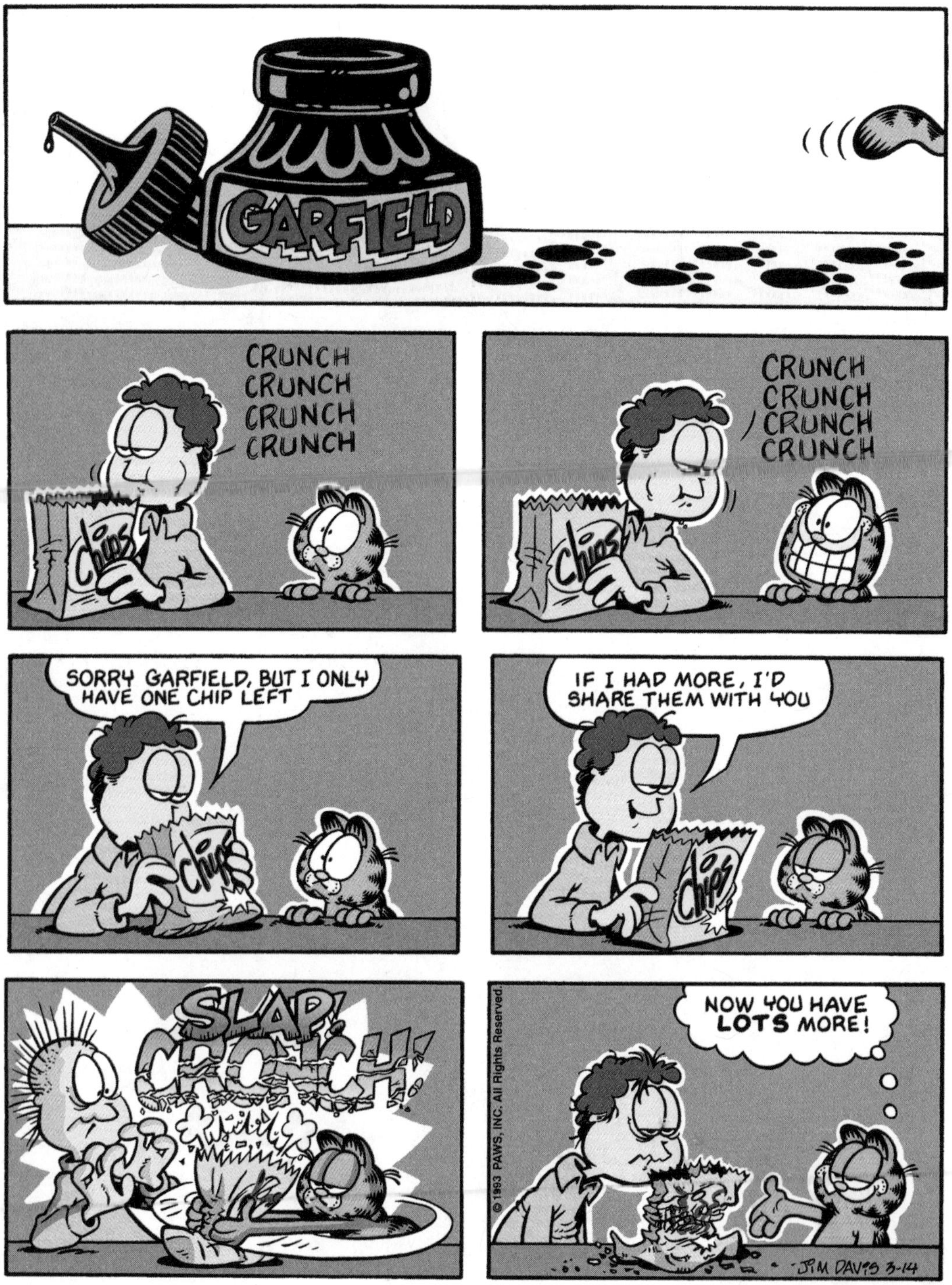
GARFIELD
CRUNCH CRUNCH CRUNCH CRUNCH
CRUNCH CRUNCH CRUNCH CRUNCH
SORRY GARFIELD, BUT I ONLY HAVE ONE CHIP LEFT
IF I HAD MORE, I'D SHARE THEM WITH YOU
SLAP! CRUNCH!
NOW YOU HAVE **LOTS** MORE!
© 1993 PAWS, INC. All Rights Reserved.
JIM DAVIS 3-14

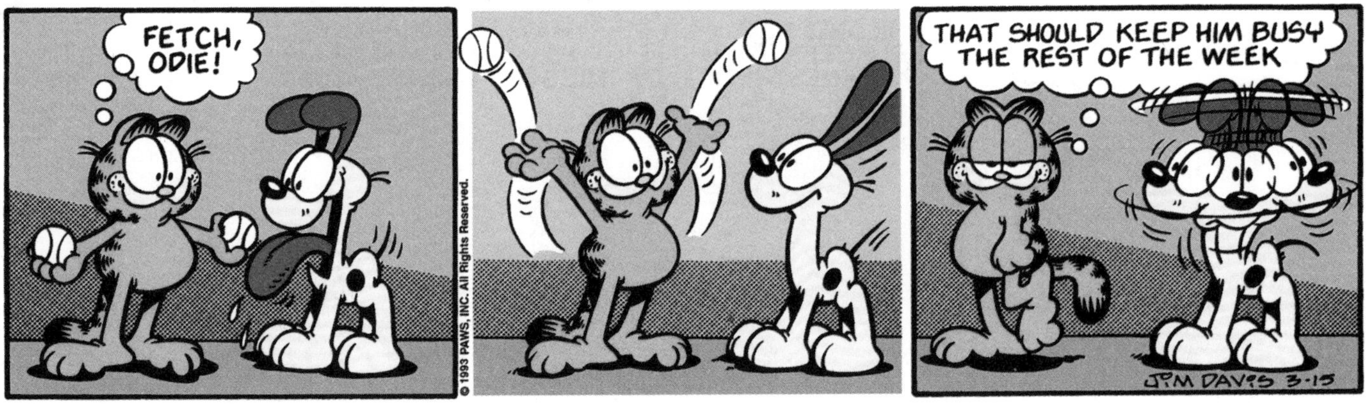
FETCH, ODIE!
© 1993 PAWS, INC. All Rights Reserved.
THAT SHOULD KEEP HIM BUSY THE REST OF THE WEEK
JIM DAVIS 3-15

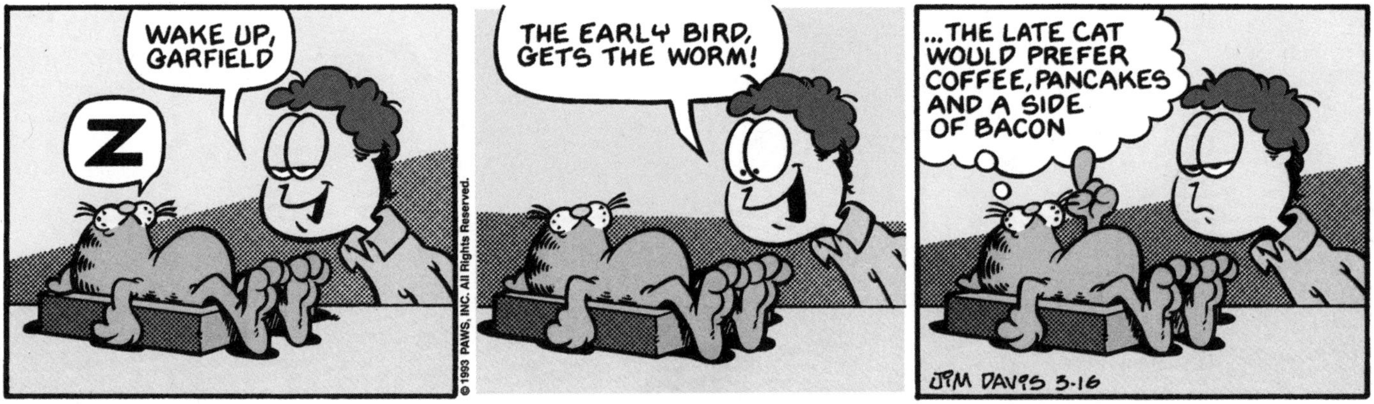
Z
WAKE UP, GARFIELD
© 1993 PAWS, INC. All Rights Reserved.
THE EARLY BIRD, GETS THE WORM!
...THE LATE CAT WOULD PREFER COFFEE, PANCAKES AND A SIDE OF BACON
JIM DAVIS 3-16

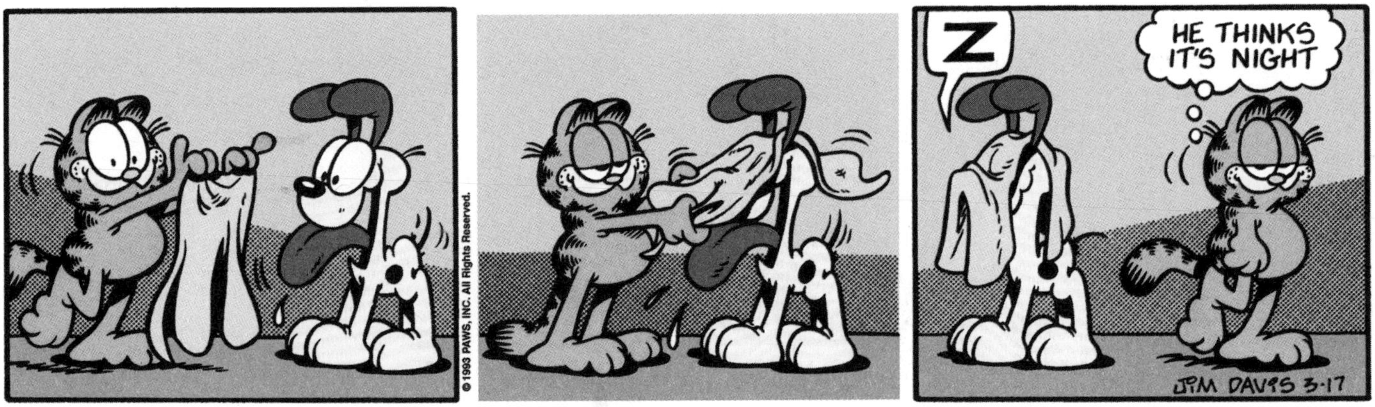
© 1993 PAWS, INC. All Rights Reserved.
Z
HE THINKS IT'S NIGHT
JIM DAVIS 3-17

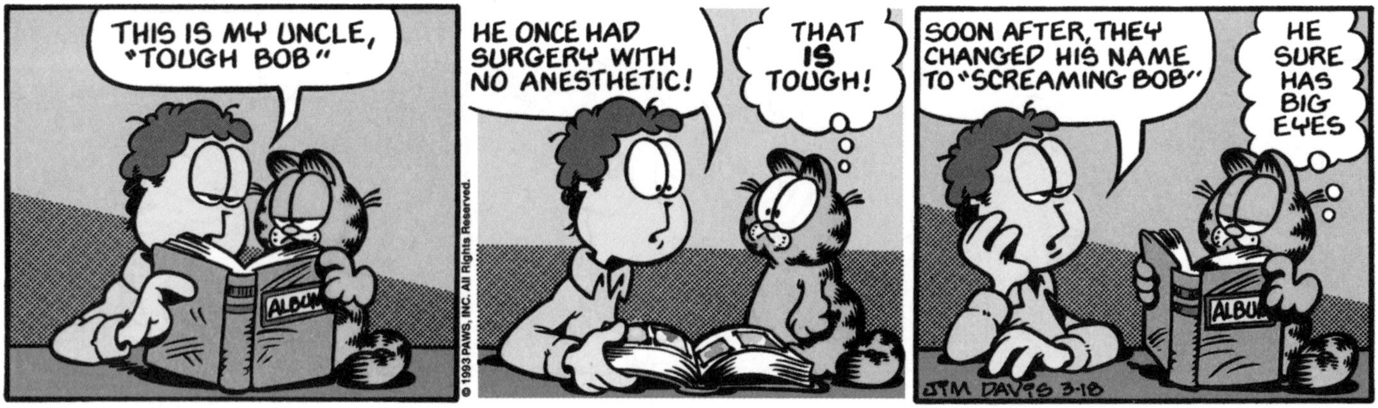
THIS IS MY UNCLE, "TOUGH BOB"
HE ONCE HAD SURGERY WITH NO ANESTHETIC!
THAT IS TOUGH!
SOON AFTER, THEY CHANGED HIS NAME TO "SCREAMING BOB"
HE SURE HAS BIG EYES
ALBUM
© 1993 PAWS, INC. All Rights Reserved.
JIM DAVIS 3-18

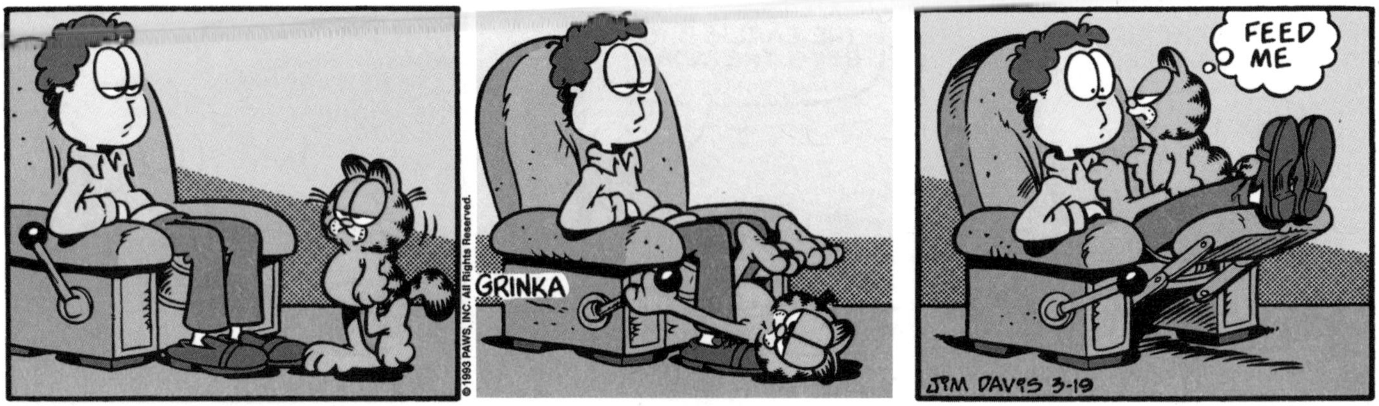
© 1993 PAWS, INC. All Rights Reserved.
GRINKA
FEED ME
JIM DAVIS 3-19

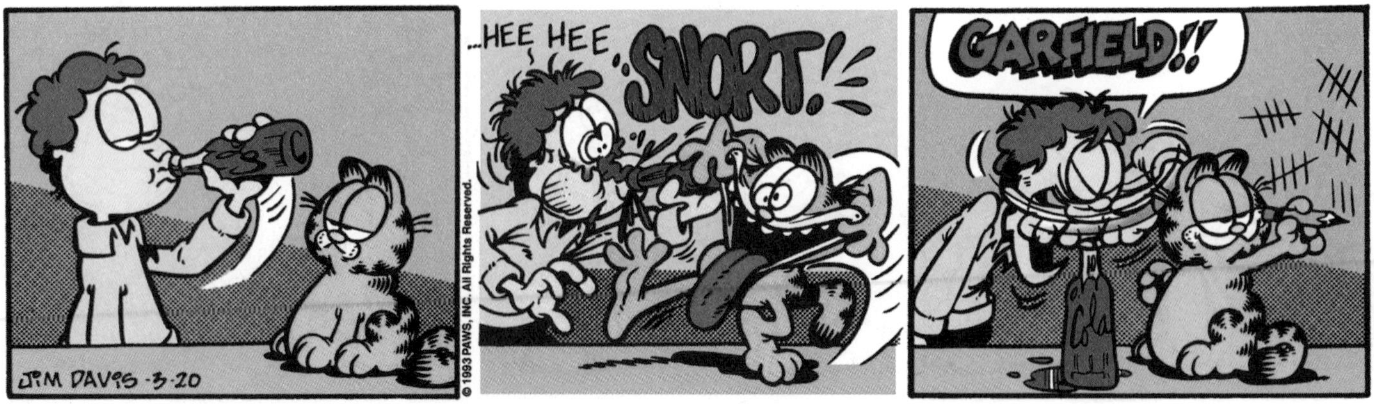
JIM DAVIS 3-20
© 1993 PAWS, INC. All Rights Reserved.
...HEE HEE
SNORT!
GARFIELD!!
Cola

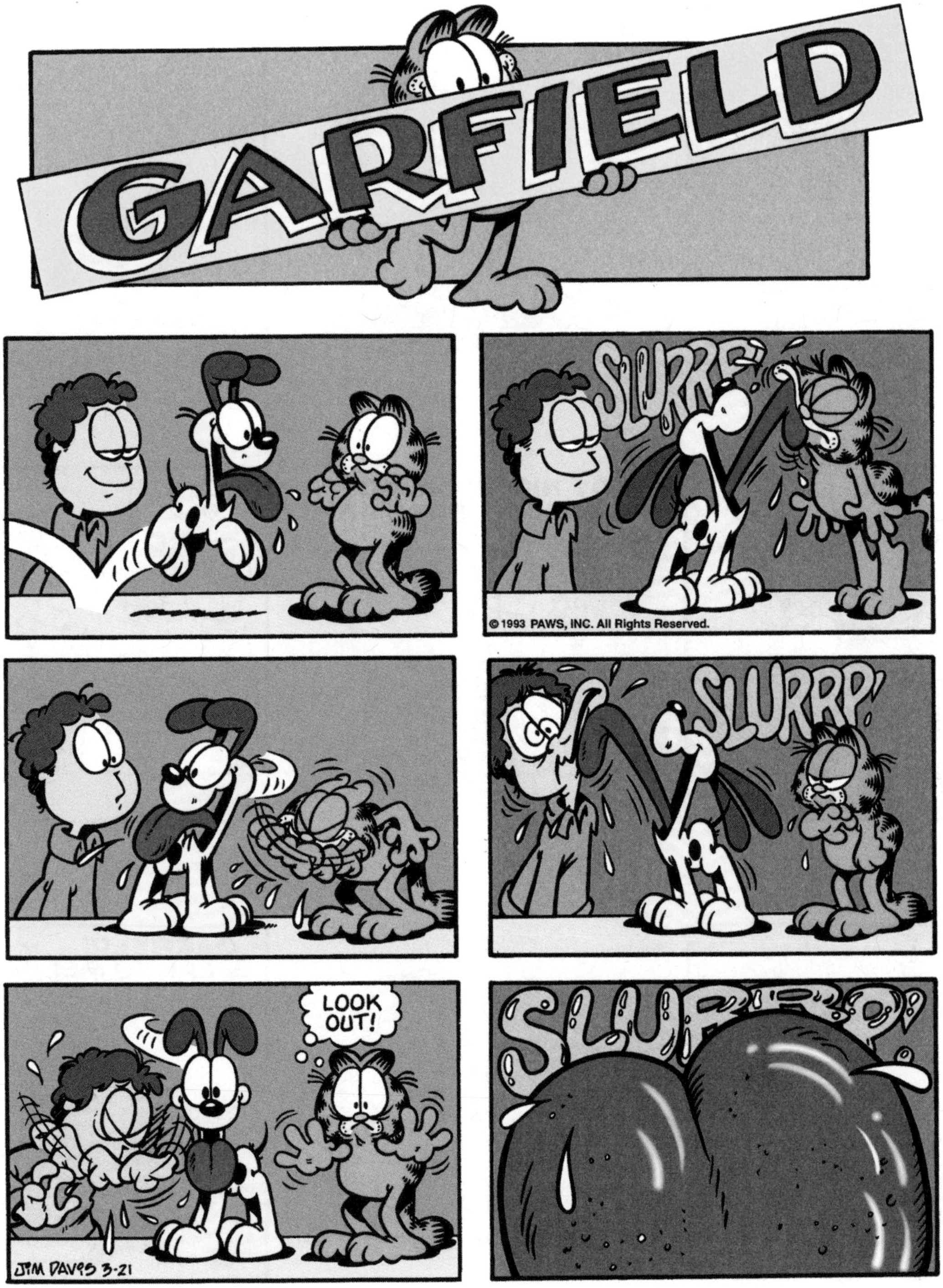
GARFIELD
SLURRP!
© 1993 PAWS, INC. All Rights Reserved.
SLURRP!
LOOK OUT!
JIM DAVIS 3-21
SLURRP!

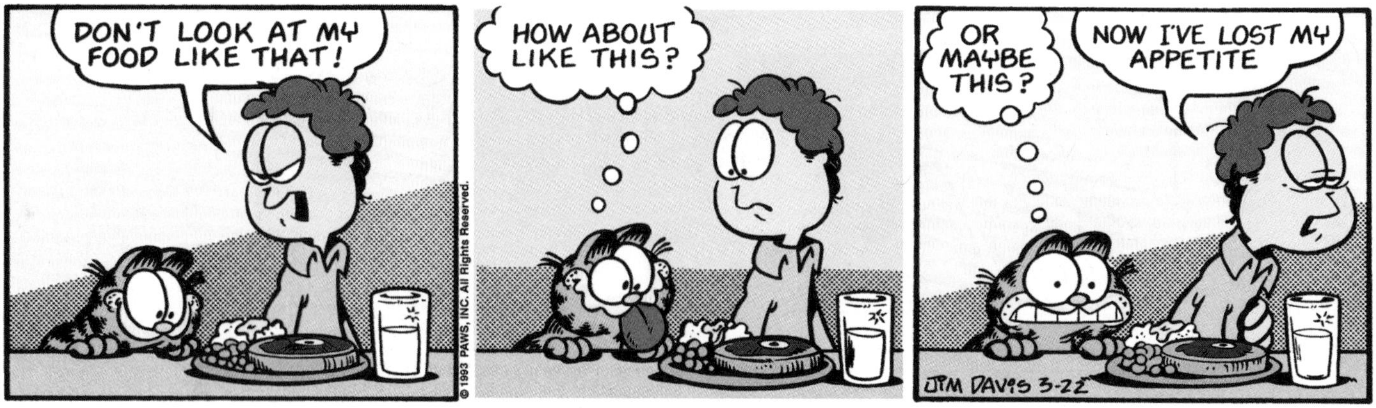
DON'T LOOK AT MY FOOD LIKE THAT!
HOW ABOUT LIKE THIS?
OR MAYBE THIS?
NOW I'VE LOST MY APPETITE
JIM DAVIS 3-22
© 1993 PAWS, INC. All Rights Reserved.

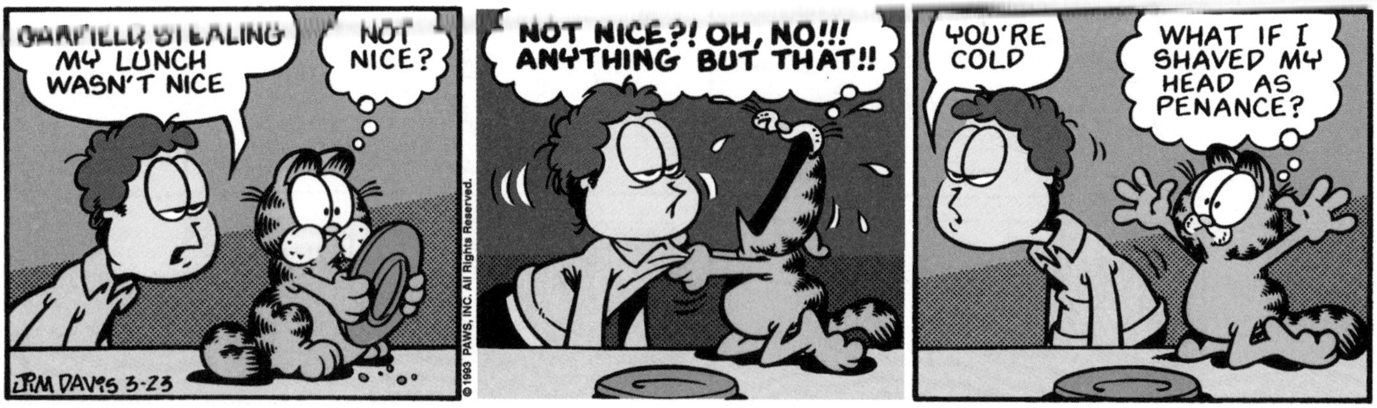
GARFIELD, STEALING MY LUNCH WASN'T NICE
NOT NICE?
NOT NICE?! OH, NO!!! ANYTHING BUT THAT!!
YOU'RE COLD
WHAT IF I SHAVED MY HEAD AS PENANCE?
JIM DAVIS 3-23
© 1993 PAWS, INC. All Rights Reserved.

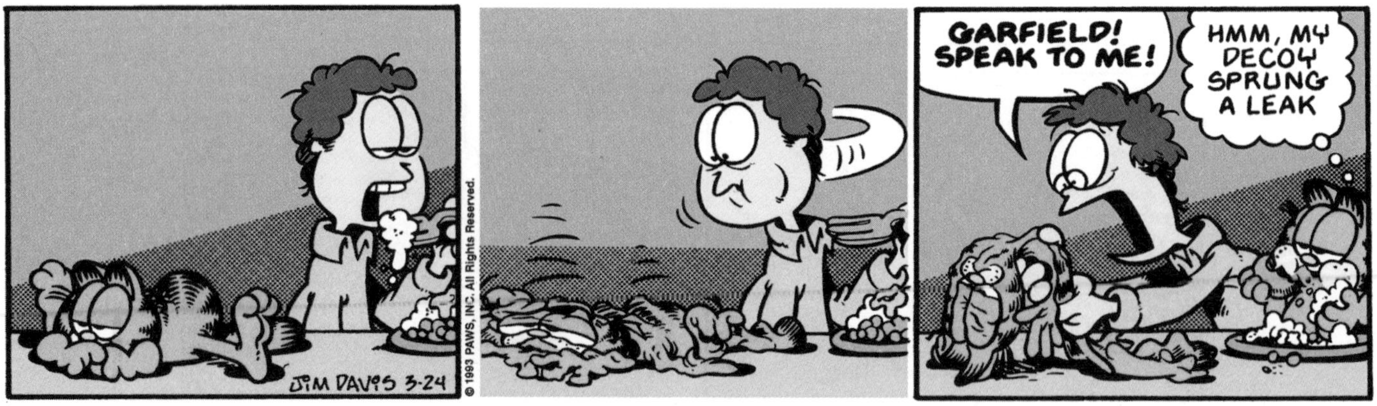
GARFIELD! SPEAK TO ME!
HMM, MY DECOY SPRUNG A LEAK
JIM DAVIS 3-24
© 1993 PAWS, INC. All Rights Reserved.

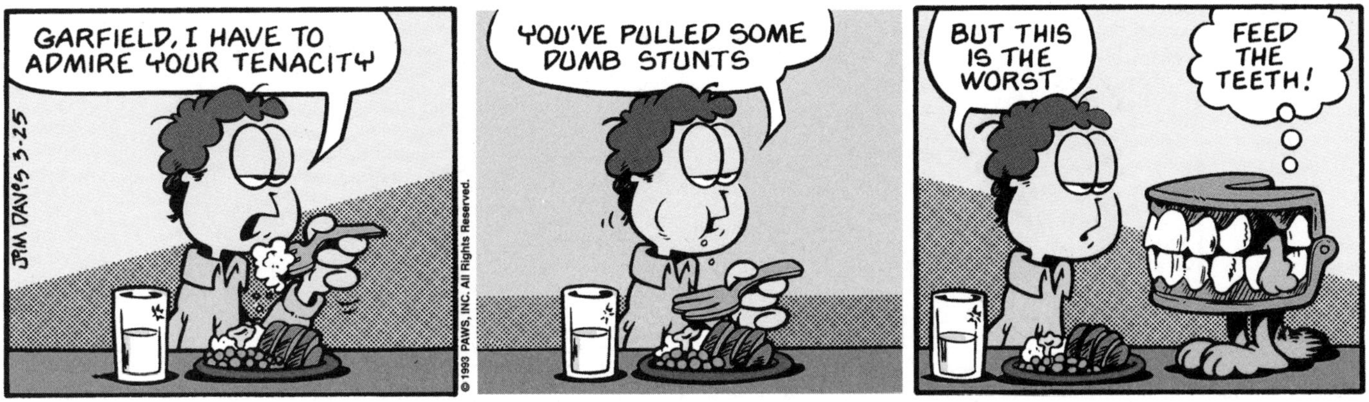
GARFIELD, I HAVE TO ADMIRE YOUR TENACITY
JIM DAVIS 3-25
YOU'VE PULLED SOME DUMB STUNTS
© 1993 PAWS, INC. All Rights Reserved.
BUT THIS IS THE WORST
FEED THE TEETH!

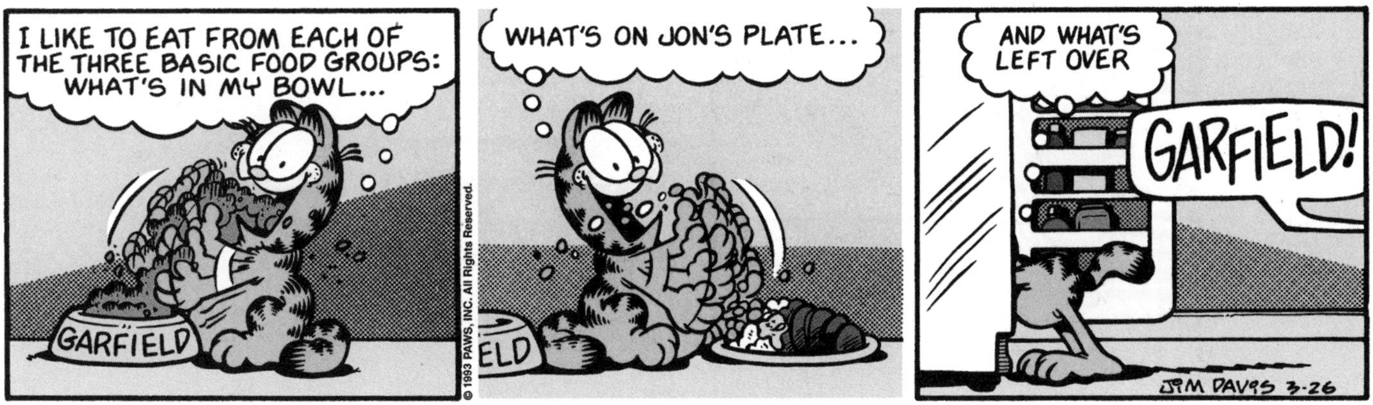
I LIKE TO EAT FROM EACH OF THE THREE BASIC FOOD GROUPS: WHAT'S IN MY BOWL...
GARFIELD
WHAT'S ON JON'S PLATE...
© 1993 PAWS, INC. All Rights Reserved.
AND WHAT'S LEFT OVER
GARFIELD!
JIM DAVIS 3-26

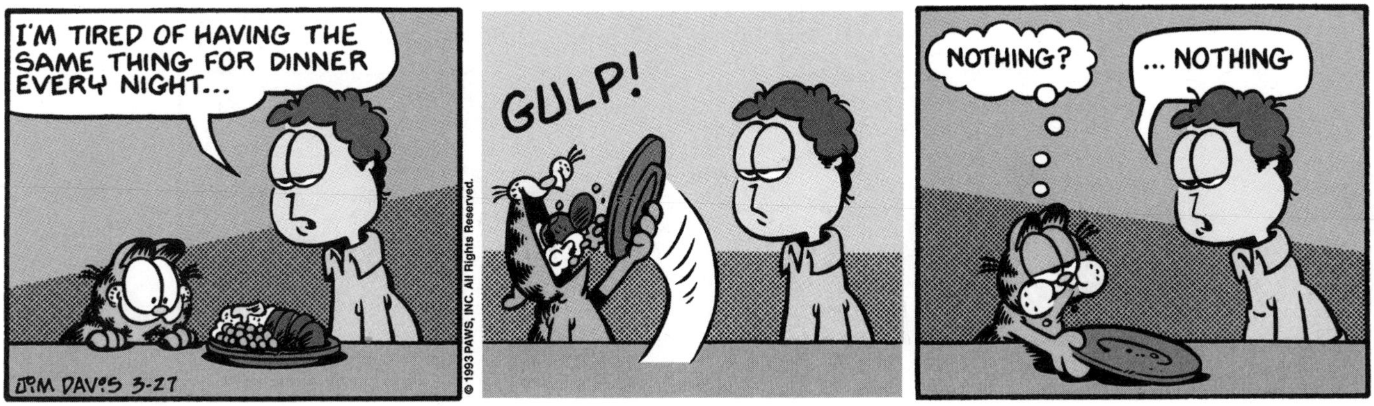
I'M TIRED OF HAVING THE SAME THING FOR DINNER EVERY NIGHT...
JIM DAVIS 3-27
GULP!
© 1993 PAWS, INC. All Rights Reserved.
NOTHING?
... NOTHING

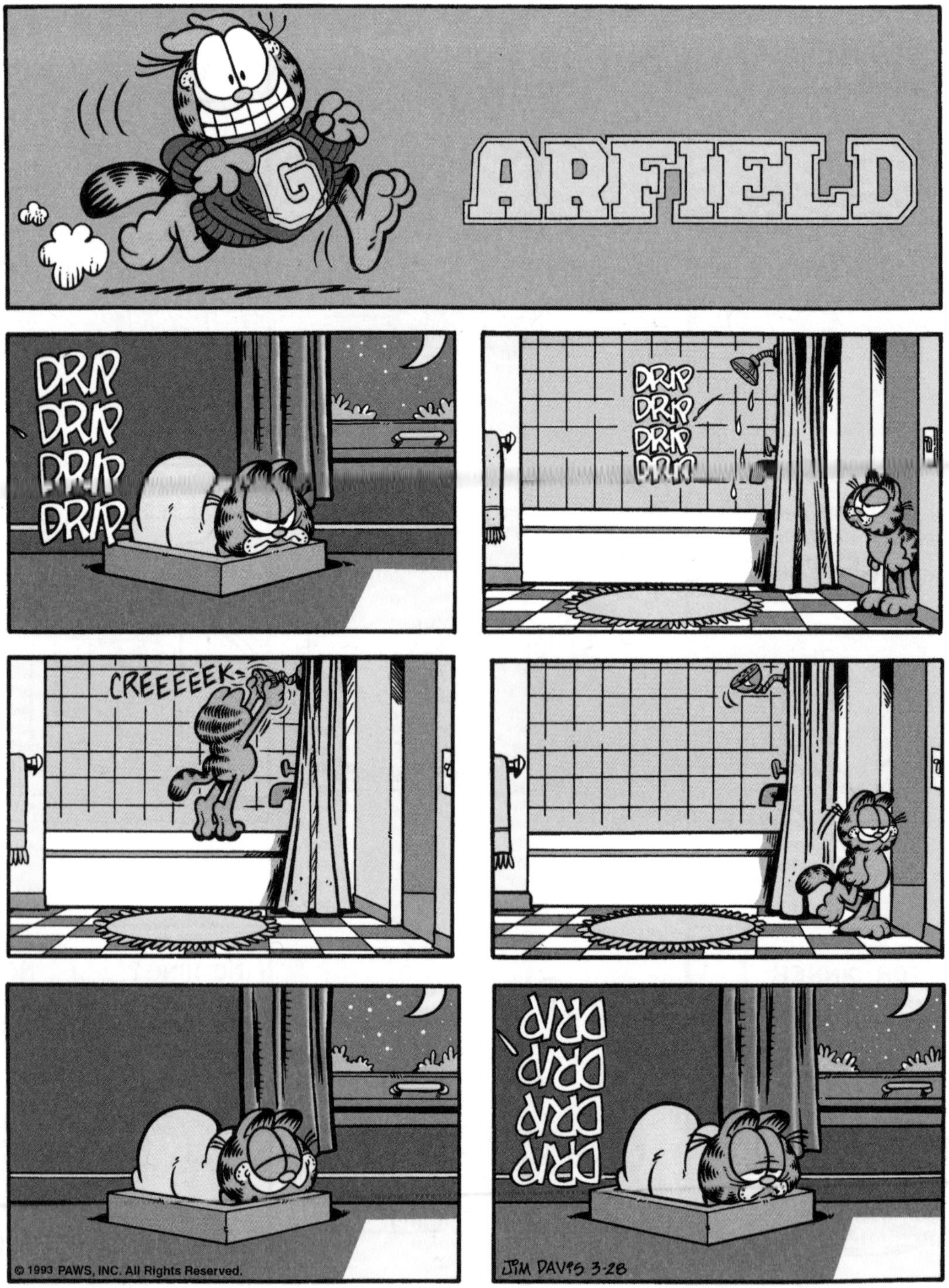
G
ARFIELD
DRIP
DRIP
DRIP
DRIP
DRIP
DRIP
DRIP
DRIP
CREEEEEK
DRIP
DRIP
DRIP
DRIP
© 1993 PAWS, INC. All Rights Reserved.
JIM DAVIS 3-28

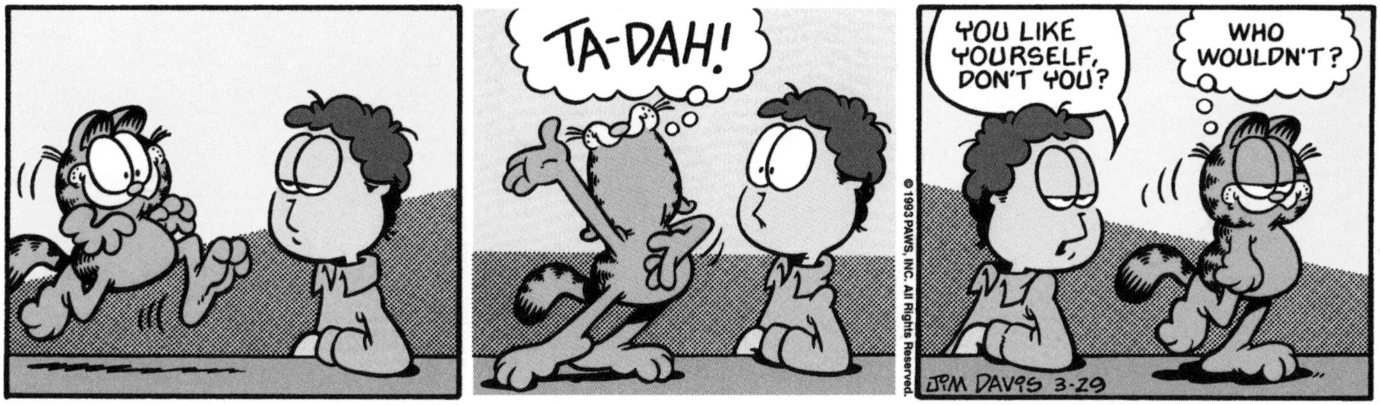
TA-DAH!
YOU LIKE YOURSELF, DON'T YOU?
WHO WOULDN'T?
© 1993 PAWS, INC. All Rights Reserved.
JIM DAVIS 3-29

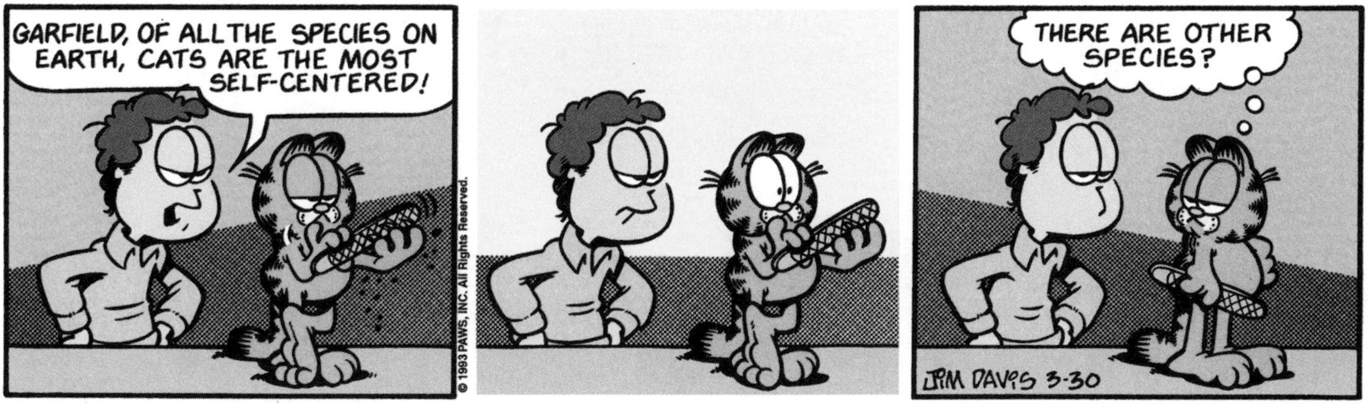
GARFIELD, OF ALL THE SPECIES ON EARTH, CATS ARE THE MOST SELF-CENTERED!
THERE ARE OTHER SPECIES?
© 1993 PAWS, INC. All Rights Reserved.
JIM DAVIS 3-30

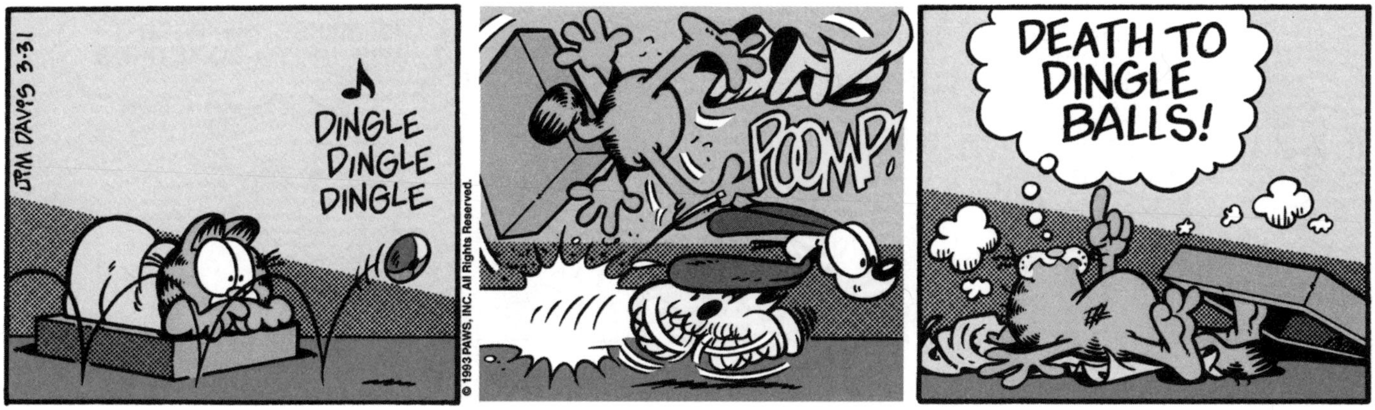
JIM DAVIS 3-31
DINGLE DINGLE DINGLE
POOMP!
DEATH TO DINGLE BALLS!
© 1993 PAWS, INC. All Rights Reserved.

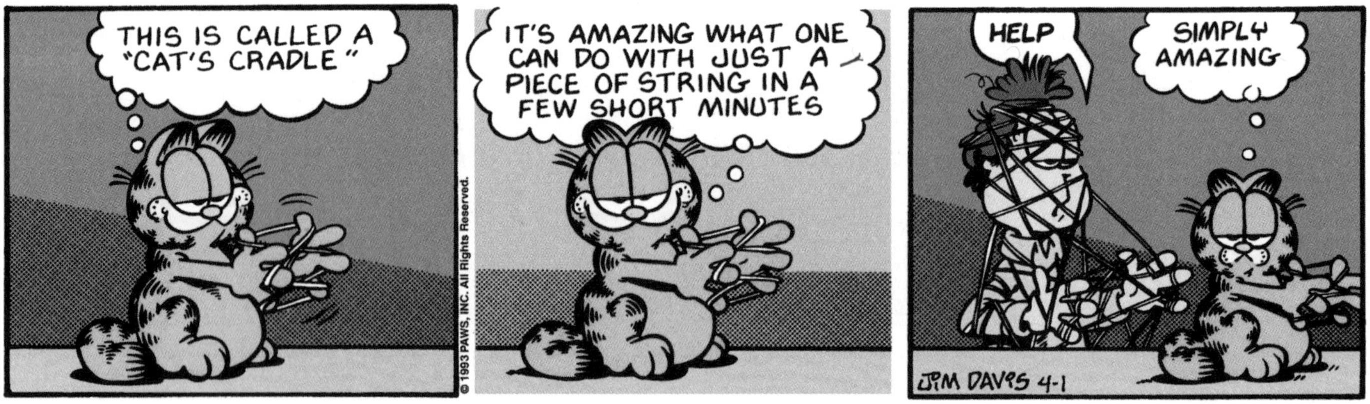
THIS IS CALLED A "CAT'S CRADLE"
© 1993 PAWS, INC. All Rights Reserved.
IT'S AMAZING WHAT ONE CAN DO WITH JUST A PIECE OF STRING IN A FEW SHORT MINUTES
HELP
SIMPLY AMAZING
JIM DAVIS 4-1

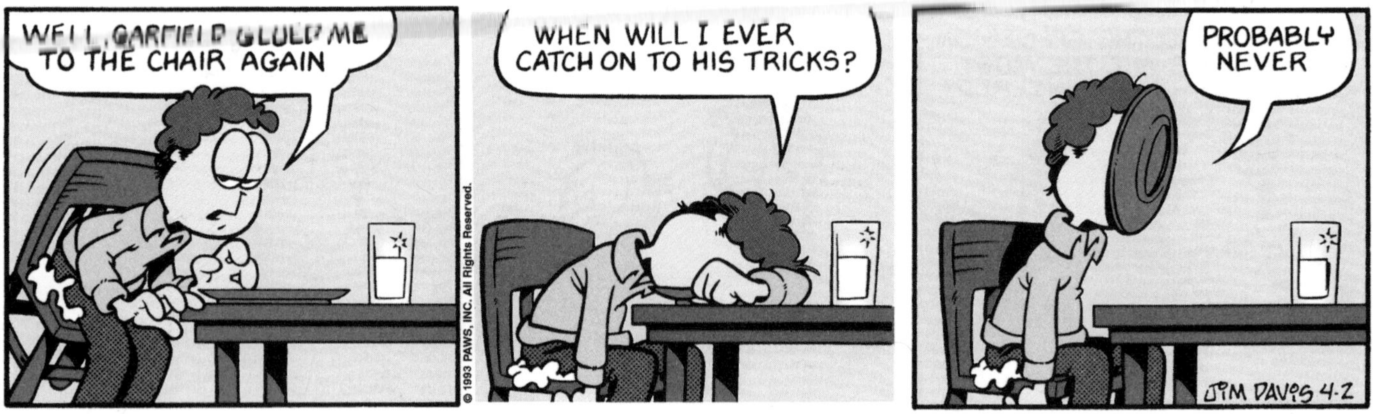
WELL, GARFIELD GLUED ME TO THE CHAIR AGAIN
© 1993 PAWS, INC. All Rights Reserved.
WHEN WILL I EVER CATCH ON TO HIS TRICKS?
PROBABLY NEVER
JIM DAVIS 4-2

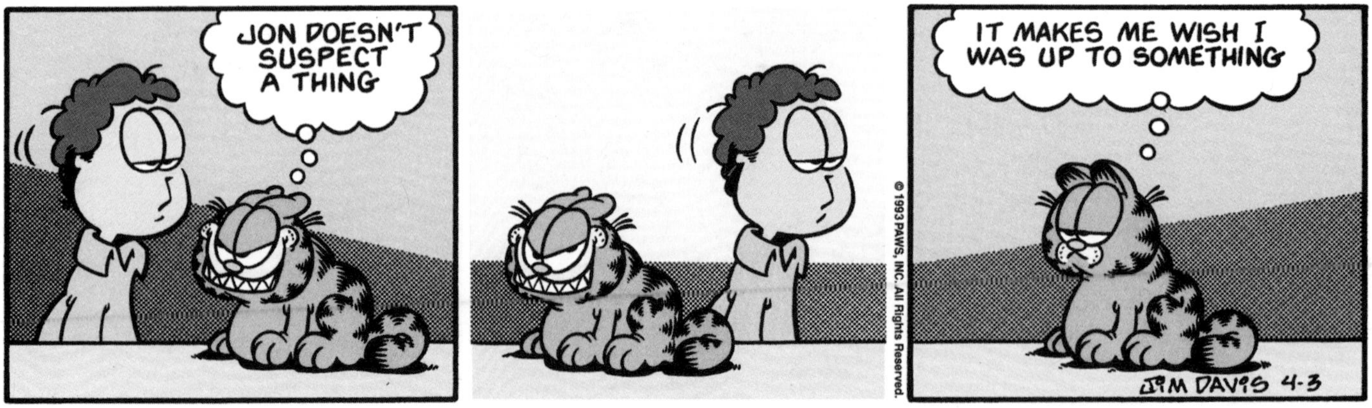
JON DOESN'T SUSPECT A THING
© 1993 PAWS, INC. All Rights Reserved.
IT MAKES ME WISH I WAS UP TO SOMETHING
JIM DAVIS 4-3

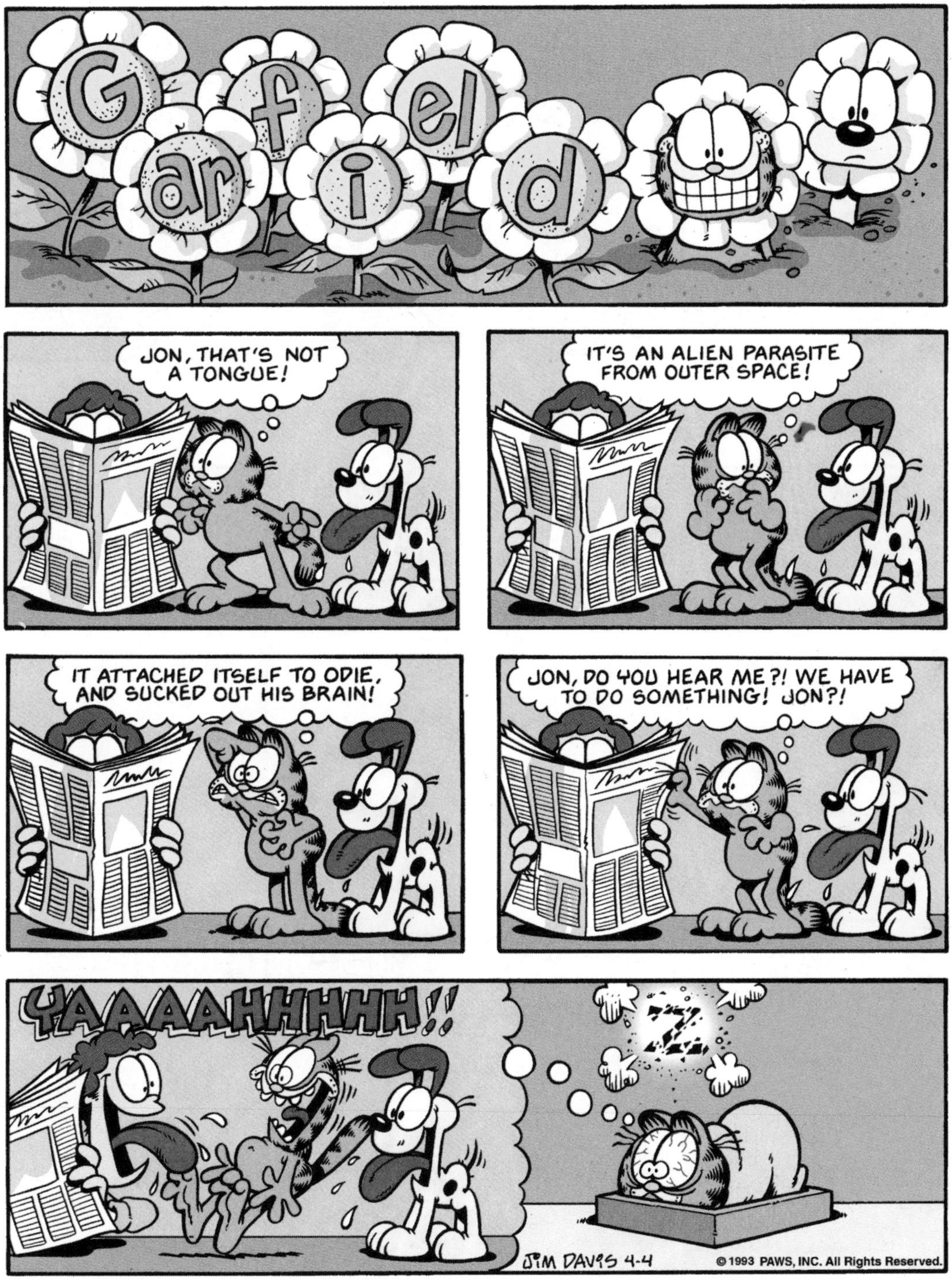
Garfield
JON, THAT'S NOT A TONGUE!
IT'S AN ALIEN PARASITE FROM OUTER SPACE!
IT ATTACHED ITSELF TO ODIE, AND SUCKED OUT HIS BRAIN!
JON, DO YOU HEAR ME?! WE HAVE TO DO SOMETHING! JON?!
YAAAAHHHHH!!
JIM DAVIS 4-4
© 1993 PAWS, INC. All Rights Reserved.

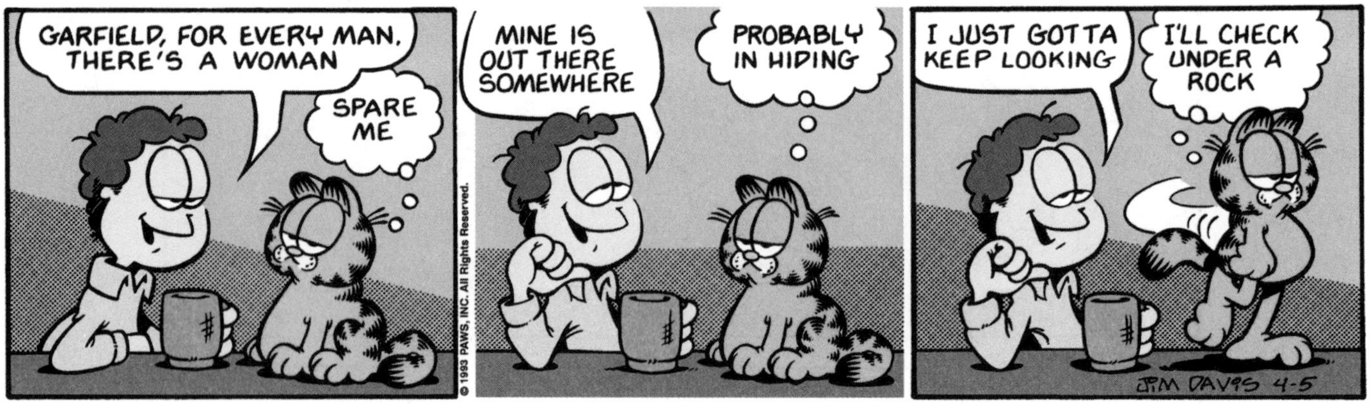
GARFIELD, FOR EVERY MAN, THERE'S A WOMAN
SPARE ME
© 1993 PAWS, INC. All Rights Reserved.
MINE IS OUT THERE SOMEWHERE
PROBABLY IN HIDING
I JUST GOTTA KEEP LOOKING
I'LL CHECK UNDER A ROCK
JIM DAVIS 4-5

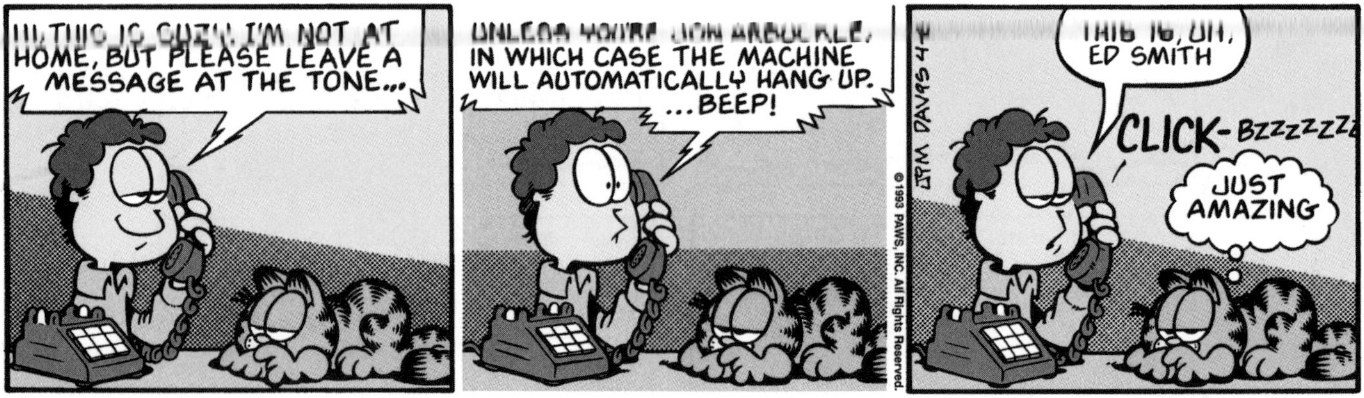
I'M NOT AT HOME, BUT PLEASE LEAVE A MESSAGE AT THE TONE...
IN WHICH CASE THE MACHINE WILL AUTOMATICALLY HANG UP. ...BEEP!
© 1993 PAWS, INC. All Rights Reserved.
JIM DAVIS 4-4
ED SMITH
CLICK-Bzzzzzzz
JUST AMAZING

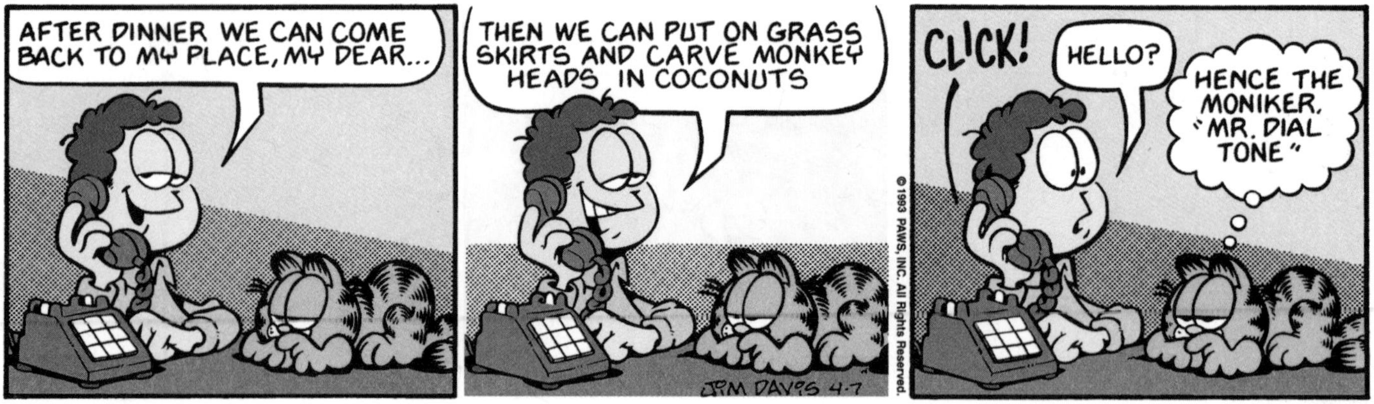
AFTER DINNER WE CAN COME BACK TO MY PLACE, MY DEAR...
THEN WE CAN PUT ON GRASS SKIRTS AND CARVE MONKEY HEADS IN COCONUTS
JIM DAVIS 4-7
© 1993 PAWS, INC. All Rights Reserved.
CLICK!
HELLO?
HENCE THE MONIKER, "MR. DIAL TONE"

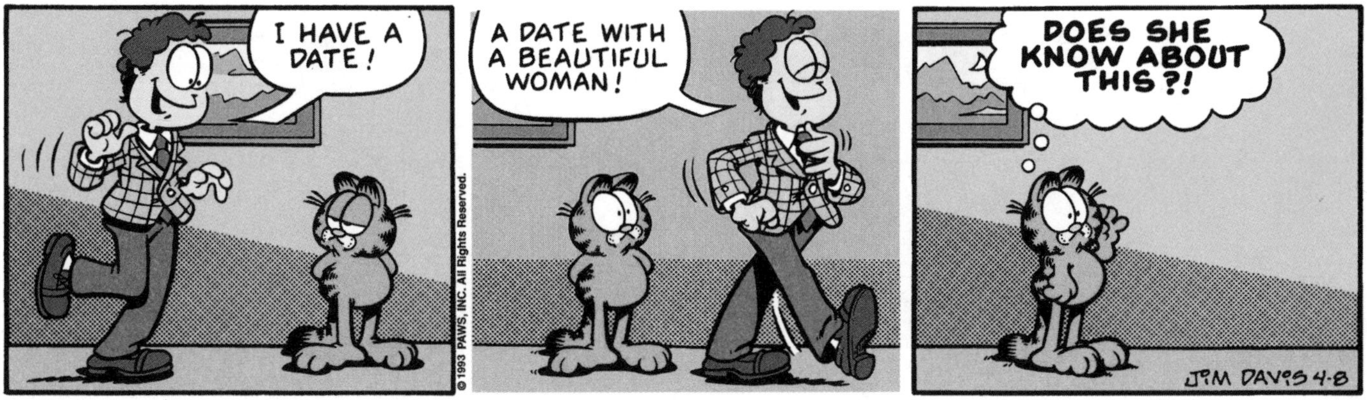
I HAVE A DATE!
A DATE WITH A BEAUTIFUL WOMAN!
DOES SHE KNOW ABOUT THIS?!
© 1993 PAWS, INC. All Rights Reserved.
JIM DAVIS 4-8

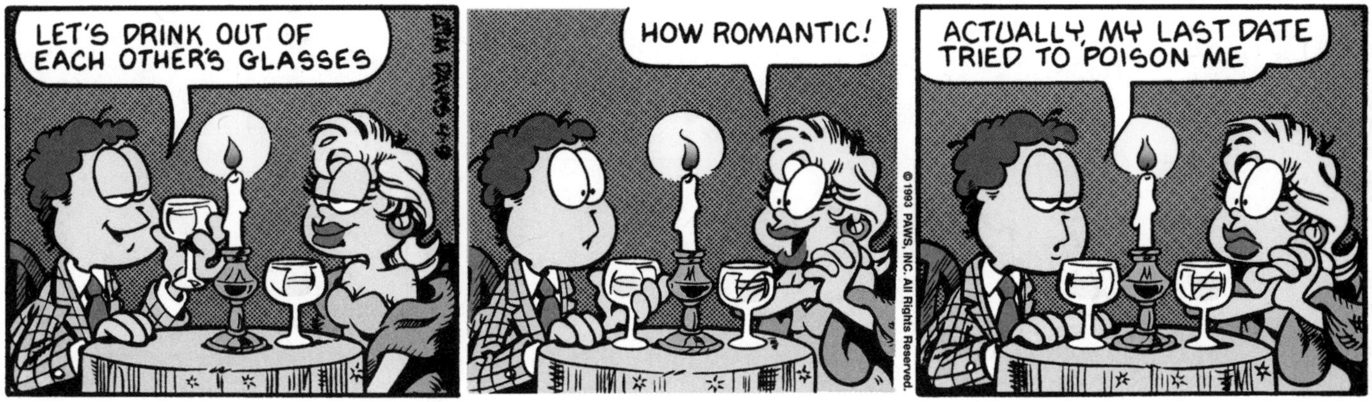
LET'S DRINK OUT OF EACH OTHER'S GLASSES
HOW ROMANTIC!
ACTUALLY, MY LAST DATE TRIED TO POISON ME
© 1993 PAWS, INC. All Rights Reserved.

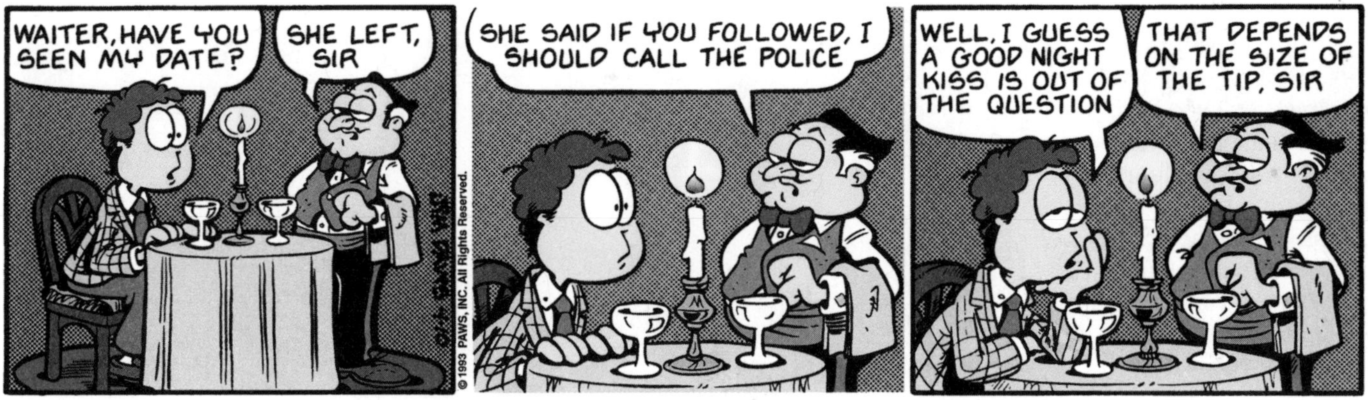
WAITER, HAVE YOU SEEN MY DATE?
SHE LEFT, SIR
SHE SAID IF YOU FOLLOWED, I SHOULD CALL THE POLICE
WELL, I GUESS A GOOD NIGHT KISS IS OUT OF THE QUESTION
THAT DEPENDS ON THE SIZE OF THE TIP, SIR
© 1993 PAWS, INC. All Rights Reserved.

The Garfield Birthday Gallery

1978

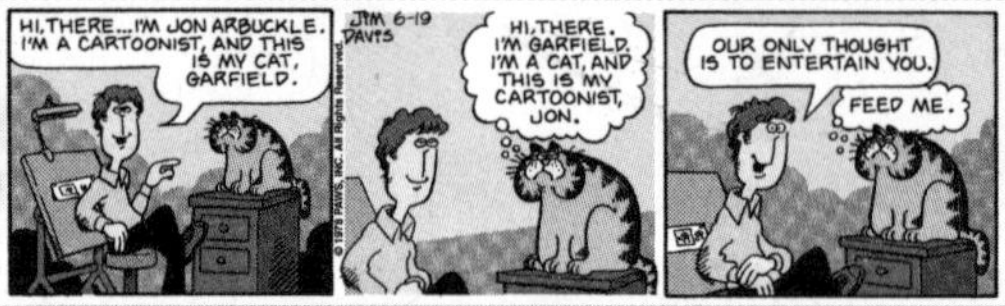

HI, THERE... I'M JON ARBUCKLE. I'M A CARTOONIST, AND THIS IS MY CAT, GARFIELD.
HI, THERE. I'M GARFIELD. I'M A CAT, AND THIS IS MY CARTOONIST, JON.
OUR ONLY THOUGHT IS TO ENTERTAIN YOU.
FEED ME.

1979

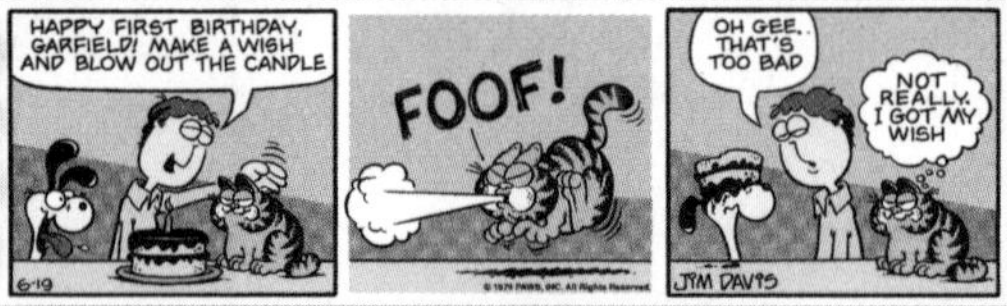

HAPPY FIRST BIRTHDAY, GARFIELD! MAKE A WISH AND BLOW OUT THE CANDLE
FOOF!
OH GEE. THAT'S TOO BAD
NOT REALLY. I GOT MY WISH

1980

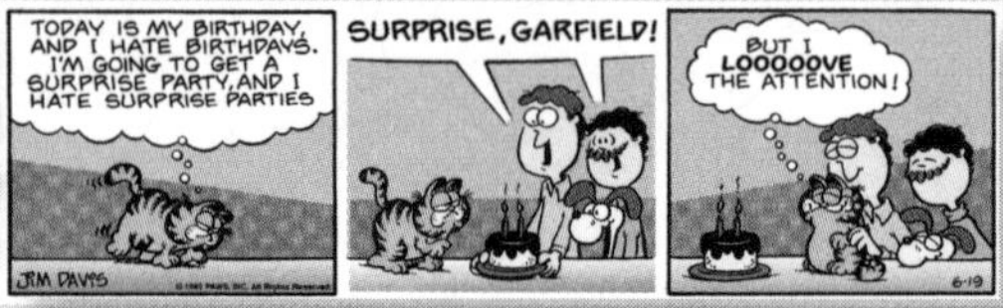

TODAY IS MY BIRTHDAY, AND I HATE BIRTHDAYS. I'M GOING TO GET A SURPRISE PARTY, AND I HATE SURPRISE PARTIES
SURPRISE, GARFIELD!
BUT I LOOOOOVE THE ATTENTION!

1981

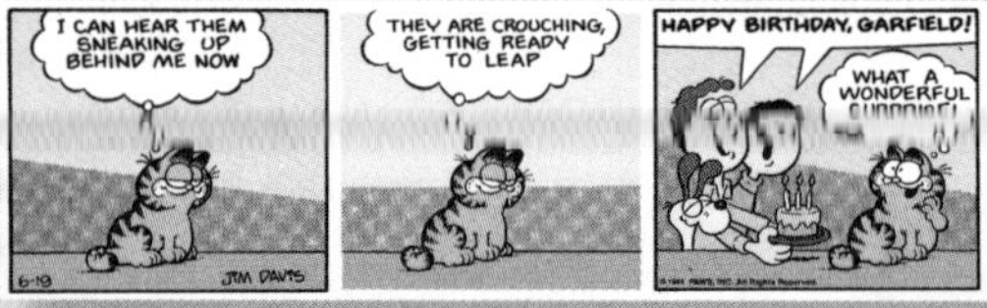

I CAN HEAR THEM SNEAKING UP BEHIND ME NOW
THEY ARE CROUCHING, GETTING READY TO LEAP
HAPPY BIRTHDAY, GARFIELD!
WHAT A WONDERFUL SURPRISE!

1982

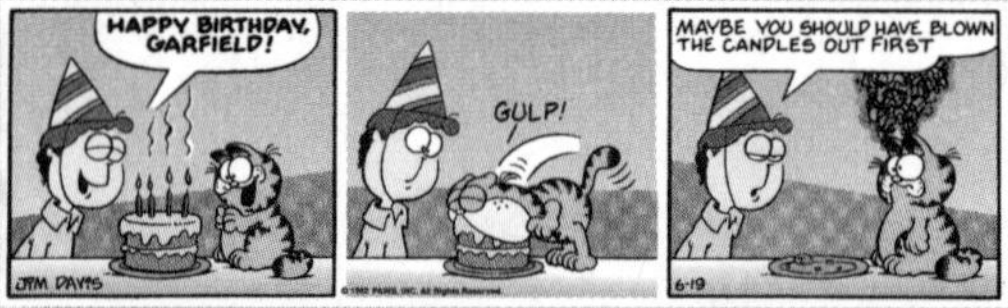

HAPPY BIRTHDAY, GARFIELD!
GULP!
MAYBE YOU SHOULD HAVE BLOWN THE CANDLES OUT FIRST

1983

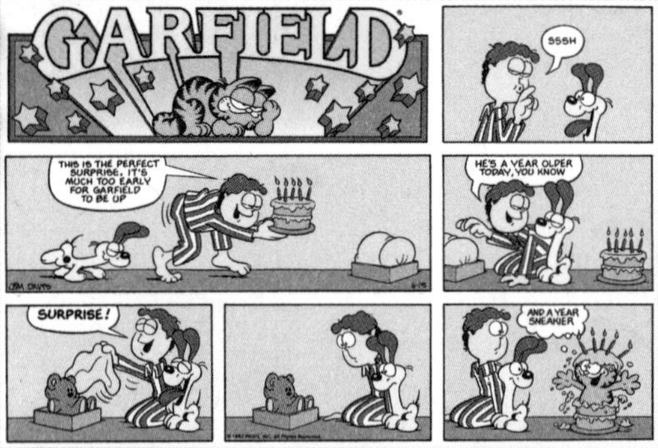

GARFIELD
SSSH
THIS IS THE PERFECT SURPRISE. IT'S MUCH TOO EARLY FOR GARFIELD TO BE UP
HE'S A YEAR OLDER TODAY, YOU KNOW
SURPRISE!
AND A YEAR SNEAKIER

1984

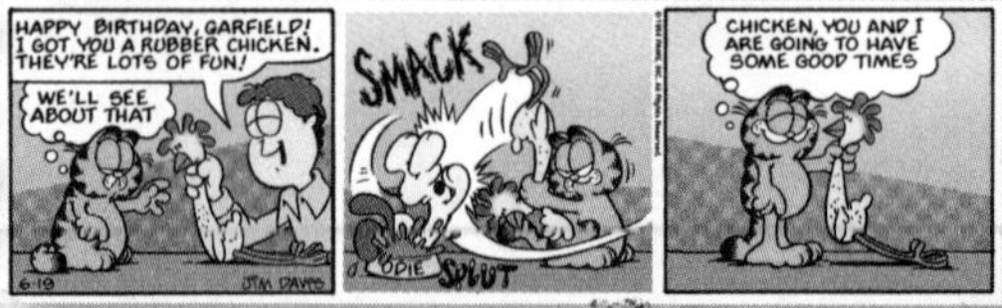

HAPPY BIRTHDAY, GARFIELD! I GOT YOU A RUBBER CHICKEN. THEY'RE LOTS OF FUN!
WE'LL SEE ABOUT THAT
SMACK
SPLUT
CHICKEN, YOU AND I ARE GOING TO HAVE SOME GOOD TIMES

1985

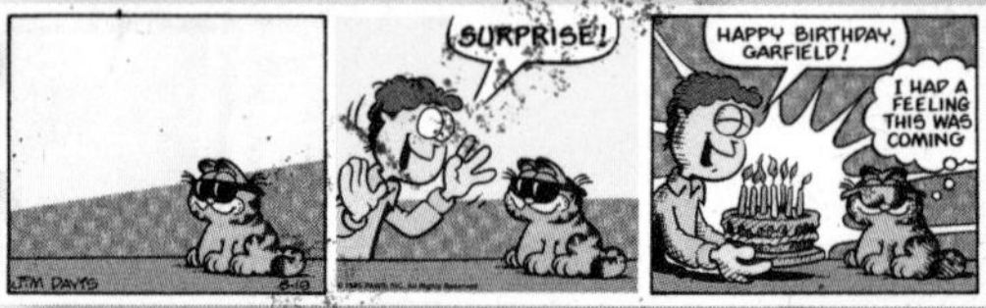

SURPRISE!
HAPPY BIRTHDAY, GARFIELD!
I HAD A FEELING THIS WAS COMING

1986

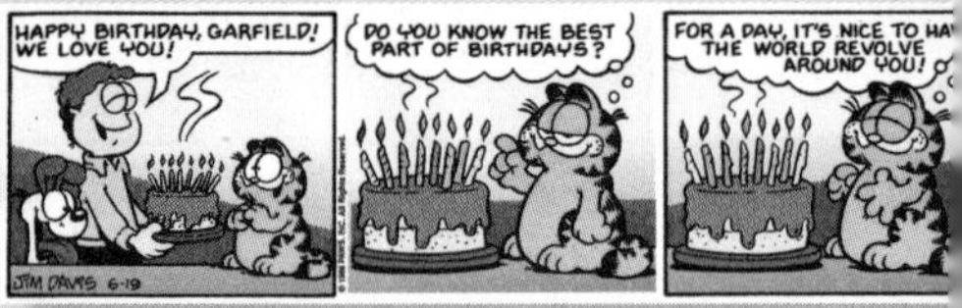

HAPPY BIRTHDAY, GARFIELD! WE LOVE YOU!
DO YOU KNOW THE BEST PART OF BIRTHDAYS?
FOR A DAY, IT'S NICE TO HAVE THE WORLD REVOLVE AROUND YOU!

1987

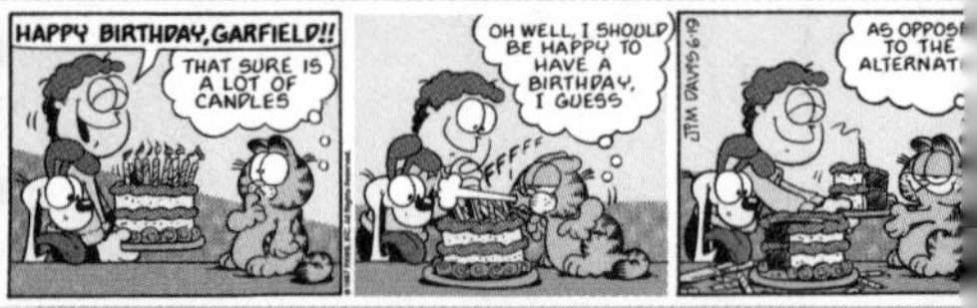

HAPPY BIRTHDAY, GARFIELD!!
THAT SURE IS A LOT OF CANDLES
OH WELL, I SHOULD BE HAPPY TO HAVE A BIRTHDAY, I GUESS

1988

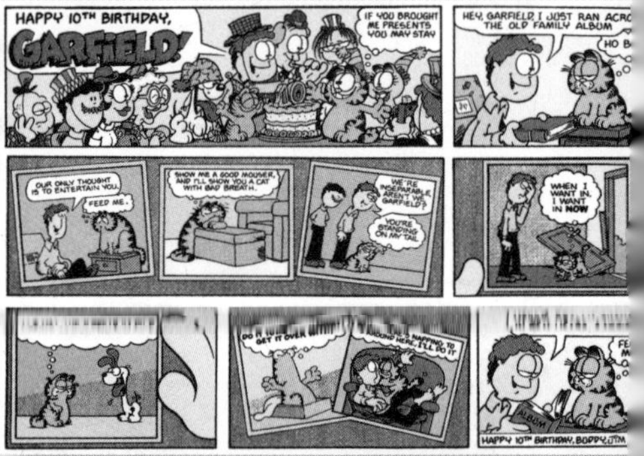

HAPPY 10TH BIRTHDAY, GARFIELD!
IF YOU BROUGHT ME PRESENTS YOU MAY STAY
OUR ONLY THOUGHT IS TO ENTERTAIN YOU.
FEED ME.
WHEN I WANT IN, I WANT IN NOW
HAPPY 10TH BIRTHDAY, BUDDY

1989

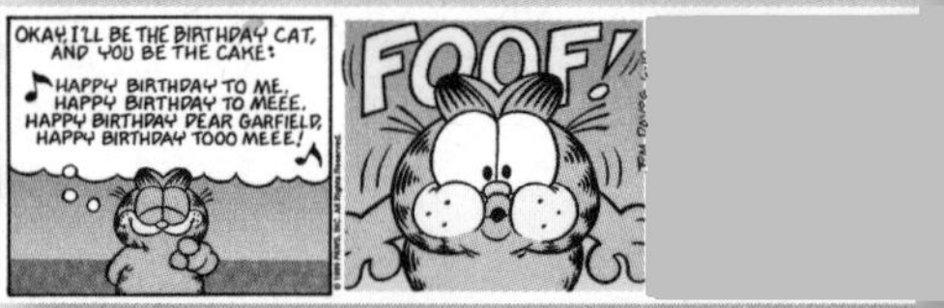

OKAY, I'LL BE THE BIRTHDAY CAT, AND YOU BE THE CAKE:
HAPPY BIRTHDAY TO ME, HAPPY BIRTHDAY TO MEEE, HAPPY BIRTHDAY DEAR GARFIELD, HAPPY BIRTHDAY TOOO MEEE!
FOOF!

1990

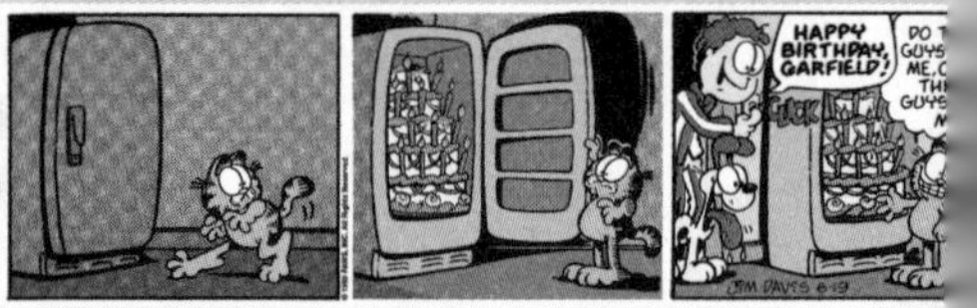

HAPPY BIRTHDAY, GARFIELD!

1991

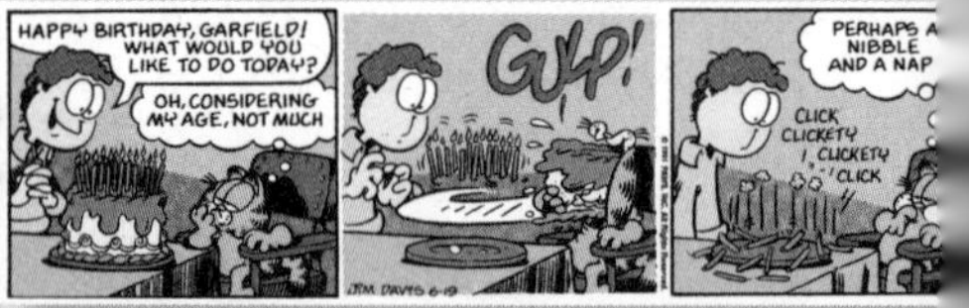

HAPPY BIRTHDAY, GARFIELD! WHAT WOULD YOU LIKE TO DO TODAY?
OH, CONSIDERING MY AGE, NOT MUCH
GULP!
CLICK CLICKETY CLICKETY CLICK

1992

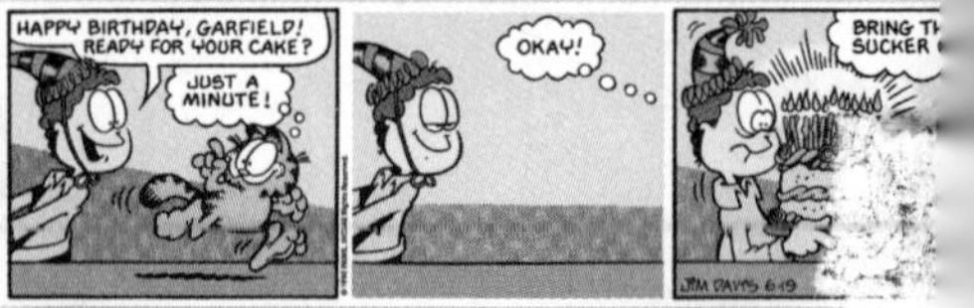

HAPPY BIRTHDAY, GARFIELD! READY FOR YOUR CAKE?
JUST A MINUTE!
OKAY!

1993

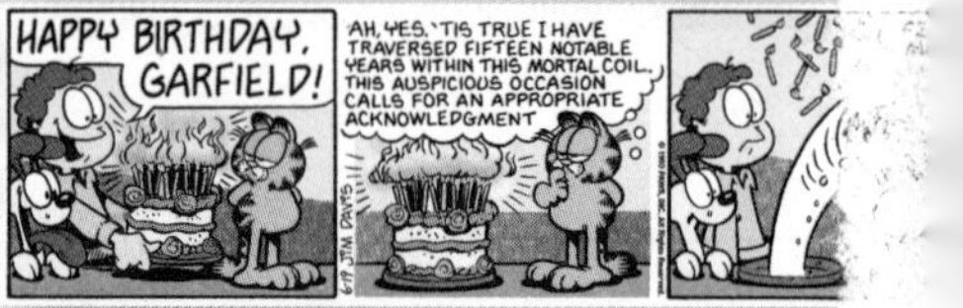

HAPPY BIRTHDAY, GARFIELD!
AH, YES. 'TIS TRUE I HAVE TRAVERSED FIFTEEN NOTABLE YEARS WITHIN THIS MORTAL COIL. THIS AUSPICIOUS OCCASION CALLS FOR AN APPROPRIATE ACKNOWLEDGMENT

Feast your eyes on the Garfield Birthday Gallery. The famished feline has been perfecting the art of eating for fifteen years now. That's a bellyful of laughs and lasagna. And rest assured that the Picasso of cats will continue to color your world with fun for many years to come.

15 CELEBRATING Fabulous Years!
1978·1993

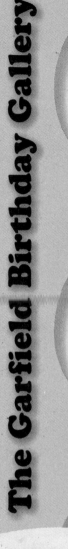

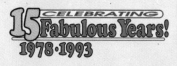

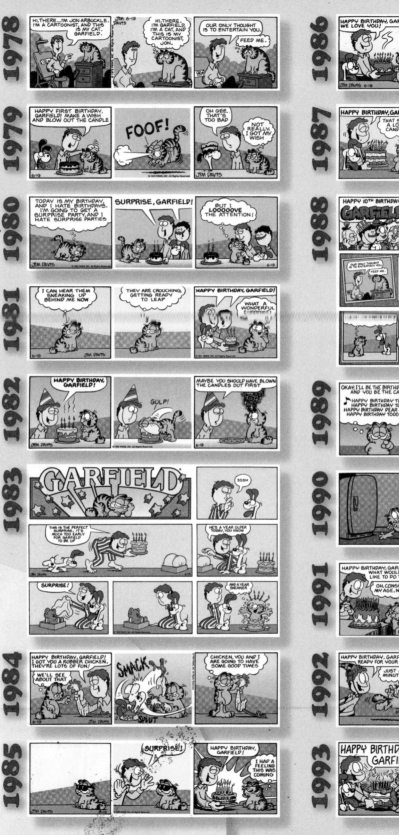